JUMBO
EASY GUITAR SONGBOOK

EASY GUITAR WITH NOTES & TAB

S0-AXD-868

ISBN 978-0-634-02567-9

HAL•LEONARD®
CORPORATION
7777 W. BLUEMOUND RD. P.O. BOX 13819 MILWAUKEE, WI 53213

Visit Hal Leonard Online at
www.halleonard.com

STRUM AND PICK PATTERNS

This chart contains the suggested strum and pick patterns that are referred to by number at the beginning
of each song in this book. The symbols ⊓ and ∨ in the strum patterns refer to down and up strokes, respectively.
The letters in the pick patterns indicate which right-hand fingers plays which strings.

p = thumb
i = index finger
m = middle finger
a = ring finger

For example; Pick Pattern 2
is played: thumb - index - middle - ring

Strum Patterns   ## Pick Patterns

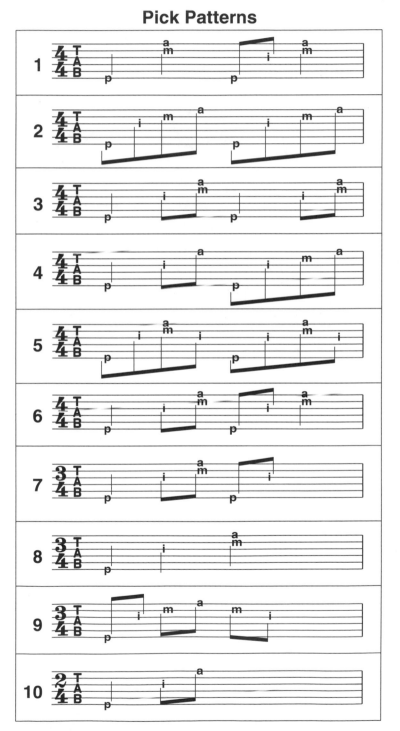

You can use the 3/4 Strum or Pick Patterns in songs written in compound meter (6/8, 9/8, 12/8, etc.).
For example, you can accompany a song in 6/8 by playing the 3/4 pattern twice in each measure.
The 4/4 Strum and Pick Patterns can be used for songs written in cut time (¢) by doubling the note
time values in the patterns. Each pattern would therefore last two measures in cut time.

A-Tisket A-Tasket

Traditional

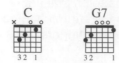

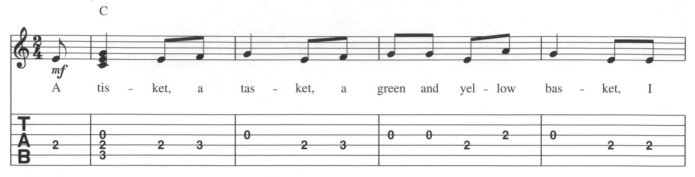

Strum Pattern: 10
Pick Pattern: 10

Moderately

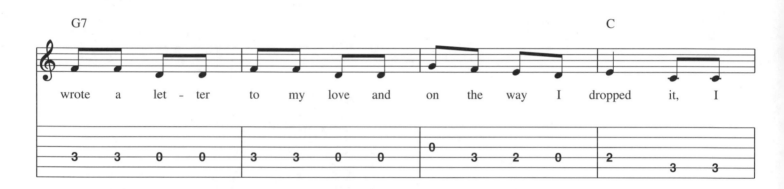

A tis - ket, a tas - ket, a green and yel - low bas - ket, I

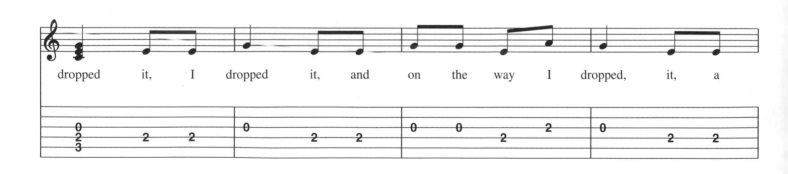

wrote a let - ter to my love and on the way I dropped it, I

dropped it, I dropped it, and on the way I dropped, it, a

lit - tle boy (girl) picked it up and put it in his (her) pock - et.

Aloha Oe

Words and Music by Queen Liliuokalani

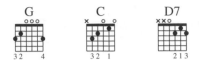

Strum Pattern: 3
Pick Pattern: 1

Slowly

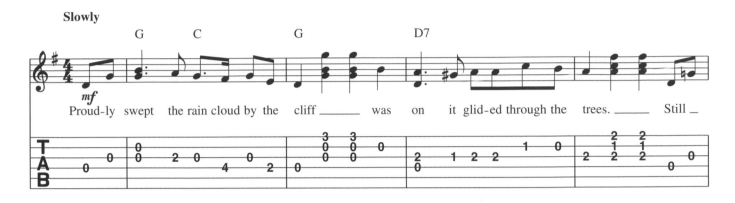

Proud-ly swept the rain cloud by the cliff _____ was on it glid-ed through the trees. _____ Still _

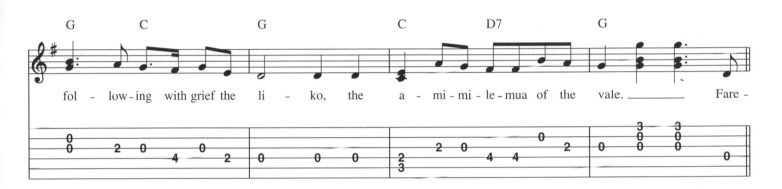

fol - low-ing with grief the li - ko, the a - mi - mi - le - mua of the vale. _____ Fare -

Chorus

well to thee, fare-well to thee, thou charm-ing one who dwells a-mong the bow - ers. One

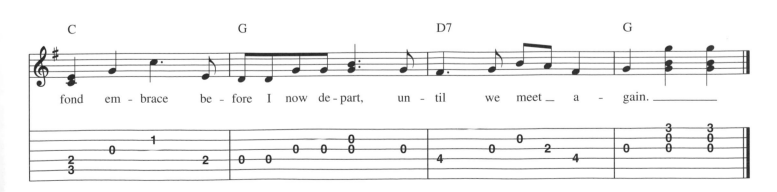

fond em - brace be - fore I now de - part, un - til we meet _ a - gain. ___

Adios Muchachos

By Julio Sanders

Strum Pattern: 2
Pick Pattern: 4

A

Moderately

After the Ball

from A TRIP TO CHINATOWN

Words and Music by Charles K. Harris

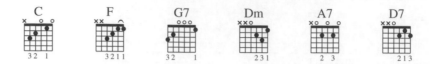

Strum Pattern: 8, 9
Pick Pattern: 8, 9

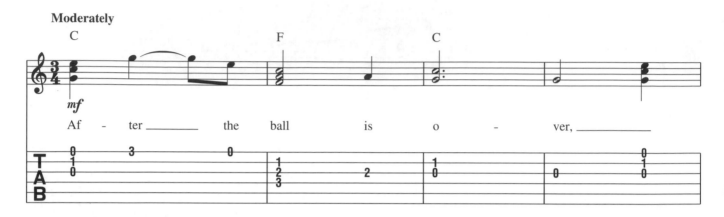

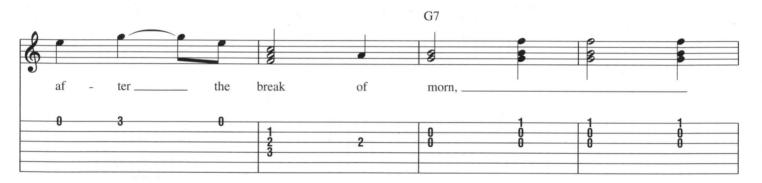

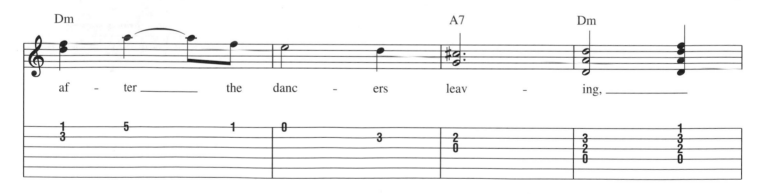

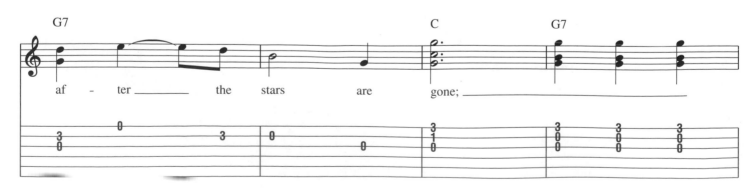

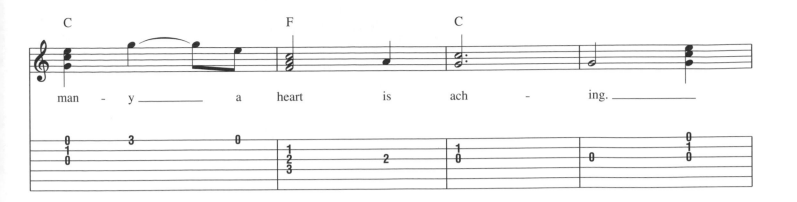

man - y _____ a heart is ach - ing. _____

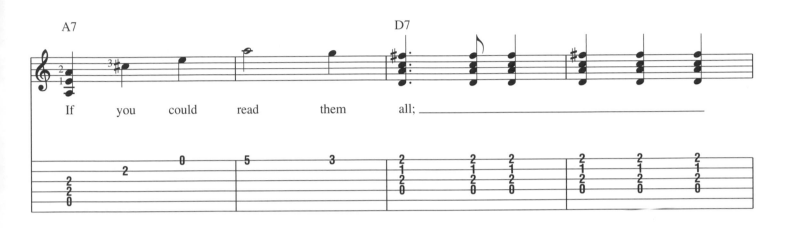

If you could read them all; _____

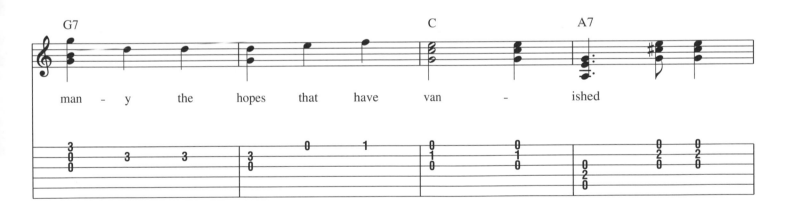

man - y the hopes that have van - ished

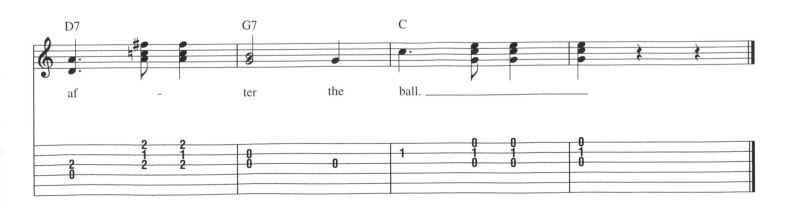

af - ter the ball. _____

After You've Gone

from One Mo' Time

Words by Henry Creamer
Music by Turner Layton

Strum Pattern: 2
Pick Pattern: 4

Verse
Moderate shuffle

1. Af - ter you've gone, _____ and left me cry - ing; af - ter you've gone, _____
2. *See additional lyrics*

there's no de - ny - ing.   You'll feel   blue, _____   you'll feel   sad, _____

you'll miss the dear - est pal you've ev - er had. _____ There'll come a time, _____

now don't for - get it, there'll come a time, _____ when you'll re - gret it.

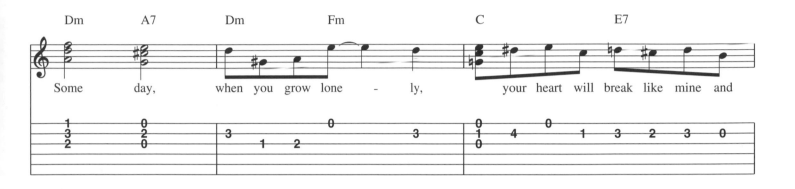

Some day, when you grow lone - ly, your heart will break like mine and

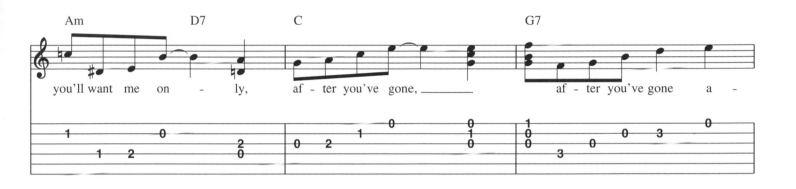

you'll want me on - ly, af - ter you've gone, _____ af - ter you've gone a -

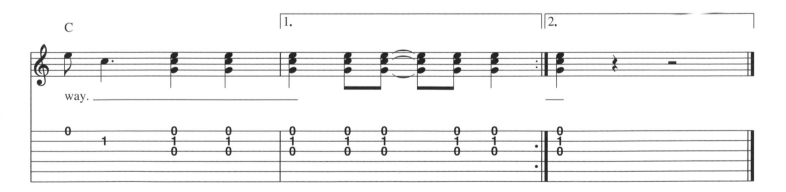

way. _____

Additional Lyrics

2. After I'm gone, after we break up;
After I'm gone, you're gonna wake up.
You will find, you were blind,
To let somebody come and change your mind.
After the years, we've been together,
Their joy and tears, all kinds of weather;
Some day, blue and downhearted,
You'll long to be with me right back where you started,
After I'm gone, after I'm gone away.

Ain't We Got Fun?

from BY THE LIGHT OF THE SILVERY MOON

Words by Gus Kahn and Raymond B. Egan
Music by Richard A. Whiting

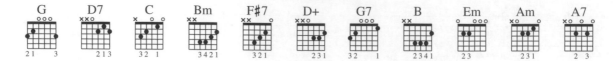

Strum Pattern: 2, 3
Pick Pattern: 3, 4

Verse
Moderately

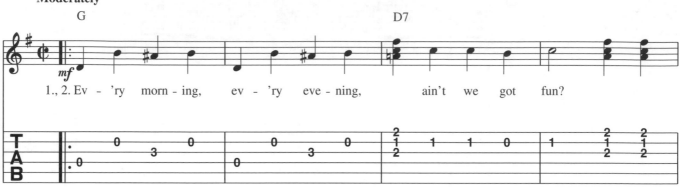

1., 2. Ev - 'ry morn - ing, ev - 'ry eve - ning, ain't we got fun?

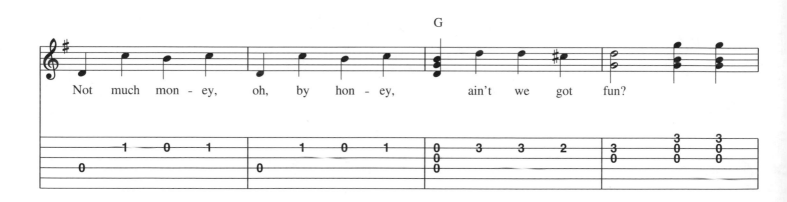

Not much mon - ey, oh, by hon - ey, ain't we got fun?

The rent's un - paid, dear, _____ we have - n't a car. _____

But an-y-way, dear, _____ we'll stay as we are.

E-ven if we owe the gro-cer, don't we have fun?

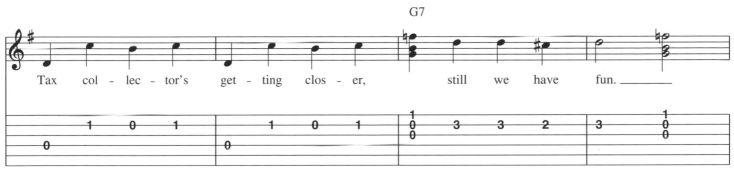

Tax col-lec-tor's get-ting clos-er, still we have fun. _____

There's noth-ing sur-er, the rich get rich and the poor get poor-er.

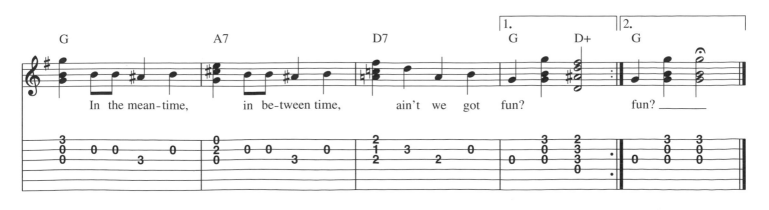

In the mean-time, in be-tween time, ain't we got fun?

fun? _____

Alabama Jubilee

Words by Jack Yellen
Music by George Cobb

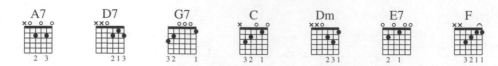

Strum Pattern: 10
Pick Pattern: 10

Lively

You ought to see Mis - ter Jones ___ when ___ he rat - tles the bones, ___

Old Colo - nel Brown ___ fool - in' 'round like a clown, ___

Miss ___ Vir - gin - ia who is past eight - y three, ___

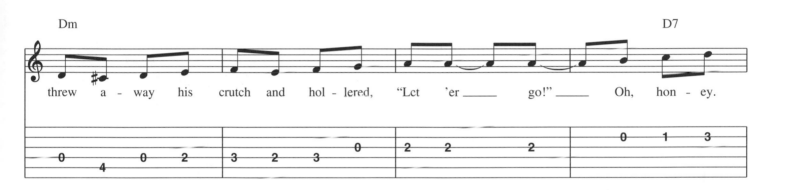

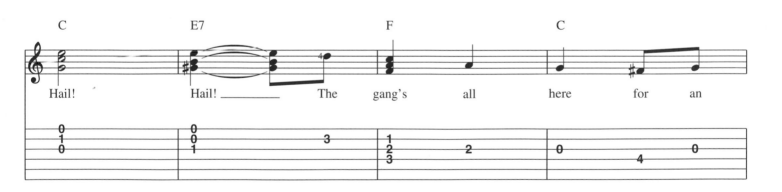

All My Trials

African-American Spiritual

Chorus

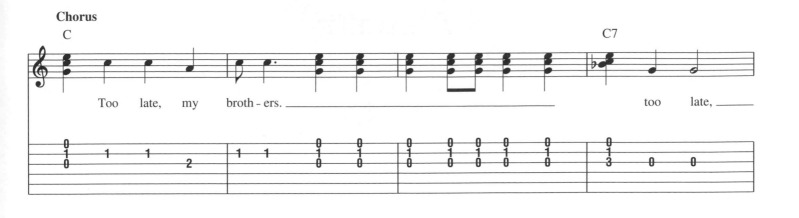

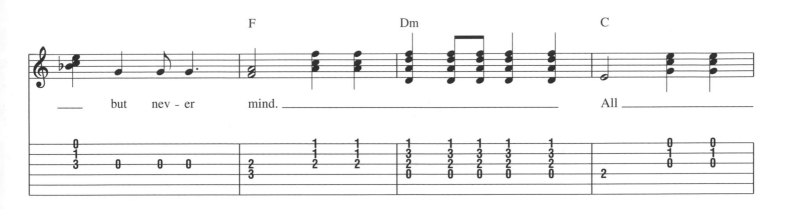

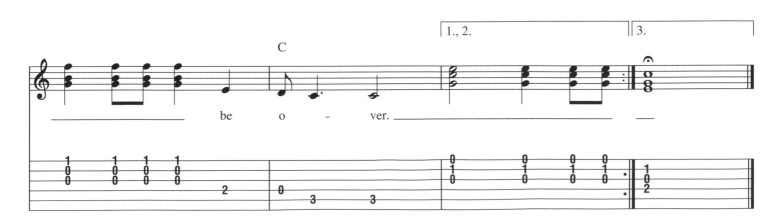

Additional Lyrics

2. If religion was a thing money could buy,
   The rich would live and the poor would die.

3. I had a little book that was given to me,
   And ev'ry page spelled liberty.

Alouette

Traditional

Strum Pattern: 10
Pick Pattern: 10

Chorus
Moderately

A - lou - et - te, gen - tille A - lou - et - te,

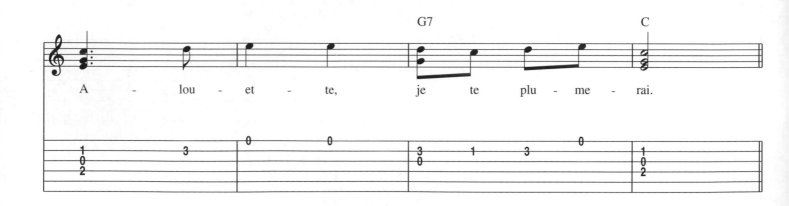

A - lou - et - te, je te plu - me - rai.

Verse

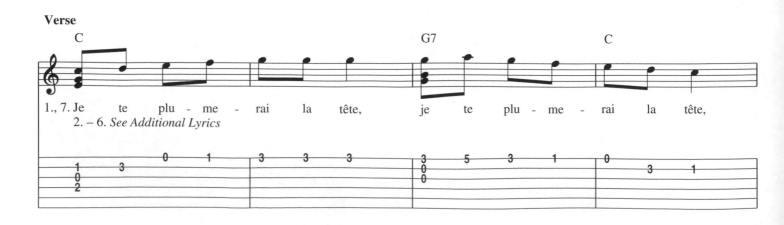

1., 7. Je te plu - me - rai la tête, je te plu - me - rai la tête,
2. – 6. *See Additional Lyrics*

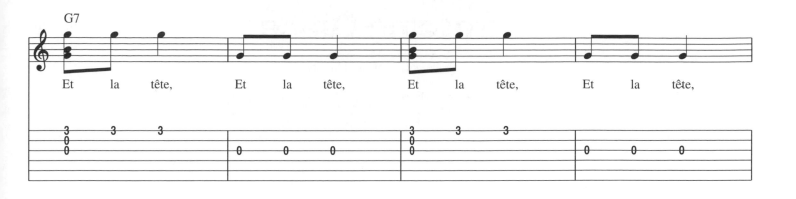

Et la tête, Et la tête, Et la tête, Et la tête,

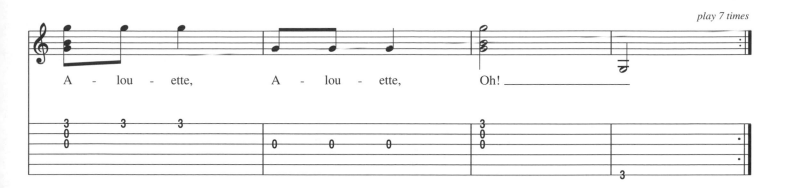

play 7 times

A - lou - ette, A - lou - ette, Oh! _____

Outro-Chorus

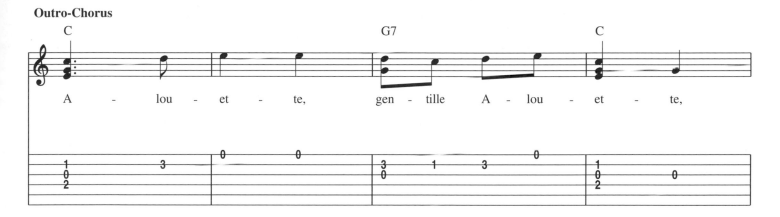

A - lou - et - te, gen - tille A - lou - et - te,

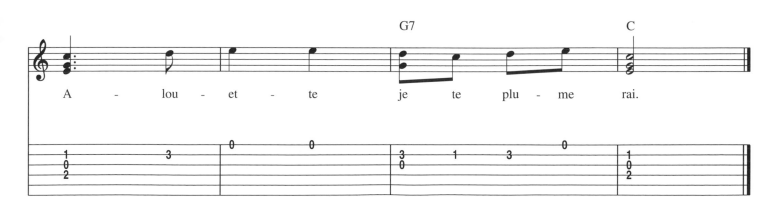

A - lou - et - te je te plu - me rai.

Additional Lyrics

2) le bec
3) le cou
4) les jambes
5) les pieds
6) les pattes

Amazing Grace

Words by John Newton
Traditional American Melody

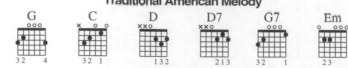

Strum Pattern: 7
Pick Pattern: 7

Additional Lyrics

2. 'Twas grace that taught my heart to fear,
   And grace my fears relieved.
   How precious did that grace appear
   The hour I first believed.

3. Through many dangers, toils and snares,
   I have already come.
   'Tis grace has brought me safe thus far,
   And grace will lead me home.

4. The Lord has promised good to me,
   His word my hope secures.
   He will my shield and portion be
   As long as life endures.

5. And when this flesh and heart shall fail,
   And mortal life shall cease.
   I shall possess within the veil
   A life of joy and peace.

6. When we've been there ten thousand years,
   Bright shining as the sun.
   We've no less days to sing God's praise
   Than when we first begun.

America the Beautiful

Words by Katherine Lee Bates
Music by Samuel A. Ward

Strum Pattern: 4
Pick Pattern: 3

Additional Lyrics

2. O beautiful for patriot dream
   That sees beyond the years,
   Thine alabaster cities gleam
   Undimmed by human tears.
   America! America!
   God shed His grace on thee,
   And crown thy good with brotherhood
   From sea to shining sea.

Anchors Aweigh

Words by Alfred Hart Miles and Royal Lovell
Music by Charles A. Zimmerman
Additional Lyric by George D. Lottman

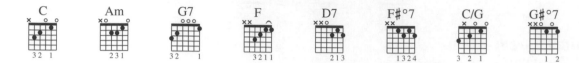

Strum Pattern: 4
Pick Pattern: 6

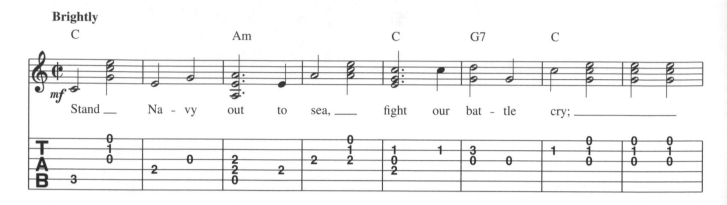

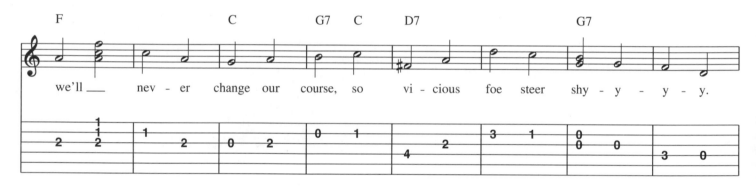

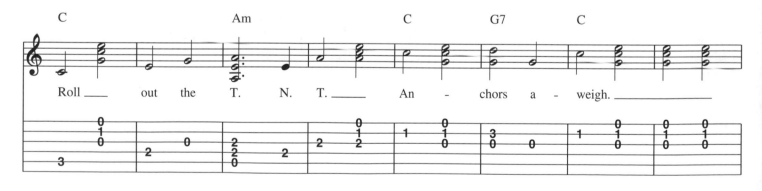

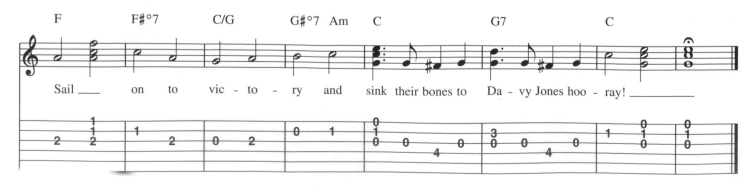

Arkansas Traveler

Southern American Folksong

Strum Pattern: 10
Pick Pattern: 10

Any Time

Words and Music by Herbert Happy Lawson

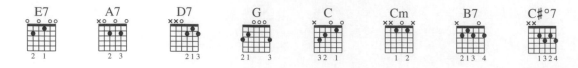

Strum Pattern: 3, 4
Pick Pattern: 1, 3

Verse
Moderately

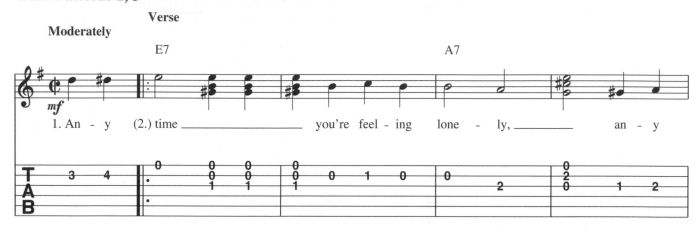

1. An - y (2.) time _____ you're feel - ing lone - ly, _____ an - y

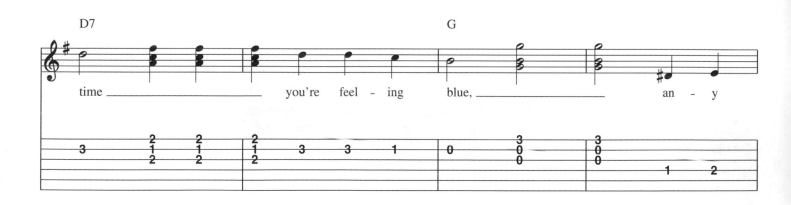

time _____ you're feel - ing blue, _____ an - y

time _____ you feel down - heart - ed, _____ that will

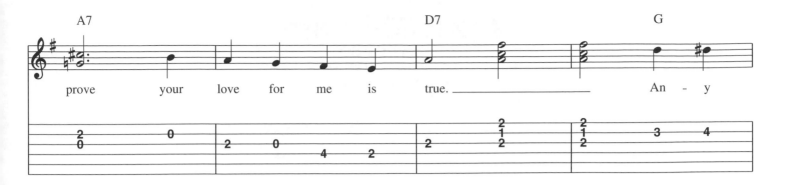

prove your love for me is true. _____ An - y

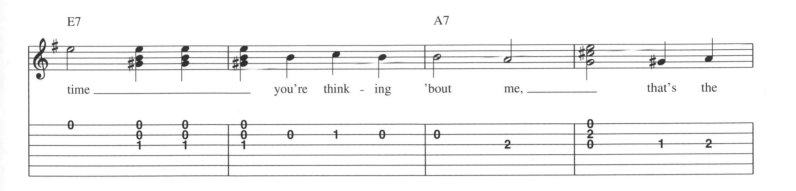

time _____ you're think - ing 'bout me, _____ that's the

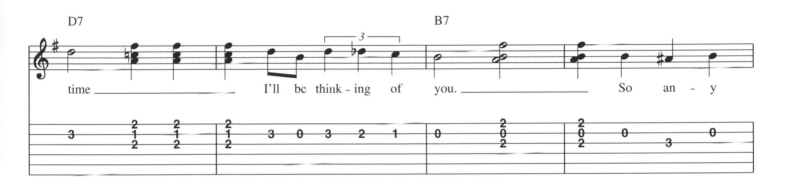

time _____ I'll be think - ing of you. _____ So an - y

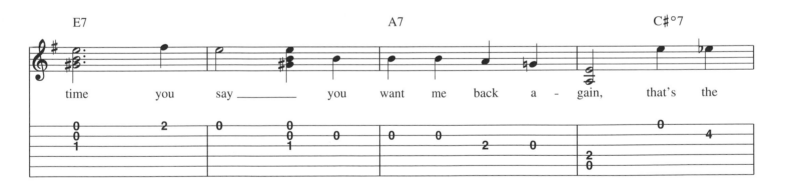

time you say _____ you want me back a - gain, that's the

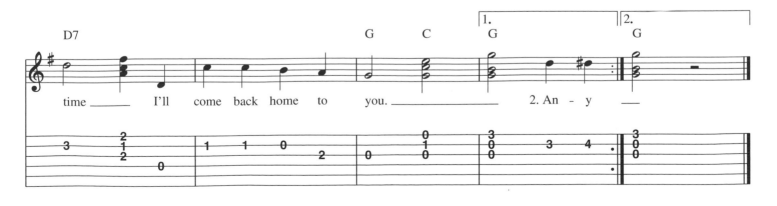

time _____ I'll come back home to you. 2. An - y ___

April Showers

from BOMBO

Words by B.G. DeSylva
Music by Louis Silvers

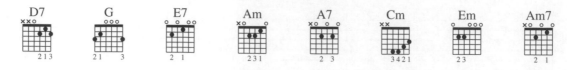

Strum Pattern: 2
Pick Pattern: 4

Moderately

Verse

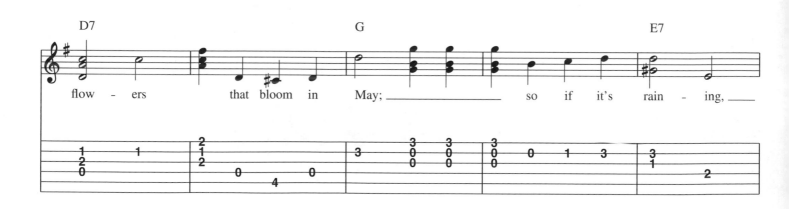

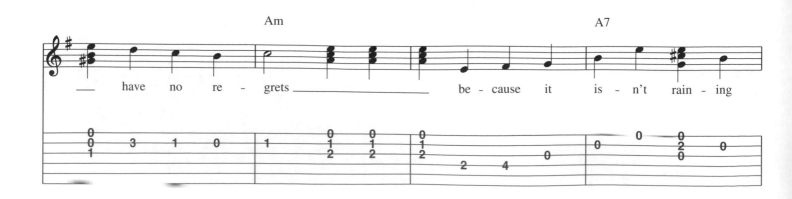

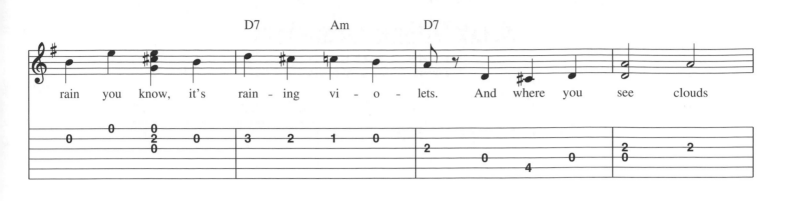

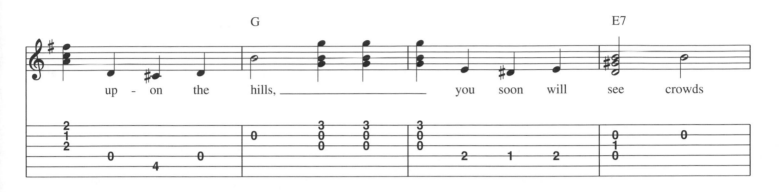

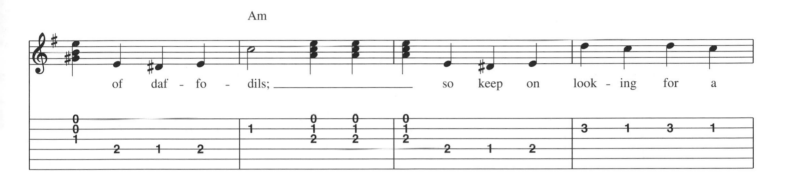

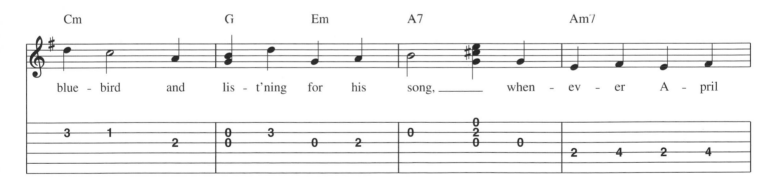

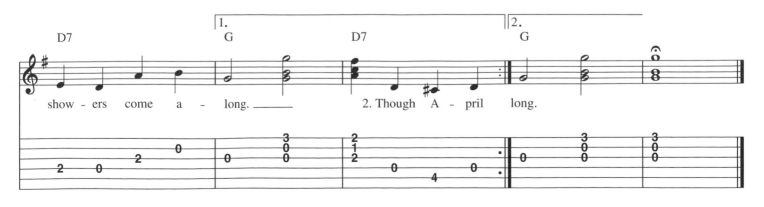

Auf Wiedersehn

Words by Herbert Reynolds
Music by Sigmund Romberg

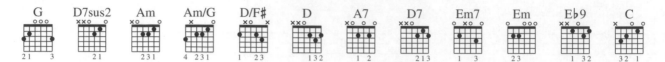

Strum Pattern: 7, 8
Pick Pattern: 7, 8

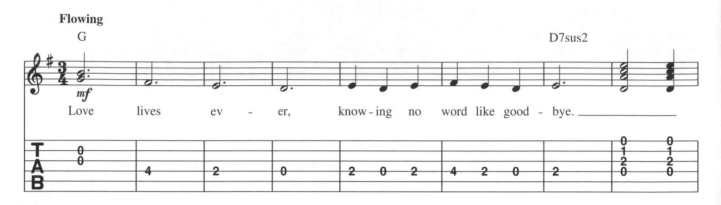

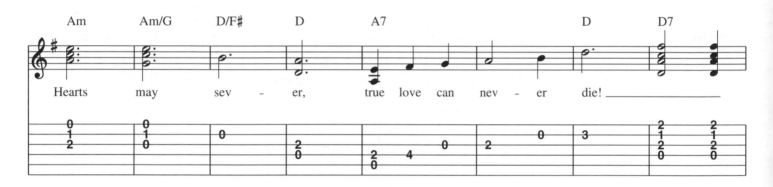

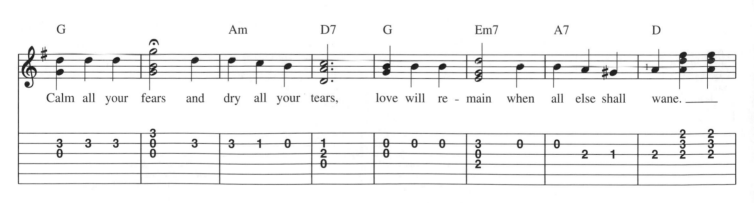

Auld Lang Syne

Words by Robert Burns
Traditional Melody

Strum Pattern: 3, 4
Pick Pattern: 2, 4

Verse
Moderately

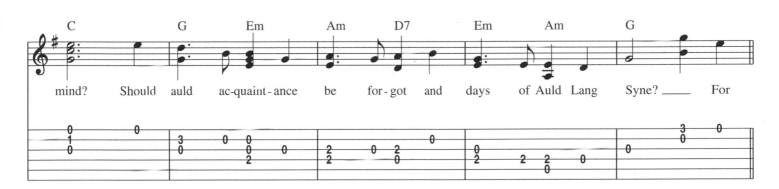

mf Should auld ac-quaint-ance be for-got and nev - er brought to

mind? Should auld ac-quaint-ance be for-got and days of Auld Lang Syne? _____ For

Chorus

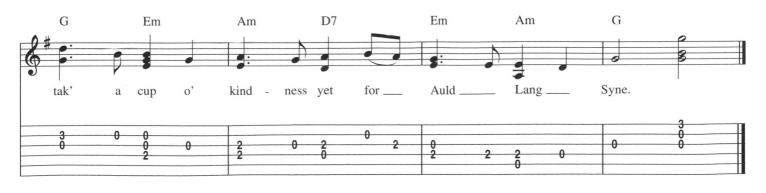

Auld _____ Lang _____ Syne, my dear, for Auld _____ Lang _____ Syne, we'll

tak' a cup o' kind - ness yet for _____ Auld _____ Lang _____ Syne.

Aura Lee

Words by W.W. Fosdick
Music by George R. Poulton

Strum Pattern: 4
Pick Pattern: 5

Verse

Slowly

1. As the black-bird in the spring, 'neath the wil-low tree _____ sat and piped I
2. *See additional lyrics*

Chorus

heard him sing, sing of Au - ra Lee. _____ Au - ra Lee, Au - ra Lee, maid of gold - en
See additional lyrics

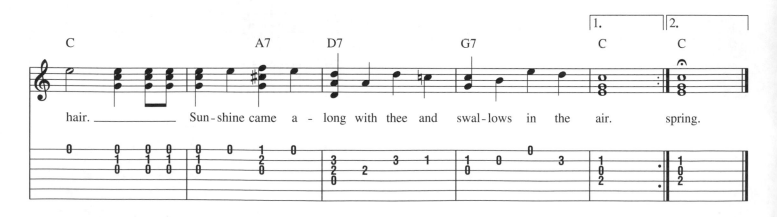

hair. _____ Sun-shine came a - long with thee and swal-lows in the air. spring.

Additional Lyrics

2. In thy blush the rose was born,
   Music when you spake,
   Though thine azure eyes the moon
   Sparkling seemed to break.

Chorus Aura Lee, Aura Lee, birds of crimson wing,
   Never song have sung to me as
   In that bright, sweet spring.

Avalon

Words by Al Jolson and B.G. DeSylva
Music by Vincent Rose

Strum Pattern: 3, 4
Pick Pattern: 1, 3

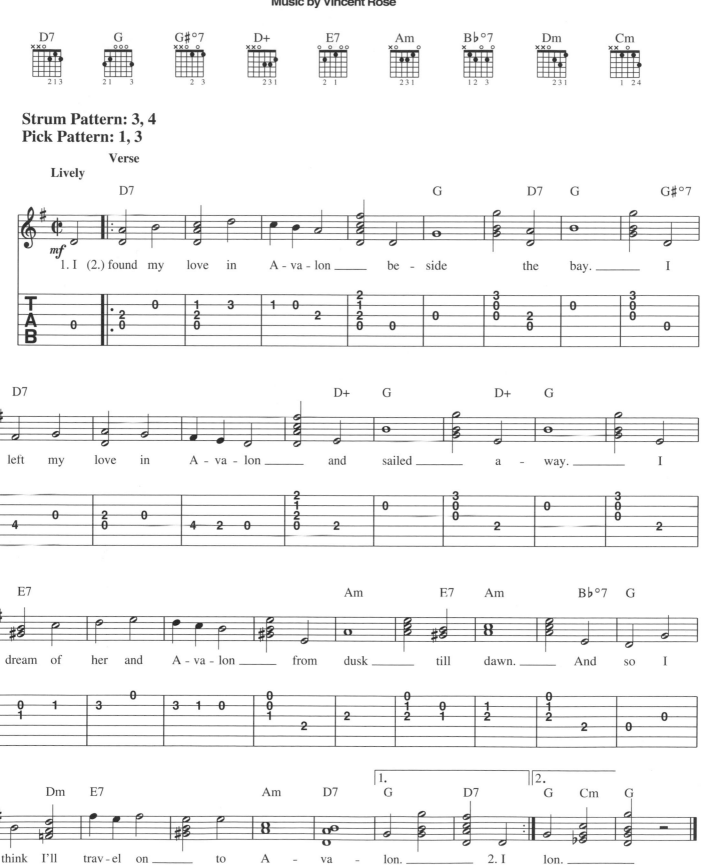

Baby, Won't You Please Come Home

Words and Music by Charles Warfield and Clarence Williams

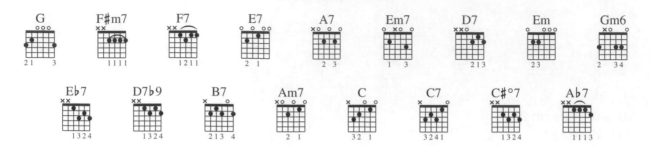

Strum Pattern: 2
Pick Pattern: 4

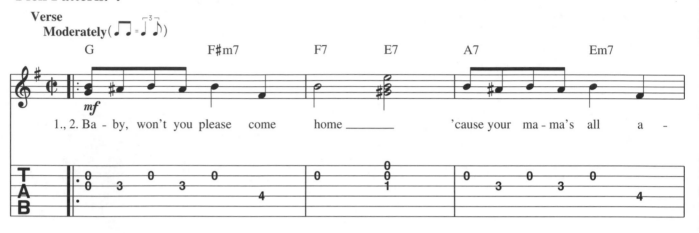

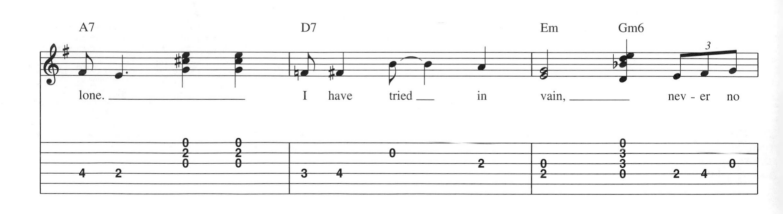

1., 2. Ba - by, won't you please come home _____ 'cause your ma - ma's all a -

lone. _____ I have tried _____ in vain, _____ nev - er no

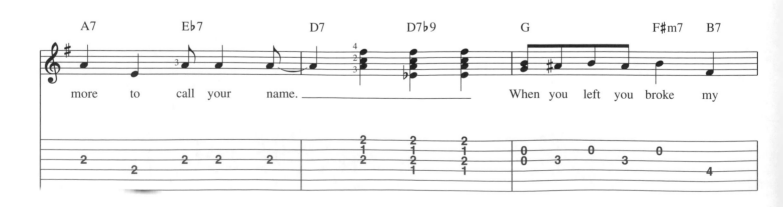

more to call your name. _____ When you left you broke my

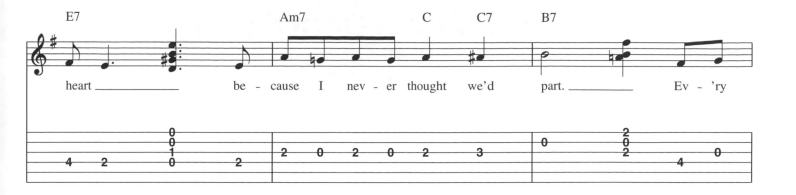

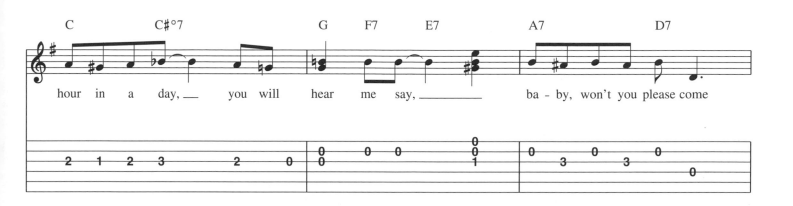

The Banana Boat Song
(Day Oh)

Jamaican Work Song

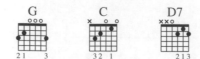

Strum Pattern: 6
Pick Pattern: 4

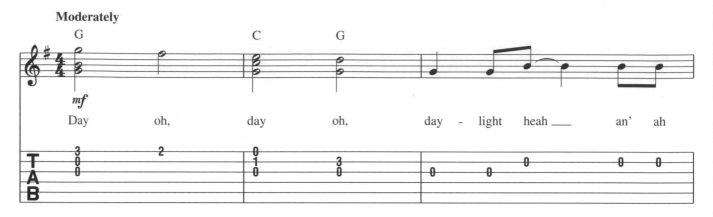

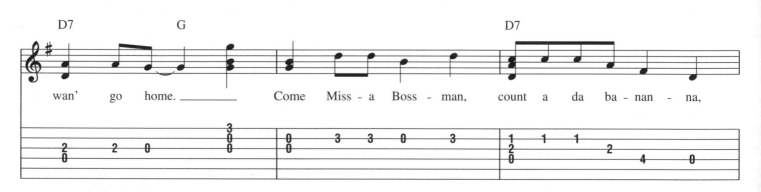

The Band Played On

Words by John E. Palmer
Music by Charles B. Ward

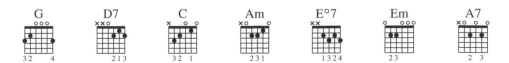

Strum Pattern: 8
Pick Pattern: 8

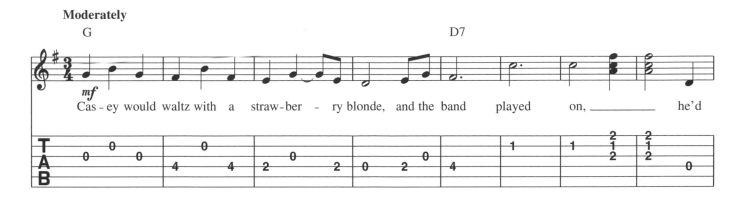

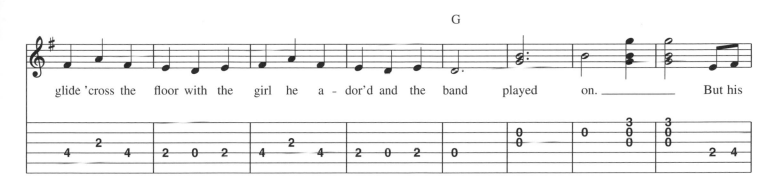

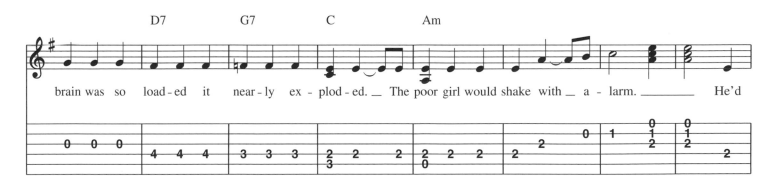

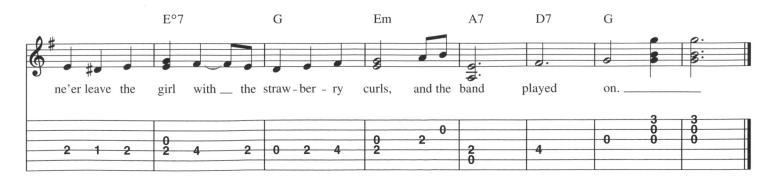

The Battle Cry of Freedom

Words and Music by George Frederick Root

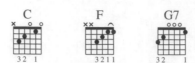

Strum Pattern: 3
Pick Pattern: 3

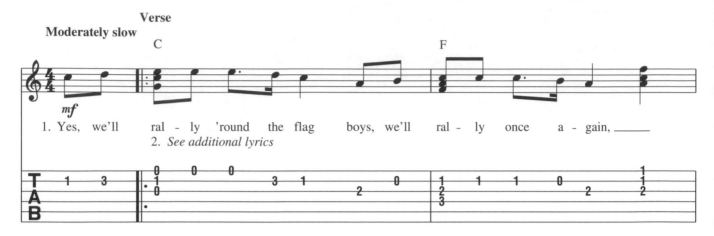

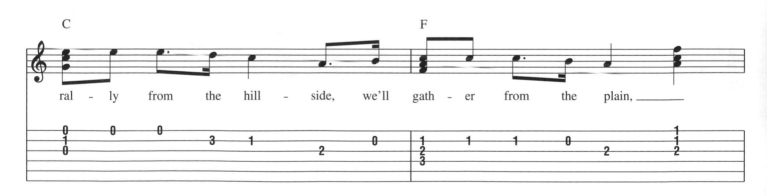

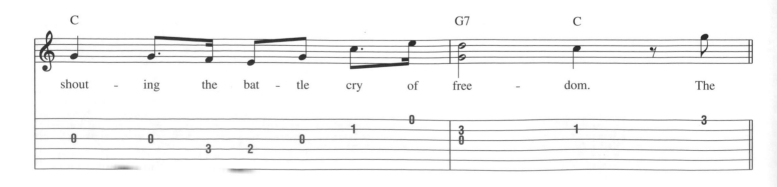

Chorus

Un - ion for - ev - er, hur - rah, boys, hur - rah!

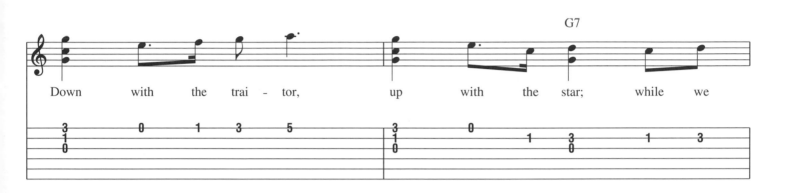

Down with the trai - tor, up with the star; while we

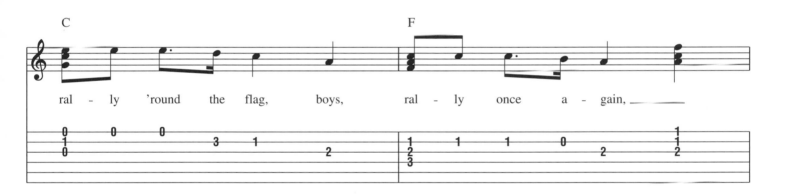

ral - ly 'round the flag, boys, ral - ly once a - gain, ___

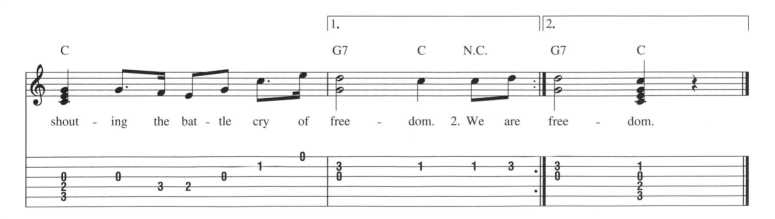

shout - ing the bat - tle cry of free - dom. 2. We are free - dom.

Additional Lyrics

2. We are springing to the call
   Of our brothers gone before,
   Shouting the battle cry of freedom.
   And we'll fill the vacant ranks
   With a million free men more,
   Shouting the battle cry of freedom.

Battle Hymn of the Republic

Words by Julia Ward Howe
Music by William Steffe

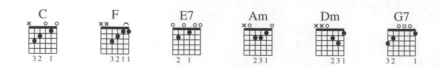

Strum Pattern: 4
Pick Pattern: 3

Verse

Moderately

1. Mine eyes have seen the glo – ry of the com – ing of the Lord; He is
2. *See additional lyrics*

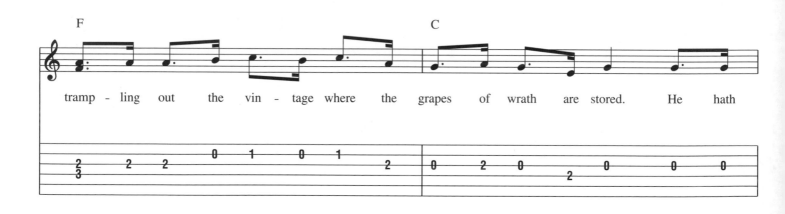

tramp – ling out the vin – tage where the grapes of wrath are stored. He hath

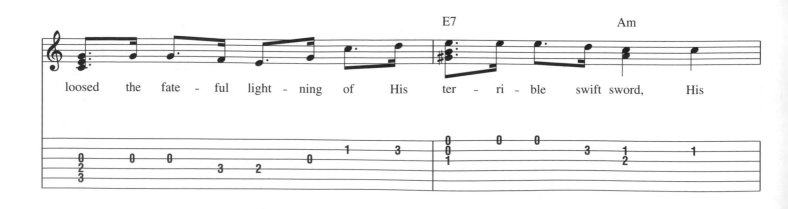

loosed the fate – ful light – ning of His ter – ri – ble swift sword, His

Additional Lyrics

2. I have seen Him in the watchfires
Of a hundred circling camps,
They have builded Him an altar
In the evening dews and damps;
I can read His righteous sentence
By the dim and flaring lamps,
His day is marching on.

Beale Street Blues

Words and Music by W.C. Handy

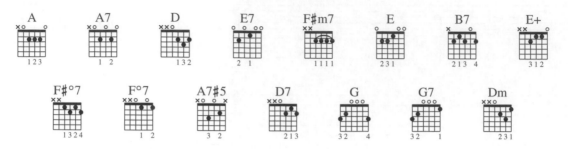

Strum Pattern: 3, 4
Pick Pattern: 1, 3

Intro
Slowly

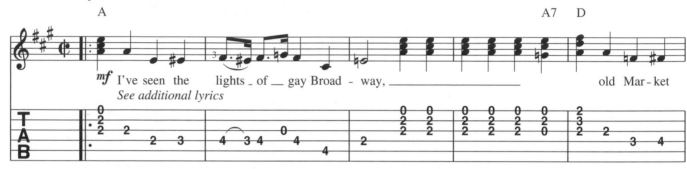

I've seen the lights _ of _ gay Broad - way, _____ old Mar-ket
See additional lyrics

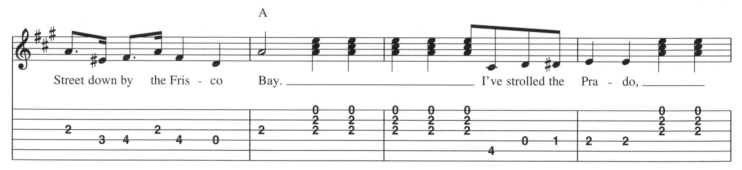

Street down by the Fris - co Bay. _____ I've strolled the Pra - do, _____

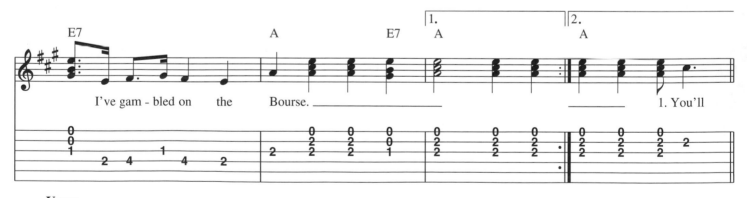

I've gam - bled on the Bourse. _____ _____ 1. You'll

see pret - ty Browns _ in beau-ti-ful gowns._ You'll see tail - or mades and hand me downs. You'll
2., 3., 4. See additional lyrics

Additional Lyrics

Intro The seven wonders of the world I've seen,
And many are the places I have been.
Take my advice folks
And see Beale Street first.

2. You'll see Hog-Nose rest'rants and Chitlin' Cafes.
You'll see jugs that tell of bygone days,
And places, once places, now just a sham.
You'll see Golden Balls enough to pave the New Jerusalem.

3. You'll see men who rank with the first in the nation,
Who come to Beale for inspiration.
Politicians call you a dub,
Unless you've been initiated in the Rickriters Club.

4. If Beale Street could talk, if Beale Street could talk
Married men would have to take their beds and walk,
Except one or two, who never drank booze
And the blind man on the corner who sings the Beale Street Blues.

Outro Go'n' to the river, maybe, bye and bye.
Go'n' to the river, and there's a reason why.
Because the river's wet
And Beale Streets done gone dry.

Beautiful Brown Eyes

Traditional

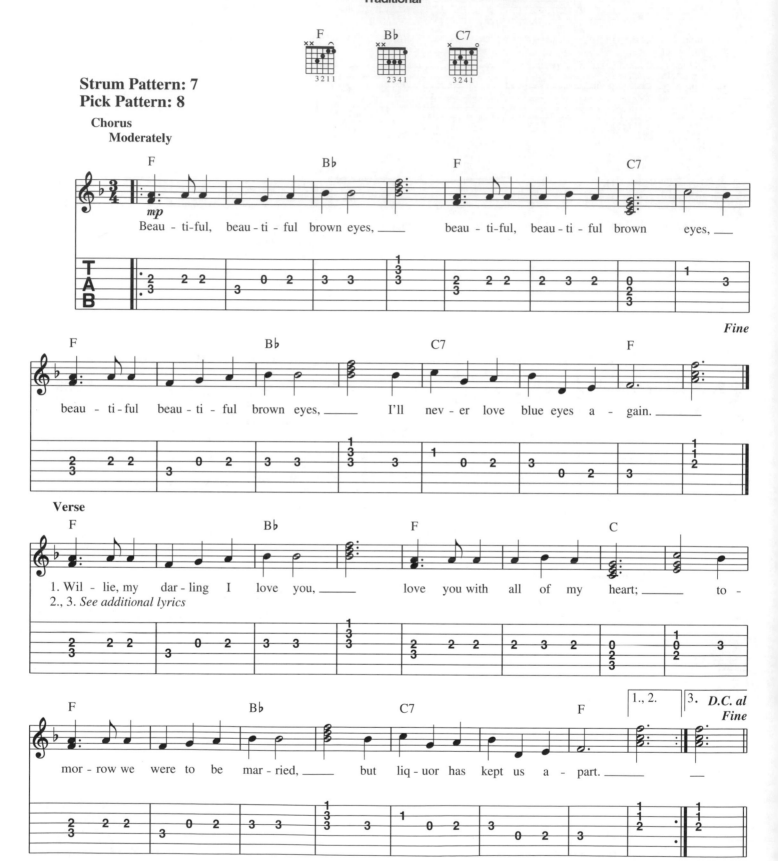

Strum Pattern: 7
Pick Pattern: 8

Chorus
Moderately

Beau - ti - ful, beau - ti - ful brown eyes, _____ beau - ti - ful, beau - ti - ful brown eyes, _____

Fine

beau - ti - ful beau - ti - ful brown eyes, _____ I'll nev - er love blue eyes a - gain. _____

Verse

1. Wil - lie, my dar - ling I love you, _____ love you with all of my heart; _____ to -
2., 3. *See additional lyrics*

mor - row we were to be mar - ried, _____ but liq - uor has kept us a - part. _____

D.C. al Fine

Additional Lyrics

2. I staggered into the barroom,
   I fell down on the floor,
   And the very last words that I uttered,
   "I'll never get drunk anymore."

3. Seven long years I've been married,
   I wish I was single again,
   A woman don't know half her troubles
   Until she has married a man.

The Bells of St. Mary's

Words by Douglas Furber
Music by A. Emmett Adams

Strum Pattern: 3, 4
Pick Pattern: 3

The Big Rock Candy Mountain

Words, Music and Arrangement by Harry K. McClintock

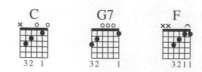

Strum Pattern: 3
Pick Pattern: 4

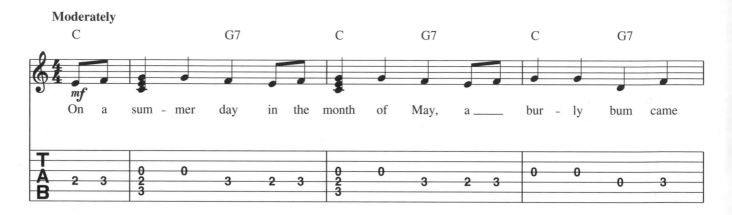

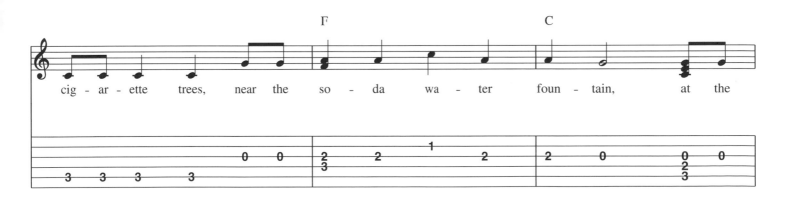

Bill Bailey, Won't You Please Come Home

Words and Music by Hughie Cannon

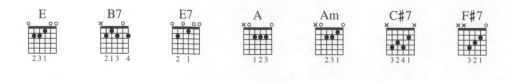

Strum Pattern: 4
Pick Pattern: 3

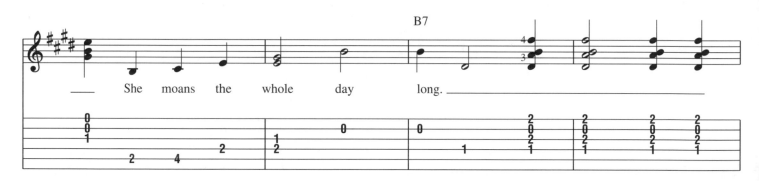

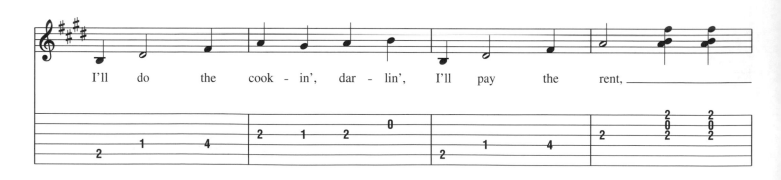

Re - mem - ber that rain - y eve - ning I drove you out _____ with

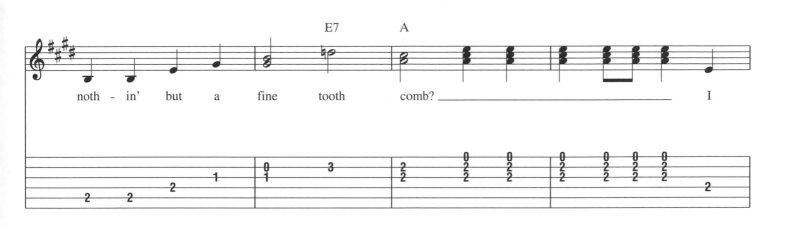

noth - in' but a fine tooth comb? _____ I

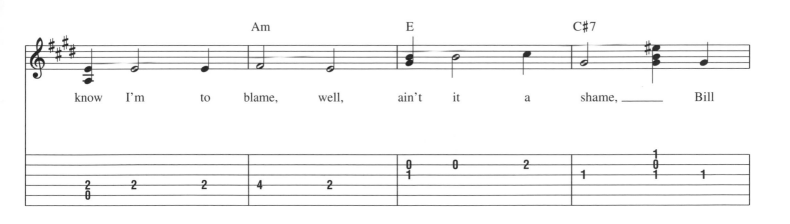

know I'm to blame, well, ain't it a shame, _____ Bill

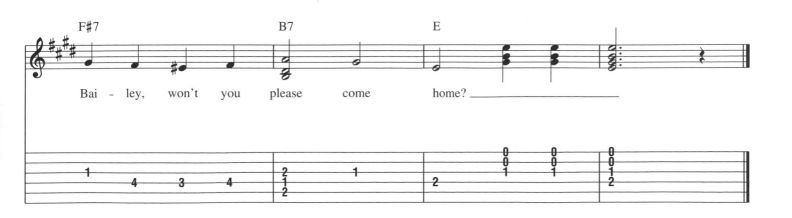

Bai - ley, won't you please come home? _____

Billboard March

By John N. Klohr

Strum Pattern: 2
Pick Pattern: 1

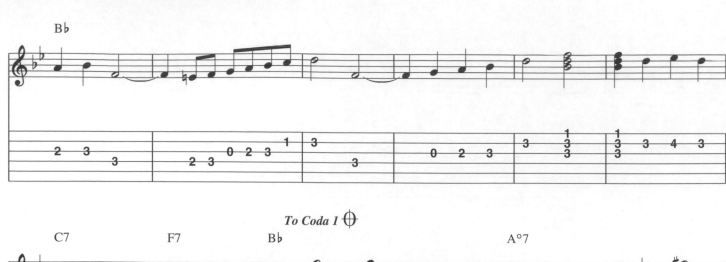

To Coda 1 ⊕

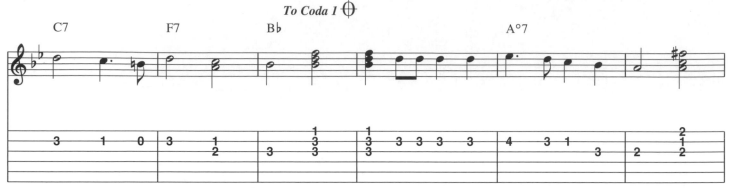

D.S. al Coda 1

⊕ **Coda 1**

D.S.S. al Coda 2
(take 2nd ending)

⊕ **Coda 2**

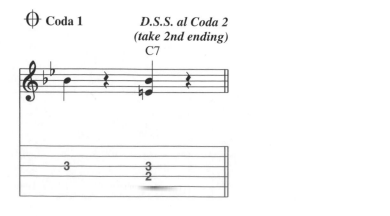
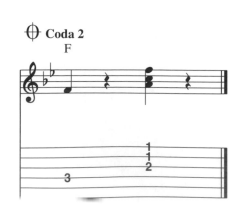

Birthday Song

Traditional

Strum Pattern: 7, 8
Pick Pattern: 8

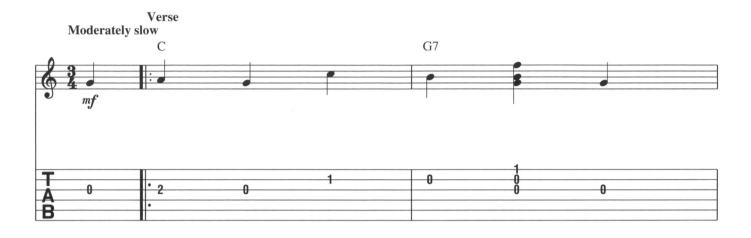

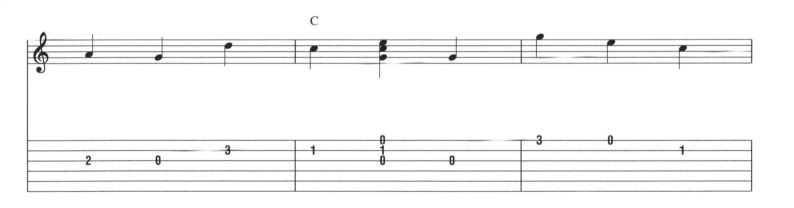

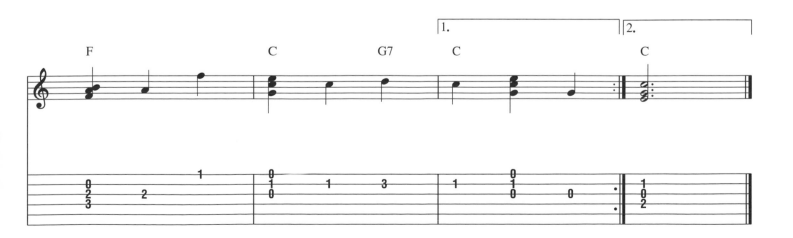

Blue Danube Waltz

Music by Johann Strauss

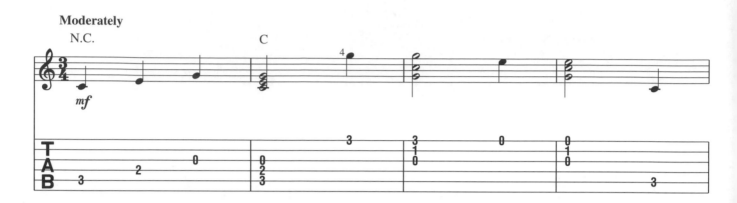

Strum Pattern: 7, 8
Pick Pattern: 8

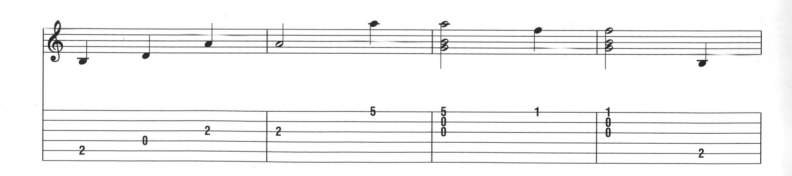

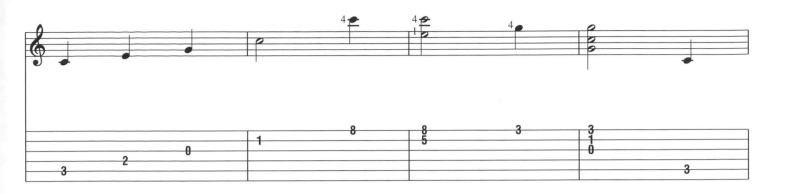

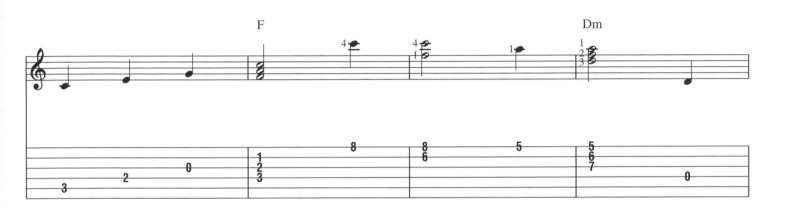

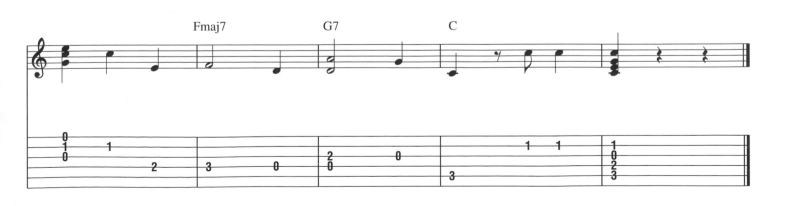

The Bluetail Fly
(Jimmy Crack Corn)

Words and Music by Daniel Decatur Emmett

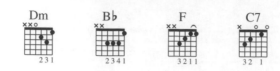

Strum Pattern: 10
Pick Pattern: 10

Additional Lyrics

2. And when he'd ride in the afternoon,
   I'd follow after with a hickory broom;
   The pony being very shy,
   When bitten by the Bluetail Fly!

3. One day while riding round the farm,
   The flies so numerous they did swarm;
   One changed to bite him on the thigh,
   The devil take the Bluetail Fly!

4. The pony run, he jump, he kick,
   He threw my Master in the ditch;
   He died and the jury wondered why,
   The verdict was the Bluetail Fly!

5. They laid him under a 'simmon tree,
   His epitaph is there to see:
   "Beneath this stone Jim forced to lie,
   A victim of the Bluetail Fly!"

Boola! Boola!

By A.M. Hirsch

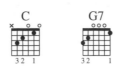

Strum Pattern: 4
Pick Pattern: 3

Moderately

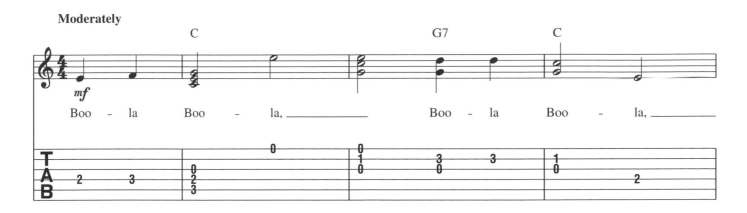

Boo - la Boo - la, _____ Boo - la Boo - la, _____

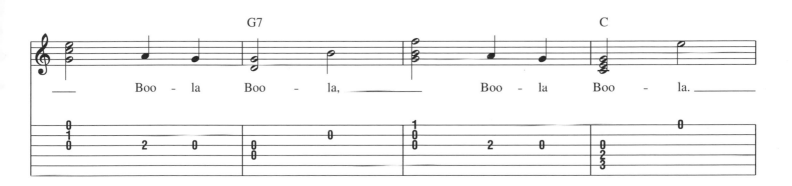

_____ Boo - la Boo - la, _____ Boo - la Boo - la. _____

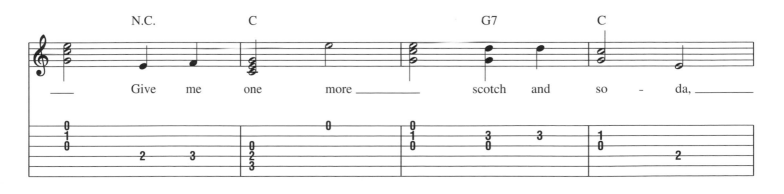

_____ Give me one more _____ scotch and so - da, _____

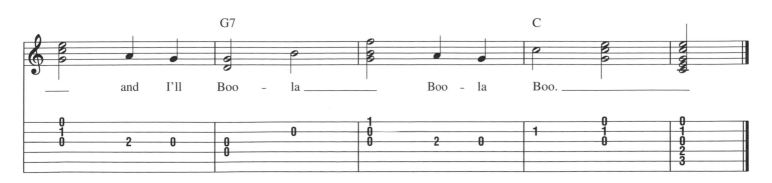

_____ and I'll Boo - la _____ Boo - la Boo.

The Bowery

Words by Charles H. Hoyt
Music by Percy Gaunt

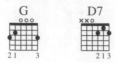

Strum Pattern: 7, 8
Pick Pattern: 7, 8

Moderately slow

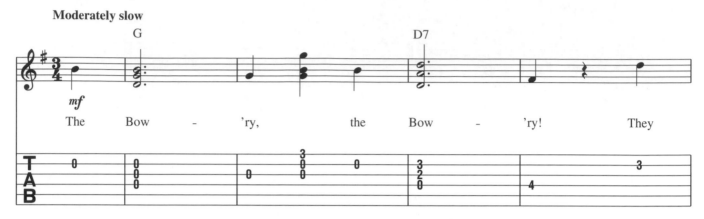

mf

The Bow - 'ry, the Bow - 'ry! They

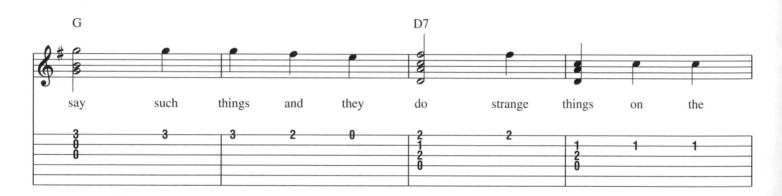

say such things and they do strange things on the

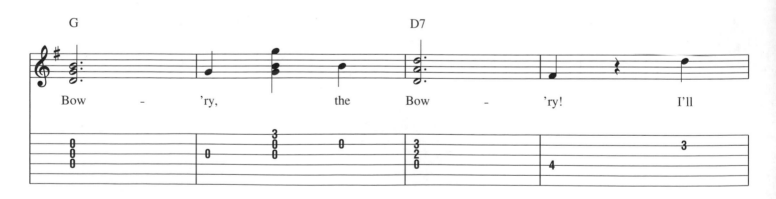

Bow - 'ry, the Bow - 'ry! I'll

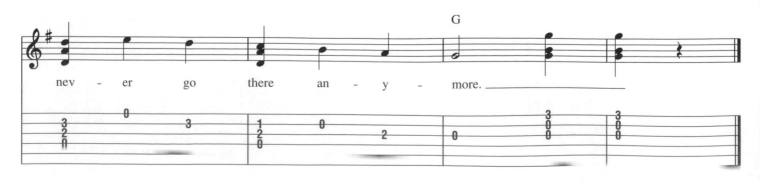

nev - er go there an - y - more.

Bridal Chorus
from LOHENGRIN
By Richard Wagner

Strum Pattern: 4
Pick Pattern: 3

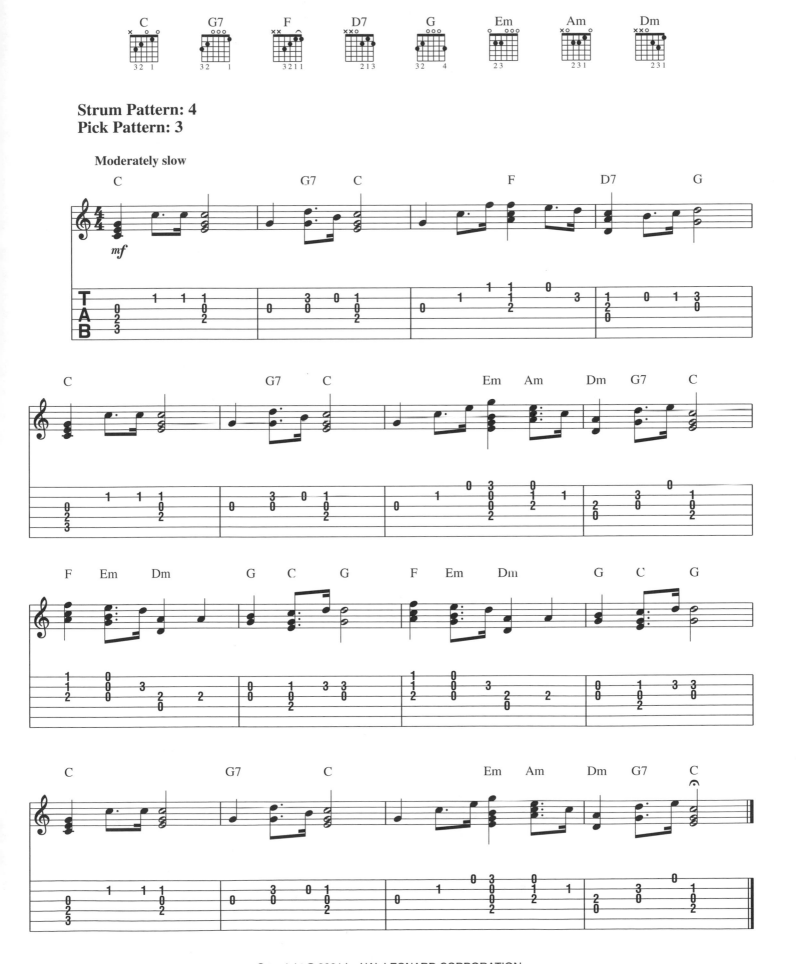

Buffalo Gals
(Won't You Come Out Tonight?)

Words and Music by Cool White (John Hodges)

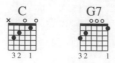

Strum Pattern: 5
Pick Pattern: 1

Verse
Lively

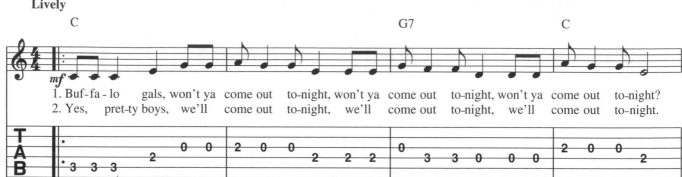

1. Buf-fa-lo gals, won't ya come out to-night, won't ya come out to-night, won't ya come out to-night?
2. Yes, pret-ty boys, we'll come out to-night, we'll come out to-night, we'll come out to-night.

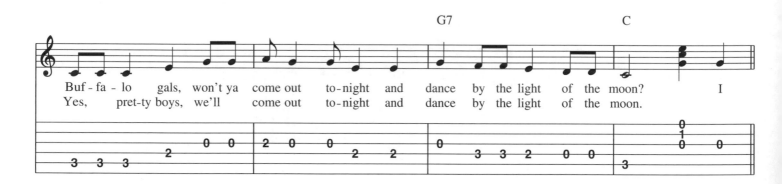

Buf-fa-lo gals, won't ya come out to-night and dance by the light of the moon? I
Yes, pret-ty boys, we'll come out to-night and dance by the light of the moon.

Chorus

danced with a gal with a hole in her stock-ing and her heel kept a-rock-in' and her toe kept a-knock-in', I

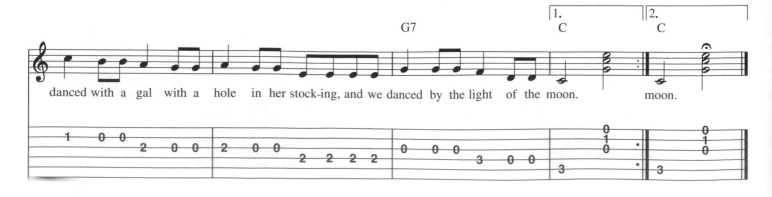

danced with a gal with a hole in her stock-ing, and we danced by the light of the moon.   moon.

Bury Me Not on the Lone Prairie

Words based on the poem "The Ocean Burial" by Rev. Edwin H. Chapin
Music by Ossian N. Dodge

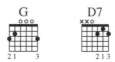

Strum Pattern: 3
Pick Pattern: 1

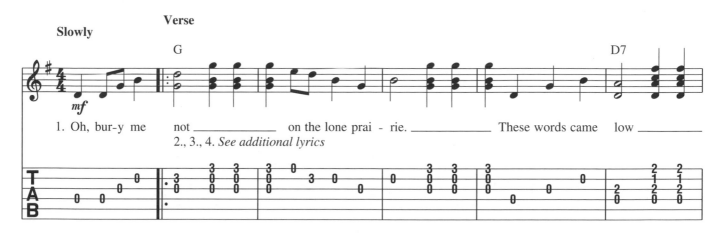

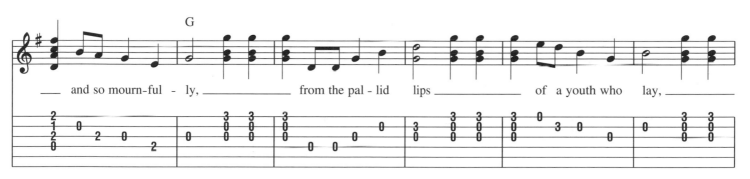

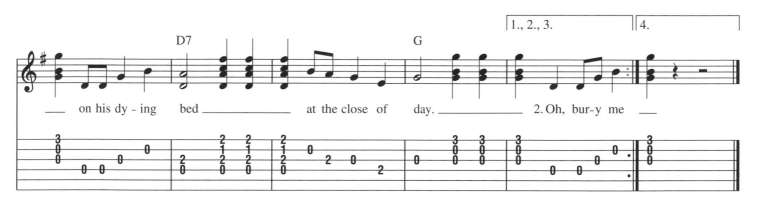

Additional Lyrics

2. Oh, bury me not on the lone prairie.
   Where the coyotes howl and the wind blows free;
   In a narrow grave just six by three.
   Oh, bury me not on the lone prairie.

3. "Oh, bury me not," and this voice failed there.
   But we took no heed of his dying prayer;
   In a narrow grave just six by three.
   We buried him there on the lone prairie.

4. Yes, we buried him there on the lone prairie.
   Where the owl all night hoots mournfully;
   And the blizzard beats and the wind blows free,
   O'er his lonely grave on the lone prairie.

By the Beautiful Sea

Words by Harold R. Atteridge
Music by Harry Carroll

Strum Pattern: 3
Pick Pattern: 6

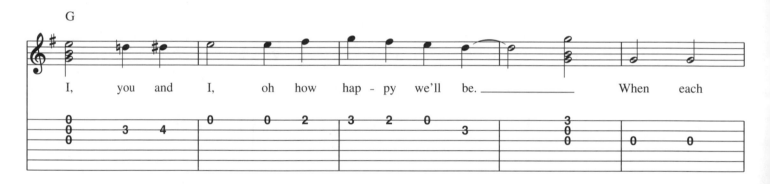

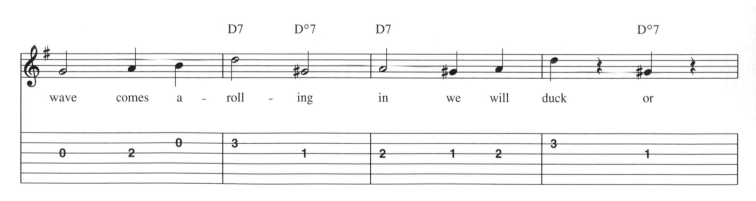

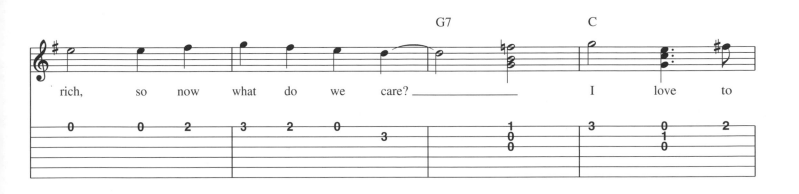

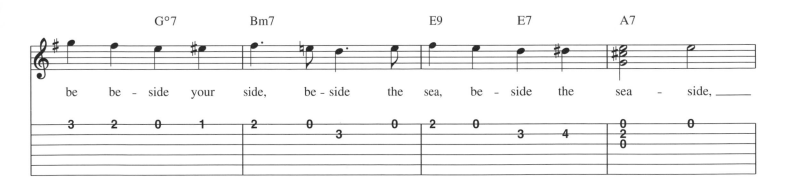

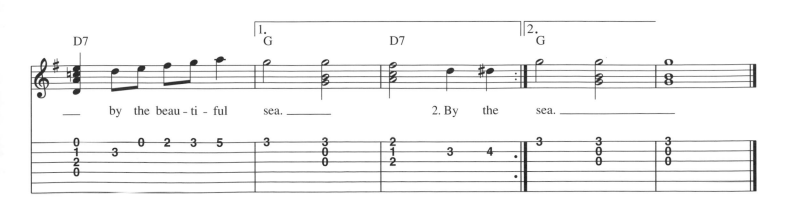

By the Light of the Silvery Moon

Lyric by Ed Madden
Music by Gus Edwards

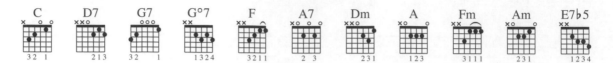

Strum Pattern: 3
Pick Pattern: 1

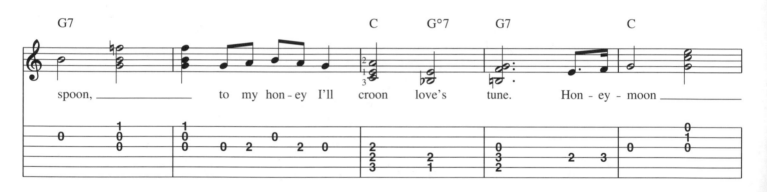

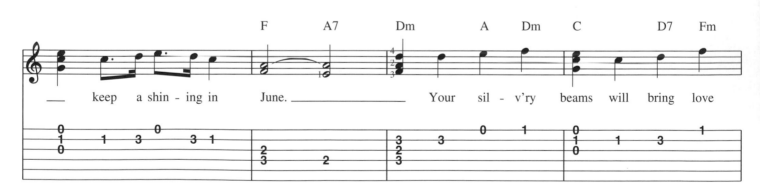

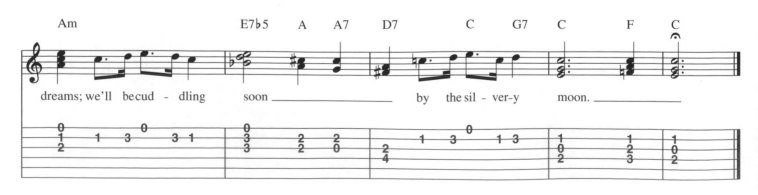

Canon in D

Music by Johann Pachelbel

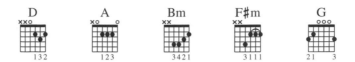

Strum Pattern: 1
Pick Pattern: 2

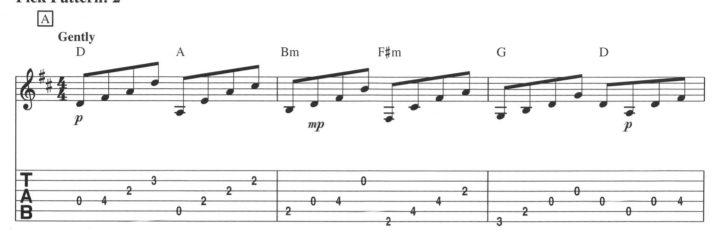

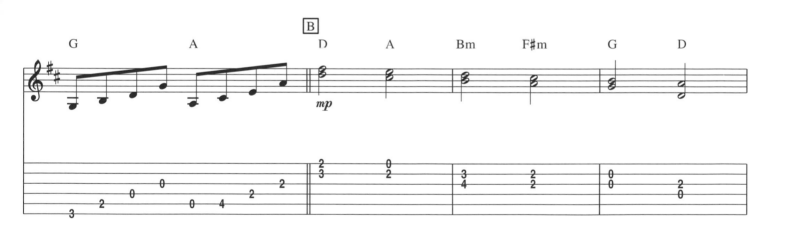

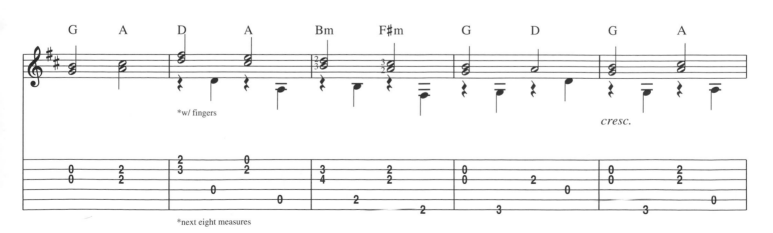

*w/ fingers

*next eight measures

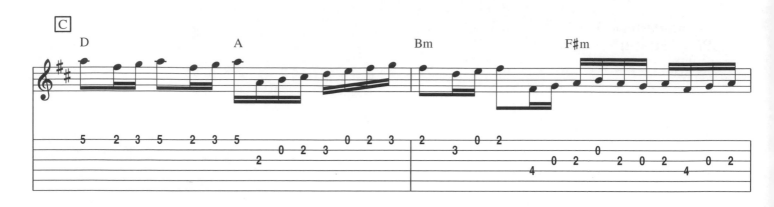

C

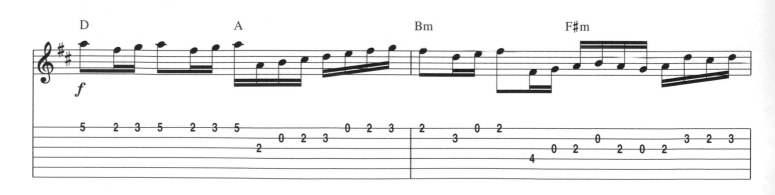

The Caissons Go Rolling Along

Words and Music by Edmund L. Gruber

Strum Pattern: 4
Pick Pattern: 3

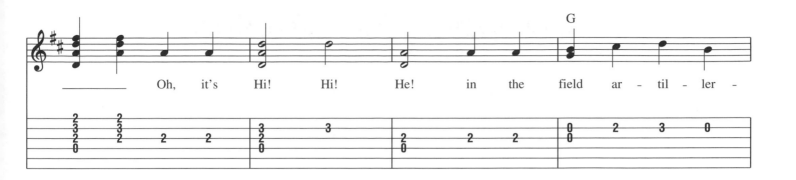

Oh, it's Hi! Hi! He! in the field ar-til-ler-

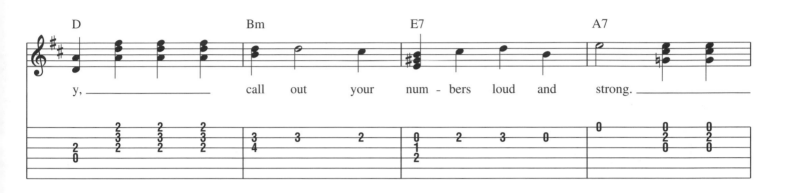

y, _____ call out your num-bers loud and strong. _____

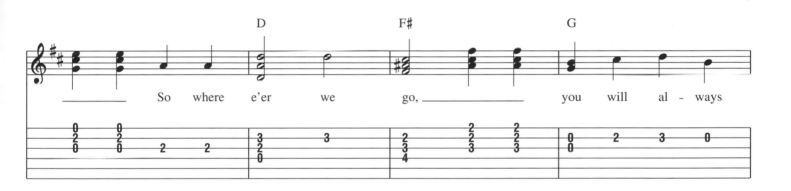

_____ So where e'er we go, _____ you will al-ways

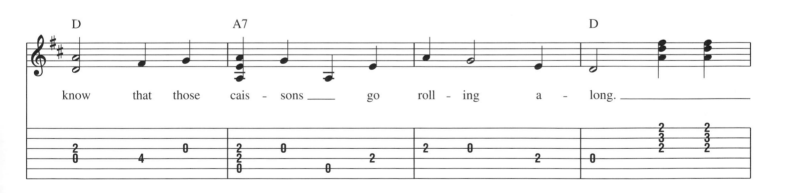

know that those cais-sons _____ go roll-ing a-long. _____

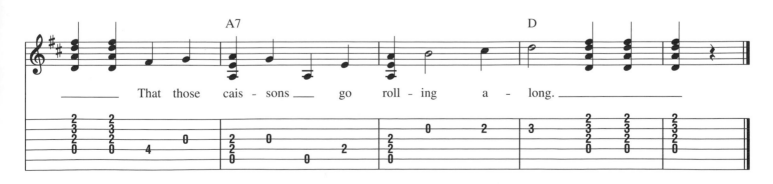

_____ That those cais-sons _____ go roll-ing a-long. _____

Campbells Are Coming

Traditional

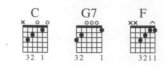

Strum Pattern: 8
Pick Pattern: 8

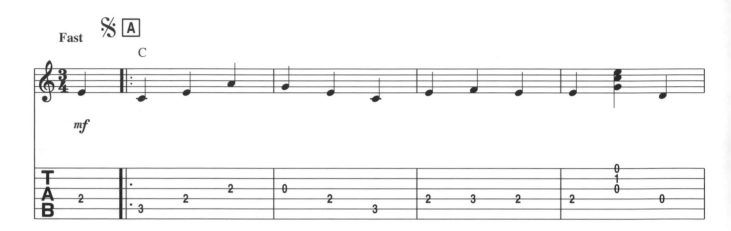

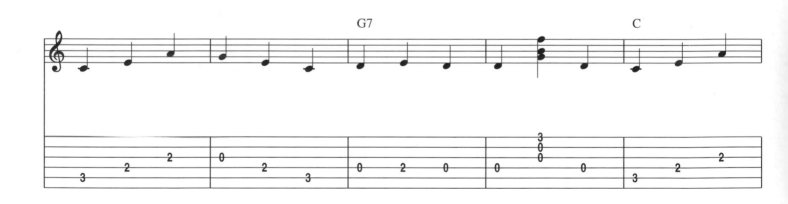

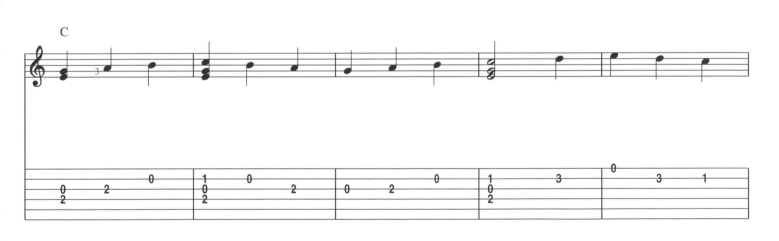

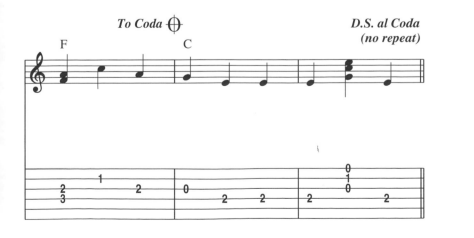

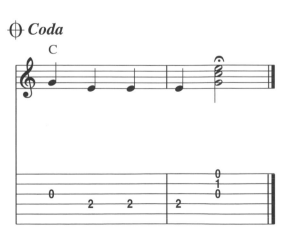

Can Can Polka

Traditional

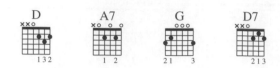

Strum Pattern: 4
Pick Pattern: 3

A

Moderately

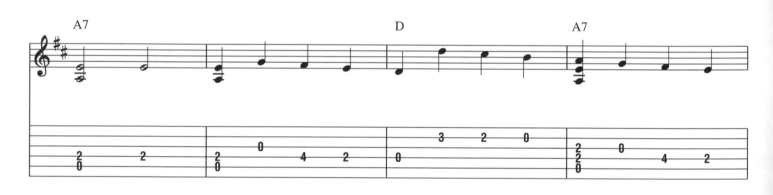

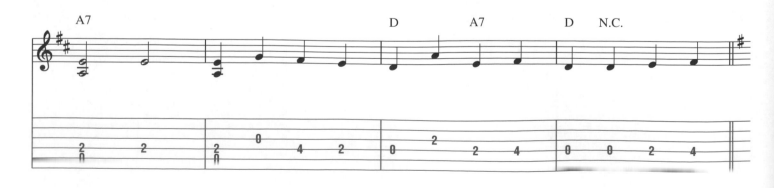

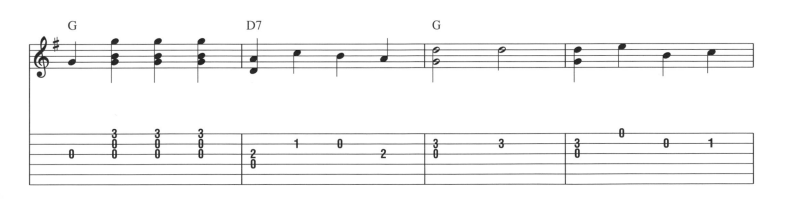

Careless Love

Anonymous

Additional Lyrics

2. I cried last night and the night before
Tonight I'll cry, then cry no more.

Carnival of Venice

Traditional

Strum Pattern: 7, 8
Pick Pattern: 8

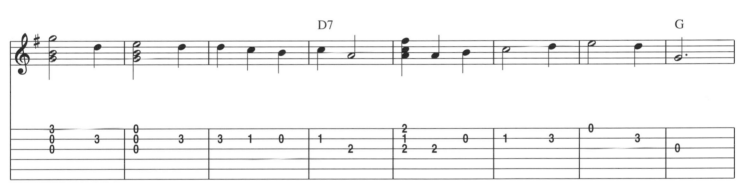

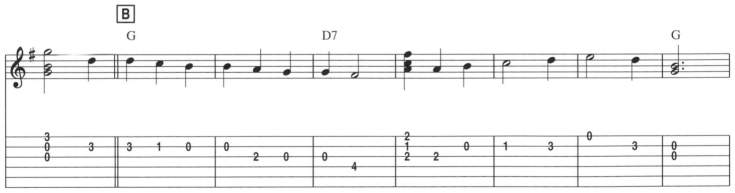

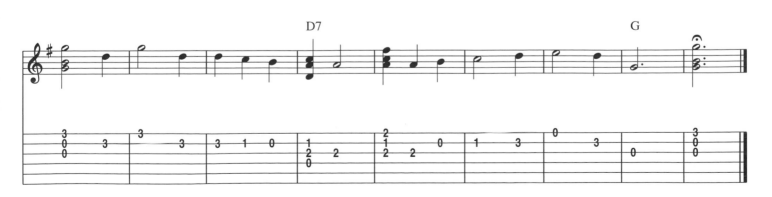

Carolina in the Morning

Lyrics by Gus Kahn
Music by Walter Donaldson

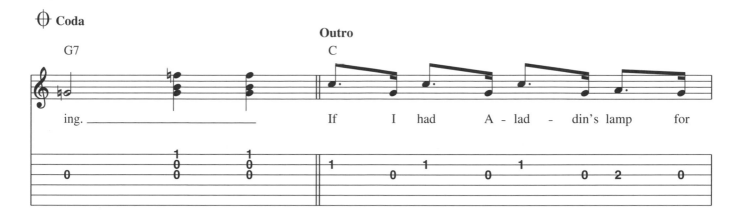

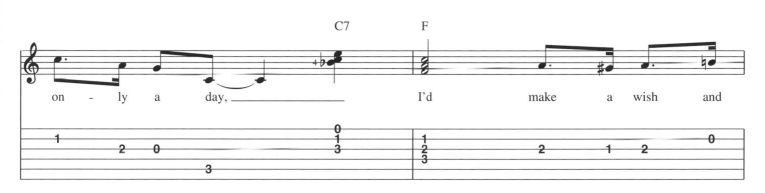

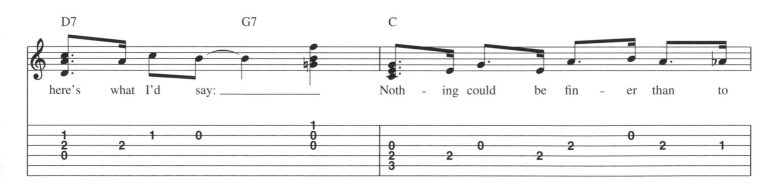

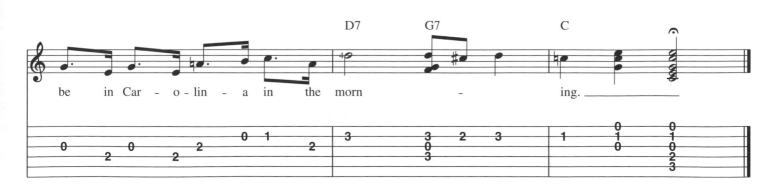

Chiapanecas

Traditional

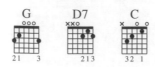

Strum Pattern: 8
Pick Pattern: 8

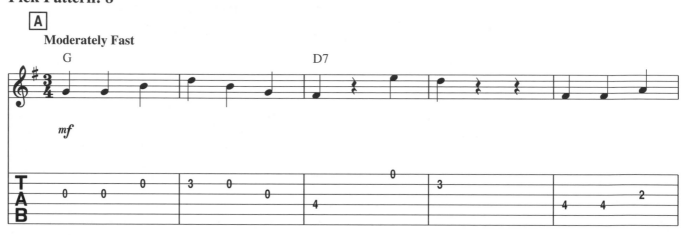

Chinatown, My Chinatown

Words by William Jerome
Music by Jean Schwartz

Strum Pattern: 10
Pick Pattern: 10

Verse
Moderately fast

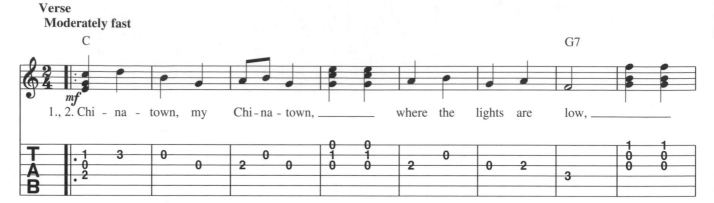

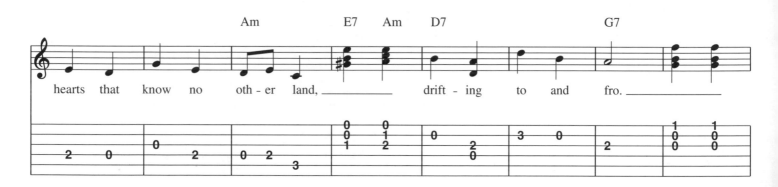

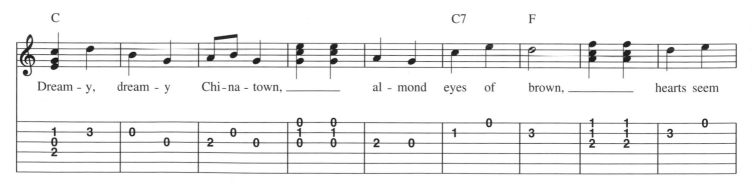

(Oh, My Darling) Clementine

Words and Music by Percy Montrose

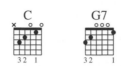

Strum Pattern: 9
Pick Pattern: 7

Verse

Moderately

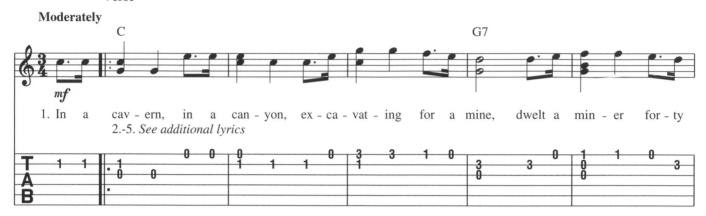

1. In a cav-ern, in a can-yon, ex-ca-vat-ing for a mine, dwelt a min-er for-ty
2.-5. *See additional lyrics*

Chorus

nin-er and his daugh-ter, Clem-en-tine. Oh, my dar-ling, oh, my dar-ling, oh my dar-ling Clem-en-

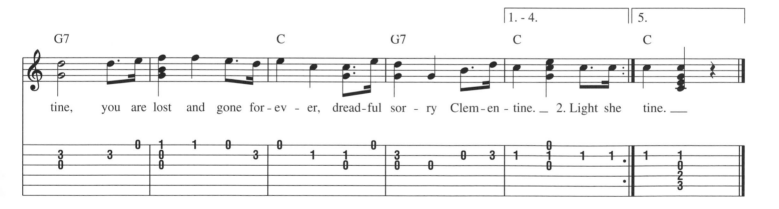

tine, you are lost and gone for-ev-er, dread-ful sor-ry Clem-en-tine. _ 2. Light she tine. _

Additional Lyrics

2. Light she was and like a fairy
   And her shoes were number nine,
   Herring boxes without topses
   Sandals were for Clementine.

3. Drove she ducklings to the water
   Ev'ry morning just at nine,
   Stubbed her toe upon a splinter
   Fell into the foaming brine.

4. Ruby lips above the water
   Blowing bubbles soft and fine,
   But alas I was no swimmer
   So I lost my Clementine.

5. There's a churchyard on the hillside
   Where the flowers grow and twine,
   There grow roses 'mongst the posies
   Fertilized by Clementine.

Church in the Wildwood

Words and Music by William S. Pitts

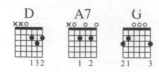

Strum Pattern: 3, 4
Pick Pattern: 1, 3

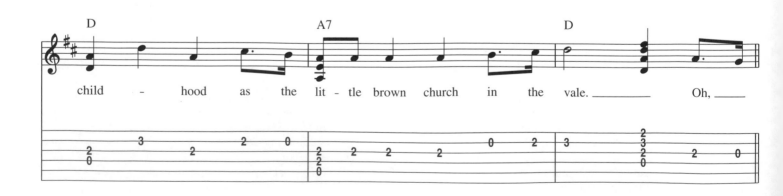

Chorus

come, come, come, come. Come to the church in the wild - wood, oh,

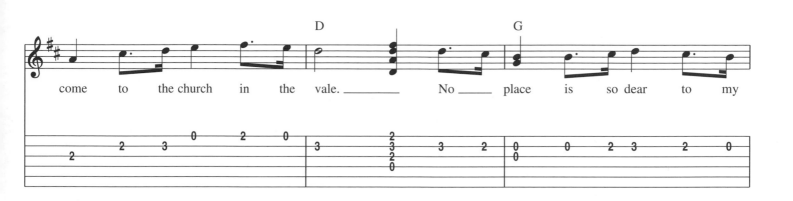

come to the church in the vale. _____ No _____ place is so dear to my

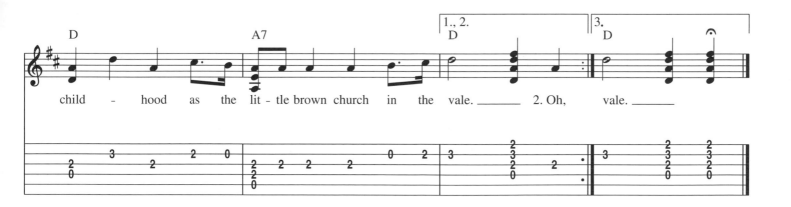

child - hood as the lit - tle brown church in the vale. _____ 2. Oh, vale. _____

Additional Lyrics

2. Oh, come to the church in the wildwood,
   To the trees where the wild flowers bloom,
   Where the parting hymn will be chanted;
   We will weep by the side of the tomb.

3. From the church in the valley by the wildwood,
   When day fades away into night,
   I would fain from this spot of my childhood;
   Winging way to the mansions of light.

Cielito Lindo
(My Pretty Darling)

By C. Fernandez

Strum Pattern: 7, 8
Pick Pattern: 8

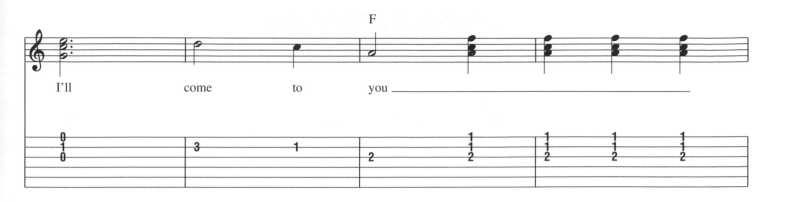

I'll come to you

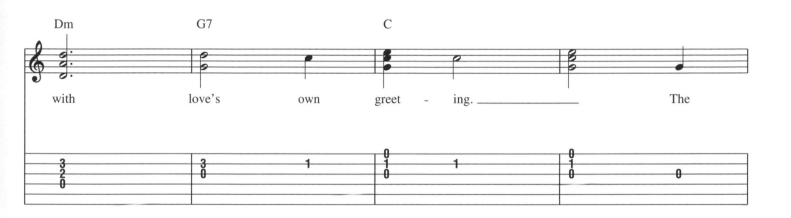

with love's own greet - ing. _____ The

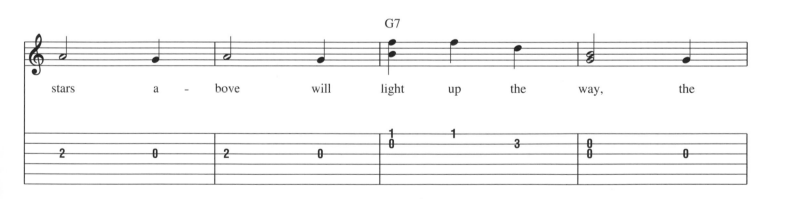

stars a - bove will light up the way, the

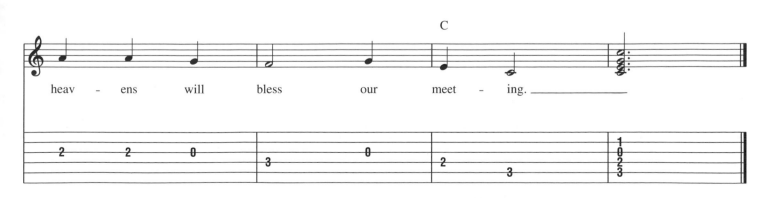

heav - ens will bless our meet - ing. _____

Clarinet Polka
Traditional

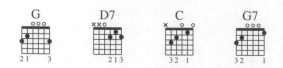

Strum Pattern: 4
Pick Pattern: 3

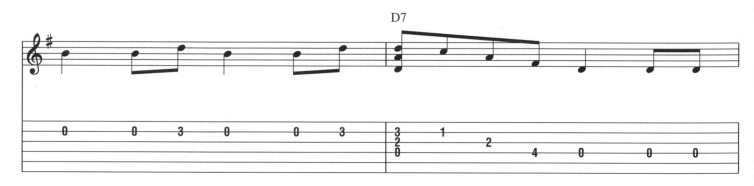

Cockles and Mussels
(Molly Malone)

Traditional Irish Folksong

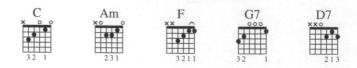

Strum Pattern: 7, 9
Pick Pattern: 9

Verse

Moderately

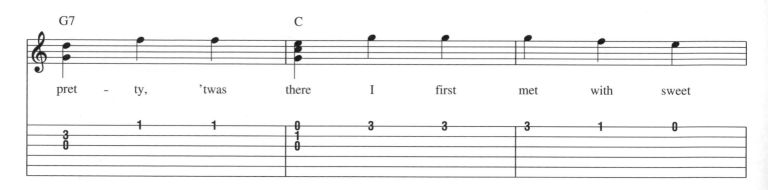

In Dub - lin cit - y where girls are so

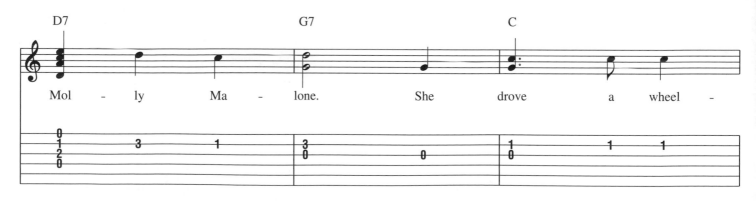

pret - ty, 'twas there I first met with sweet

Mol - ly Ma - lone. She drove a wheel -

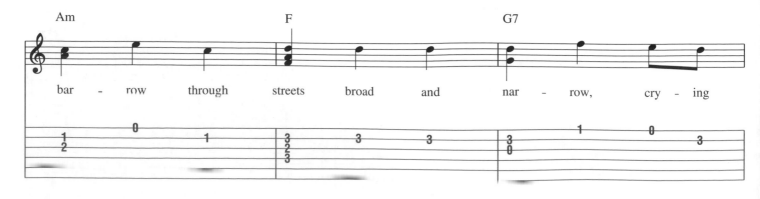

bar - row through streets broad and nar - row, cry - ing

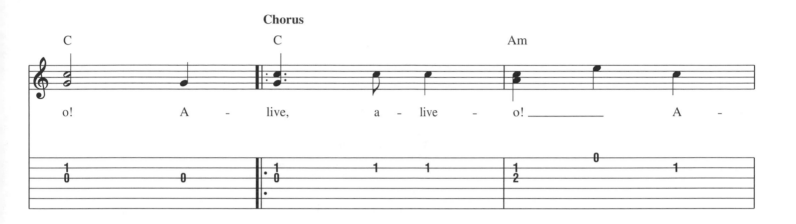

Chorus

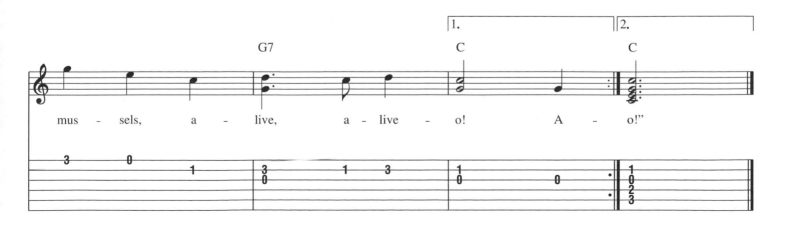

Columbia, The Gem of the Ocean
(The Red, White and Blue)

By David T. Shaw

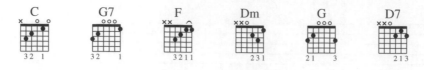

Strum Pattern: 4
Pick Pattern: 3

Moderately

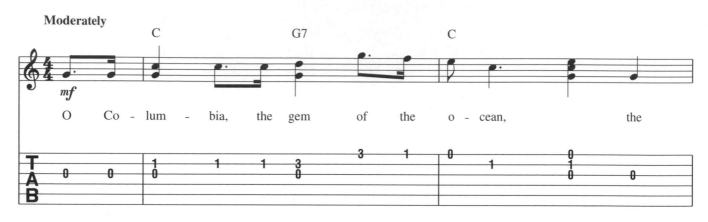

O Co - lum - bia, the gem of the o - cean, the

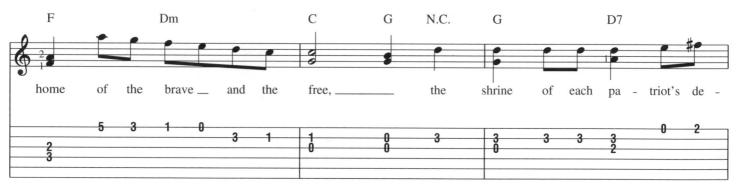

home of the brave ___ and the free, _____ the shrine of each pa - triot's de -

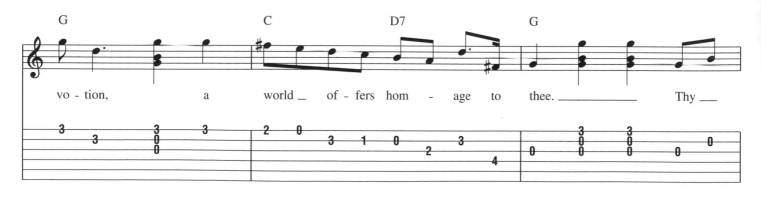

vo - tion, a world ___ of - fers hom - age to thee. _____ Thy ___

man - dates make he - roes as - sem - ble, when ___ Lib - er - ty's form ___ stands in

Come Back to Sorrento

Traditional

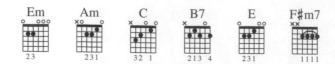

Strum Pattern: 7, 9
Pick Pattern: 8, 9

Intro
Moderately

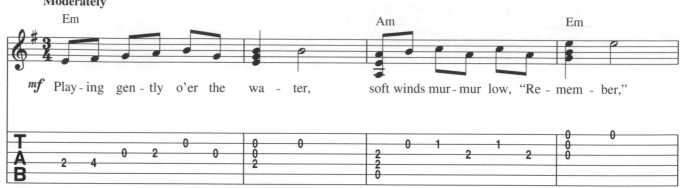

Play - ing gen - tly o'er the wa - ter, soft winds mur - mur low, "Re - mem - ber,"

and en - chant - ed, I lie dream - ing, sigh - ing, long - ing, dear for you. ___

Verse

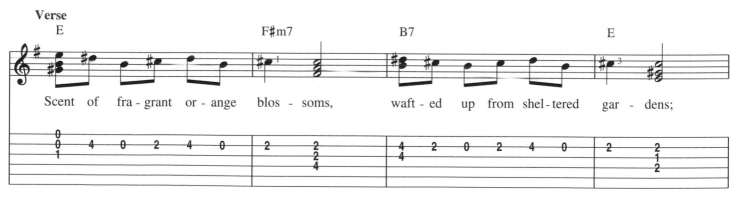

Scent of fra - grant or - ange blos - soms, waft - ed up from shel - tered gar - dens;

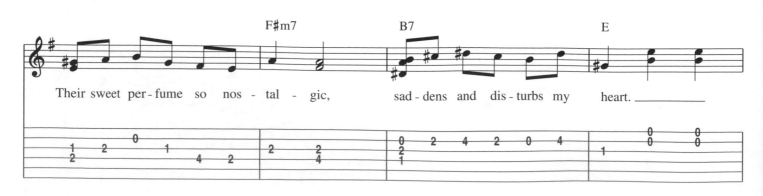

Their sweet per - fume so nos - tal - gic, sad - dens and dis - turbs my heart. ___

Outro

Italian Lyrics

Guardail mare comé bello, spira tauto sentimento,
Come tuo soave accento cheme desto, fa sognar.
Senti come lieve sale dei giardini odor daranci;
Un profumo non v'haeguale per chi palpita d'a mor!
E tu dici "Io parto addio!"
T'allontani dal mio core; questa terra dell' a more
Hai la forza di lasciar?
Ma non mi fugir, non darmi piu' tormento,
Torna a Surriento, non farmi morir!

Comin' Through the Rye

Traditional

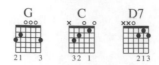

Strum Pattern: 9
Pick Pattern: 8, 9

Verse
Stately

1. If a bod - y meet a bod - y com - in' through the Rye. _____
2. *See Additional Lyrics*

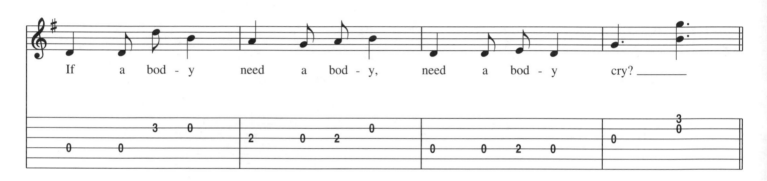

If a bod - y need a bod - y, need a bod - y cry? _____

Chorus

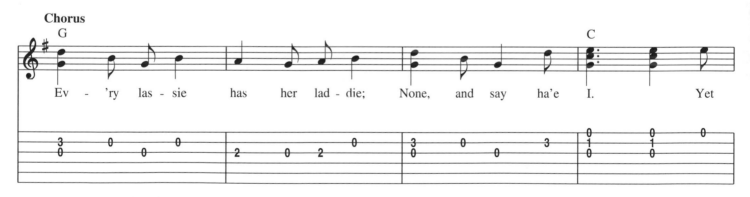

Ev - 'ry las - sie has her lad - die; None, and say ha'e I. Yet

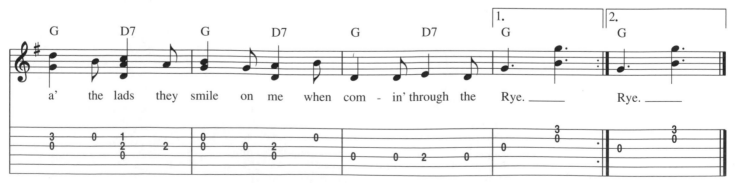

a' the lads they smile on me when com - in' through the Rye. _____ Rye. _____

Additional Lyrics

2. If a body meet a body comin' frae the town.
If a body greet a body, need a body frown?

Cripple Creek

American Fiddle Tune

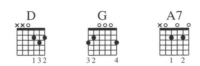

Strum Pattern: 3
Pick Pattern: 1

Verse
Fast

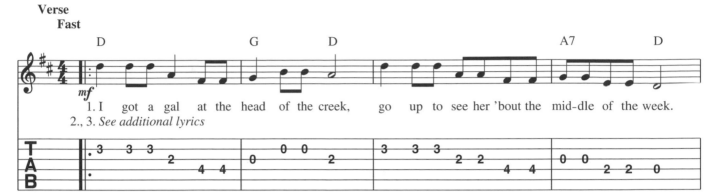

1. I got a gal at the head of the creek, go up to see her 'bout the mid-dle of the week.
2., 3. *See additional lyrics*

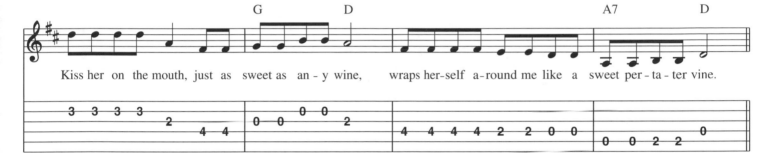

Kiss her on the mouth, just as sweet as an - y wine, wraps her-self a-round me like a sweet per - ta - ter vine.

Chorus

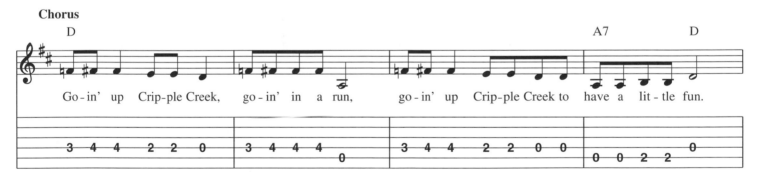

Go-in' up Crip-ple Creek, go - in' in a run, go - in' up Crip-ple Creek to have a lit - tle fun.

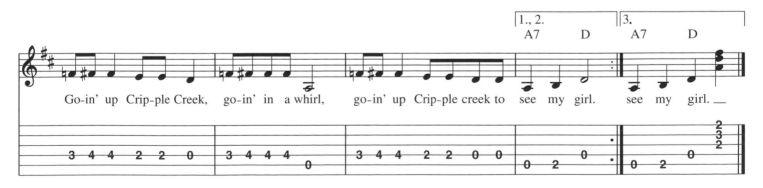

Go-in' up Crip-ple Creek, go-in' in a whirl, go-in' up Crip-ple creek to see my girl. see my girl. __

Additional Lyrics

2. Girls on the Cripple Creek 'bout half grown,
   Jump on a boy like a dog on a bone.
   Roll my britches up to my knees,
   I'll wade old Cripple Creek when I please.

3. Cripple Creek's wide and Cripple Creek's deep,
   I'll wade old Cripple Creek afore I sleep,
   Roads are rocky and the hillside's muddy,
   And I'm so drunk that I can't stand study.

Danny Boy (Londonderry Air)

Words by Frederick Edward Weatherly
Traditional Irish Folk Melody

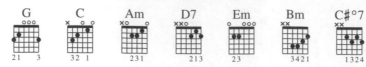

Strum Pattern: 4
Pick Pattern: 4

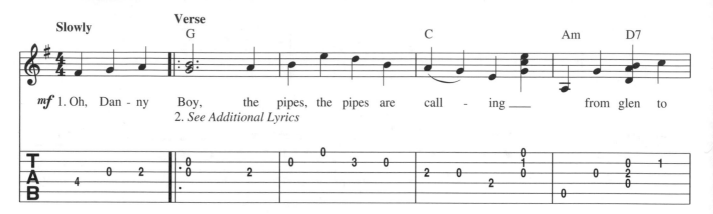

1. Oh, Dan-ny Boy, the pipes, the pipes are call-ing ___ from glen to
2. *See Additional Lyrics*

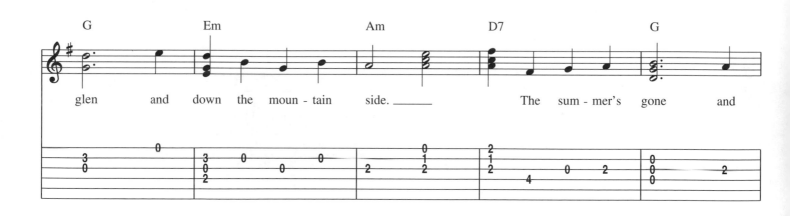

glen and down the moun-tain side. ___ The sum-mer's gone and

all the ros-es fall-ing. ___ 'Tis you, 'tis you must go and I must

Additional Lyrics

2. And when ye come and all the flowers are dying,
   If I am dead, and dead I well may be,
   You'll come and find the place where I am lying,
   And kneel and say an Ave there for me.

Chorus And I shall hear, tho' soft you tread above me.
   And all my grave will warmer, sweeter be.
   If you will bend and tell me that you love me
   Then I shall sleep in peace until you come to me.

Dark Eyes

Traditional

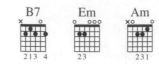

Strum Pattern: 7
Pick Pattern: 8

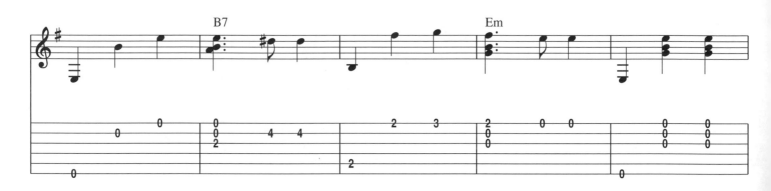

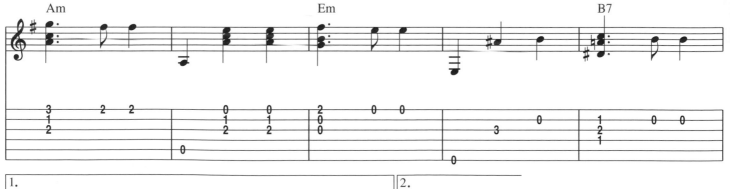

Down in the Valley

Traditional American Folksong

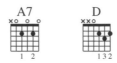

Strum Pattern: 7
Pick Pattern: 9

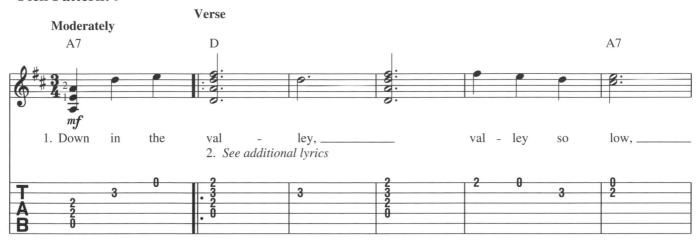

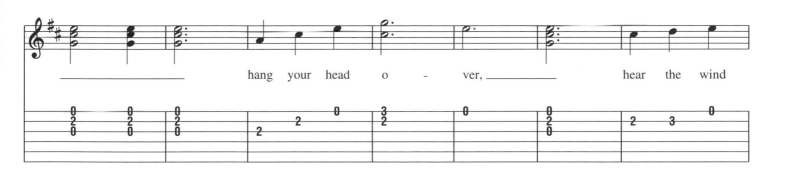

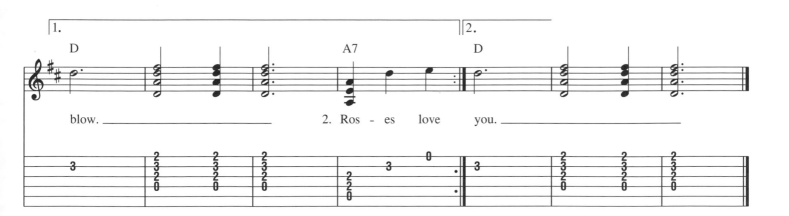

Additional Lyrics

2. Roses love sunshine,
   Violets love dew,
   Angels in heaven
   Know I love you.

(I Wish I Was In) Dixie

Words and Music by Daniel Decatur Emmett

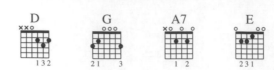

Strum Pattern: 3
Pick Pattern: 4

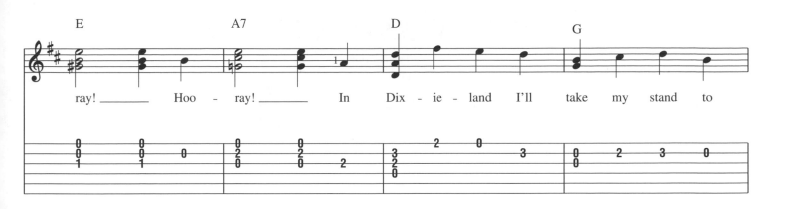

ray! _____ Hoo - ray! _____ In Dix - ie - land I'll take my stand to

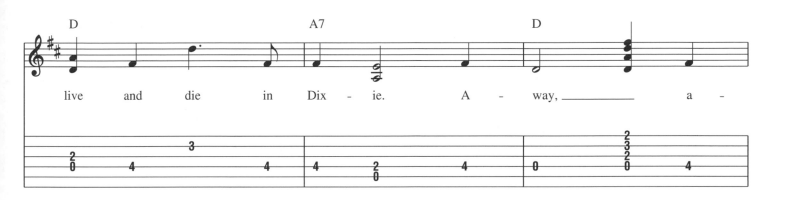

live and die in Dix - ie. A - way, _____ a -

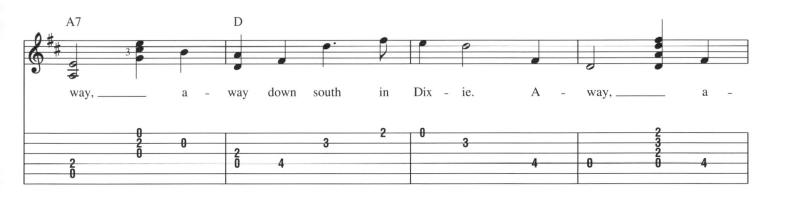

way, _____ a - way down south in Dix - ie. A - way, _____ a -

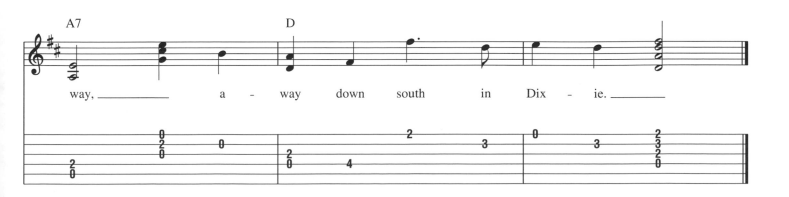

way, _____ a - way down south in Dix - ie. _____

Additional Lyrics

2. In Dixieland where I was born,
   In early on one frosty mornin'.
   Look away! Look away!
   Look away! Dixieland.

Do Lord

Traditional

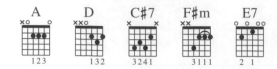

Strum Pattern: 3, 4
Pick Pattern: 1, 3

Verse
Joyfully

1. I've got a home in glo - ry land that out - shines the sun, _____
2. *See Additional Lyrics*

I've got a home in glo - ry land that out - shines the sun, _____

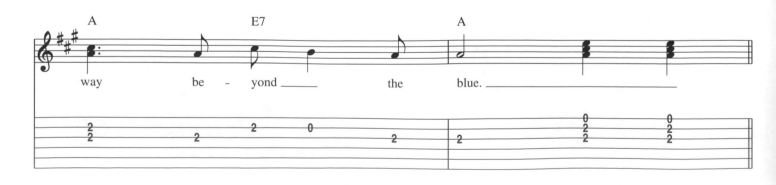

way be - yond _____ the blue. _____

Chorus

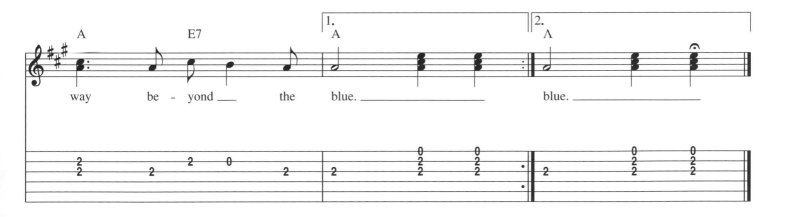

Additional Lyrics

2. I took Jesus as my Savior; you take Him, too.
   I took Jesus as my Savior; you take Him, too.
   I took Jesus as my Savior; you take Him, too.
   While He's calling you.

Down by the Old Mill Stream

Words and Music by Tell Taylor

Strum Pattern: 8
Pick Pattern: 8

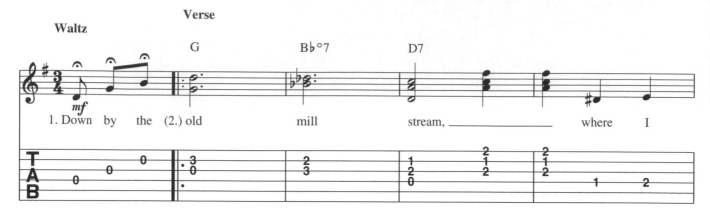

1. Down by the (2.) old mill stream, _____ where I

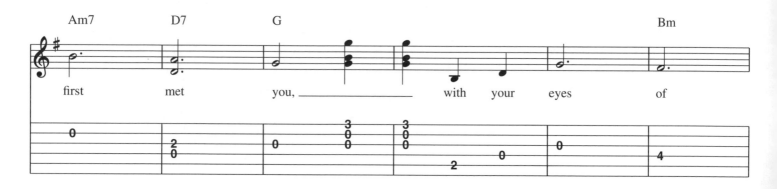

first met you, _____ with your eyes of

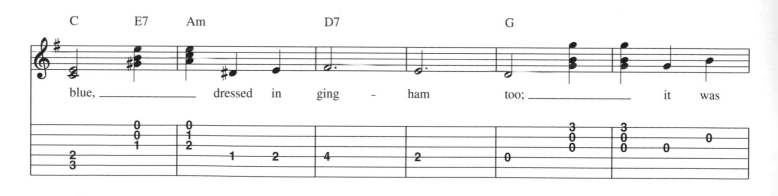

blue, _____ dressed in ging - ham too; _____ it was

there I knew _____ that you loved me

true. _____ You were six - teen, _____ my vil - lage queen, _____ by the

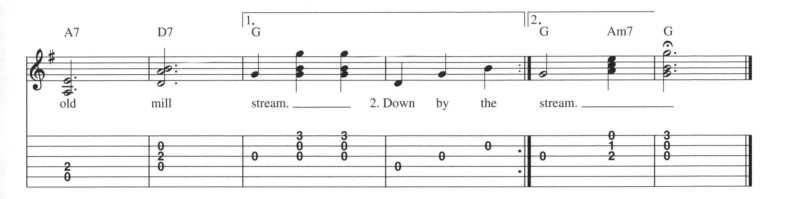

old   mill   stream. _____ 2. Down   by   the   stream. _____

Down by the Riverside

African American Spiritual

Strum Pattern: 3
Pick Pattern: 6

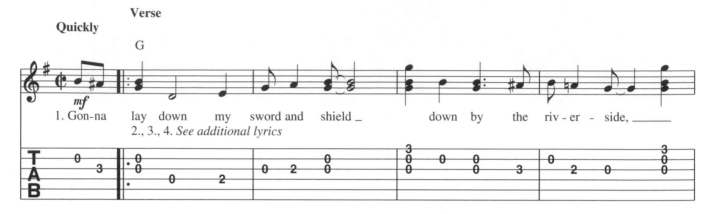

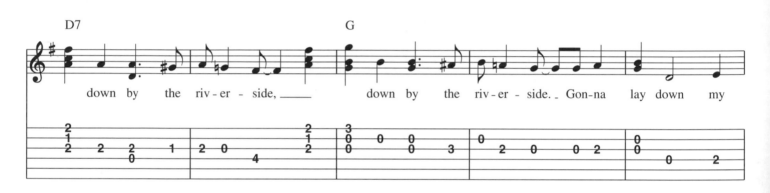

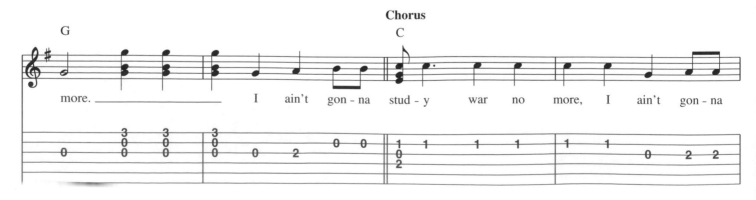

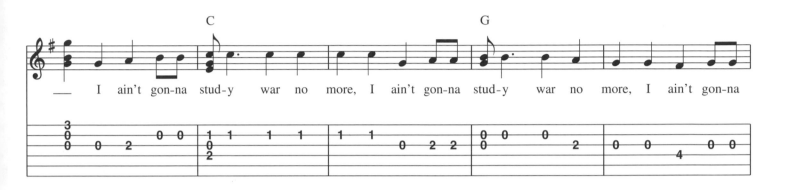

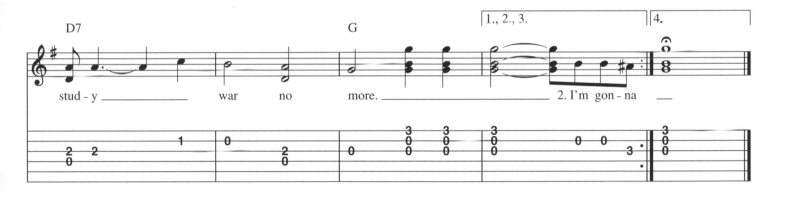

Additional Lyrics

2. I'm gonna join hands with everyone,
Down by the riverside, down by the riverside,
Down by the riverside.
I'm gonna join hands with everyone,
Down by the riverside,
And study war no more.

3. I'm gonna put on my long white robe,
Down by the riverside, down by the riverside,
Down by the riverside.
I'm gonna put on my long white robe,
Down by the riverside,
And study war no more.

4. I'm gonna walk with the Prince of Peace,
Down by the riverside, down by the riverside,
Down by the riverside.
I'm gonna walk with the Prince of Peace,
Down by the riverside,
And study war no more.

Down Yonder

Words and Music by L. Wolfe Gilbert

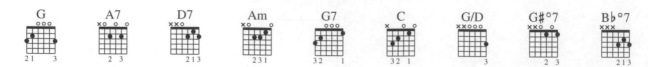

Strum Pattern: 10
Pick Pattern: 10

Verse
Moderately fast

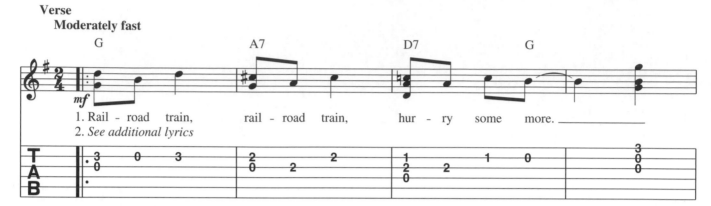

1. Rail - road train, rail - road train, hur - ry some more. ___
2. *See additional lyrics*

Put a lit - tle steam on just like nev - er be - fore. ___ Hus - tle on,

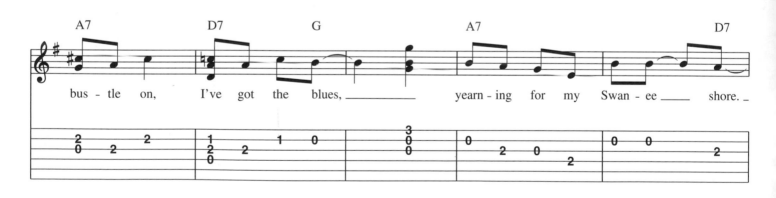

bus - tle on, I've got the blues, ___ yearn - ing for my Swan - ee ___ shore.

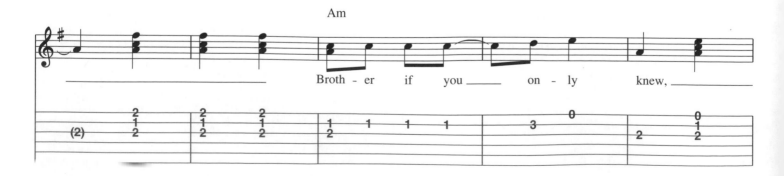

Broth - er if you ___ on - ly knew, ___

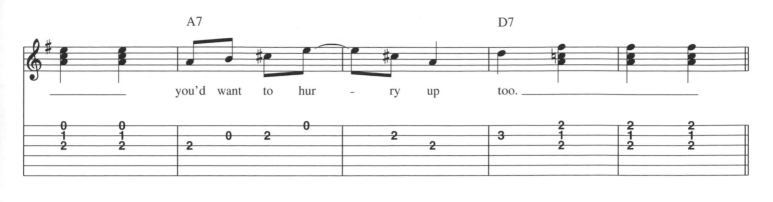

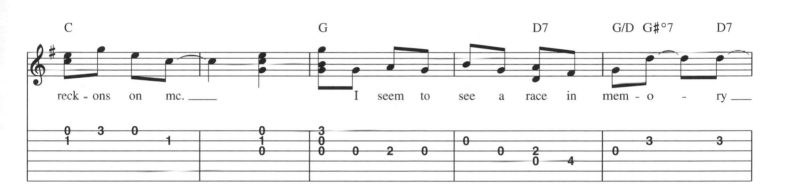

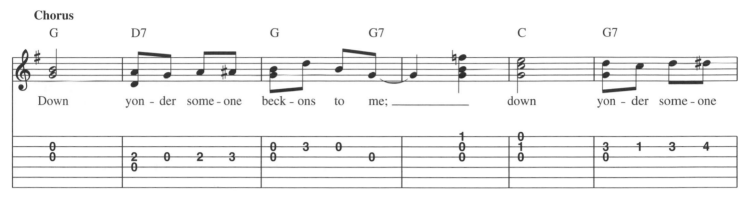

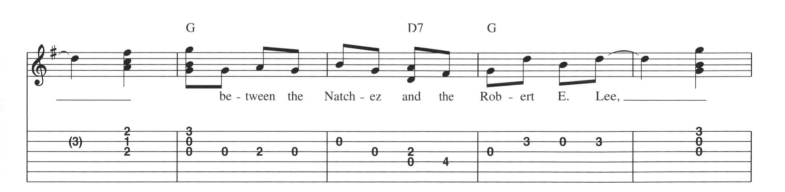

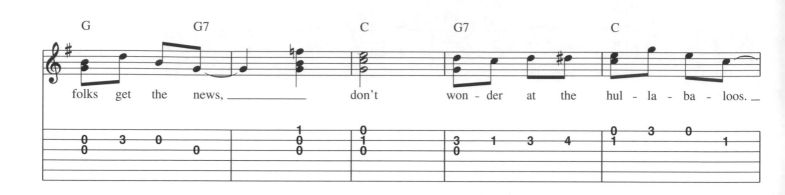

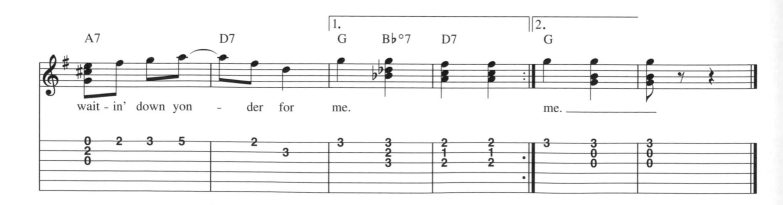

Additional Lyrics

2. Summer night, fields of white, bright cotton moon.
   My but I feel glad, I'm gonna see you all soon.
   'Lasses cakes, Mammy bakes, I taste them now.
   I can hear the darkies croon.
   I'll see my sweetie once more.
   There's lots of kissing in store.

Dry Bones
Traditional

F C7 F# G Ab A Bb F7

Strum Pattern: 3
Pick Pattern: 3

Chorus
Rhythmically

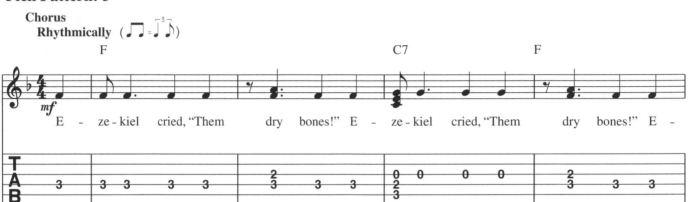

E - ze - kiel cried, "Them dry bones!" E - ze - kiel cried, "Them dry bones!" E -

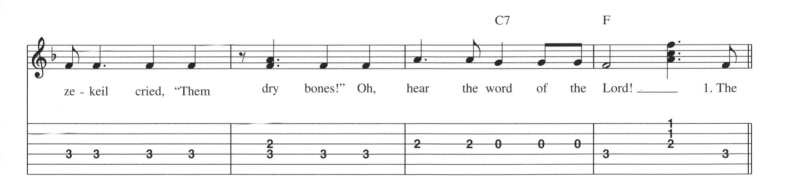

ze - keil cried, "Them dry bones!" Oh, hear the word of the Lord! _____ 1. The

Verse

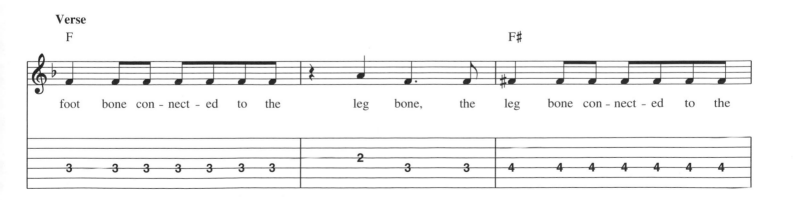

foot bone con - nect - ed to the leg bone, the leg bone con - nect - ed to the

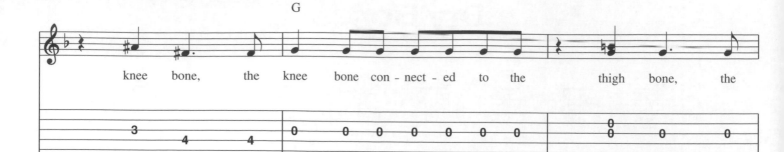

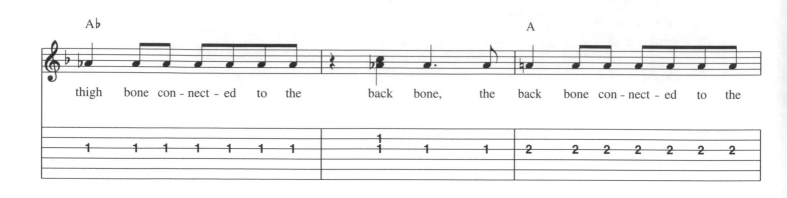

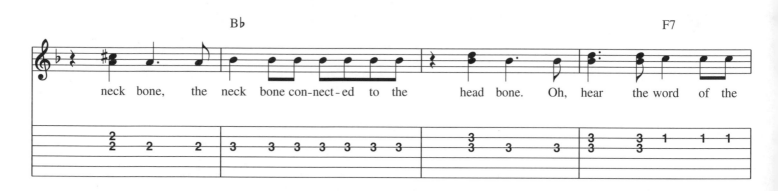

Chorus

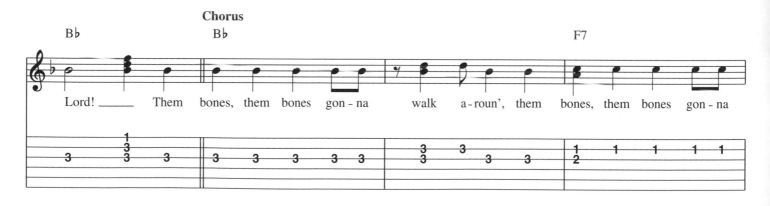

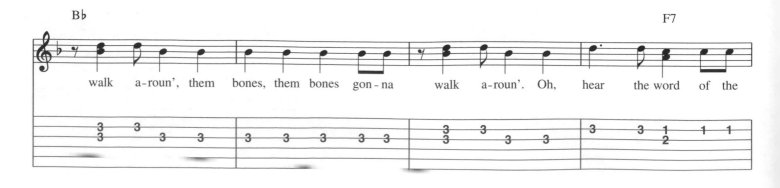

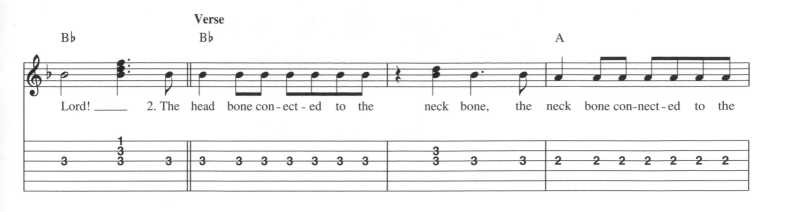

Verse

Lord! _____ 2. The head bone con-ect-ed to the neck bone, the neck bone con-nect-ed to the

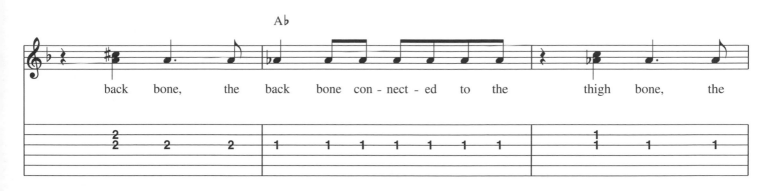

back bone, the back bone con-nect-ed to the thigh bone, the

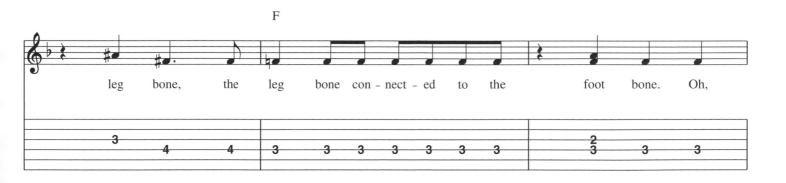

thigh bone con-nect-ed to the knee bone, the knee bone con-nect-ed to the

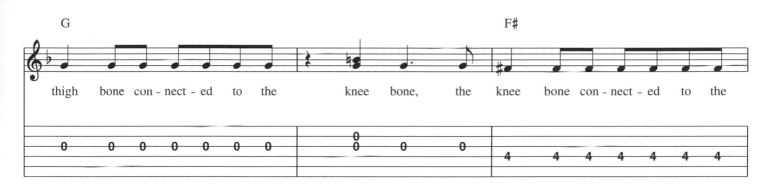

leg bone, the leg bone con-nect-ed to the foot bone. Oh,

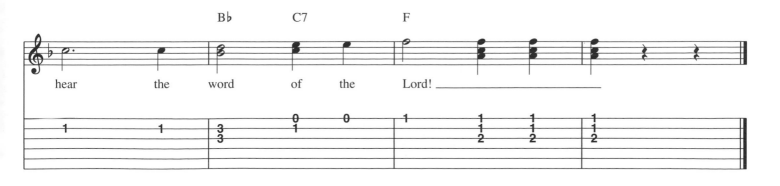

hear the word of the Lord! _____

Du, Du Liegst Mir Im Herzen
(You, You Weigh on My Heart)

German Folksong

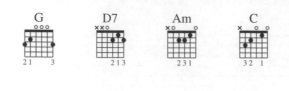

Strum Pattern: 7, 8
Pick Pattern: 7, 8

Moderately

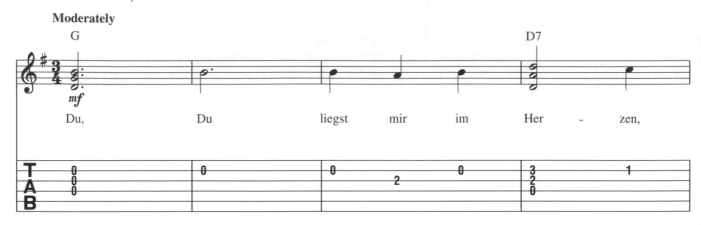

Du, Du liegst mir im Her - zen,

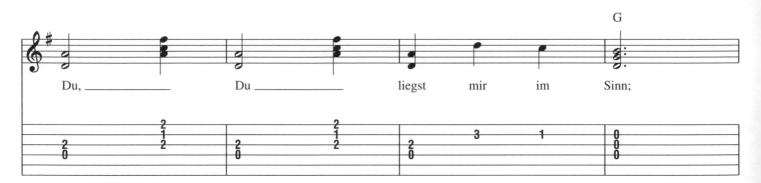

Du, _____ Du _____ liegst mir im Sinn;

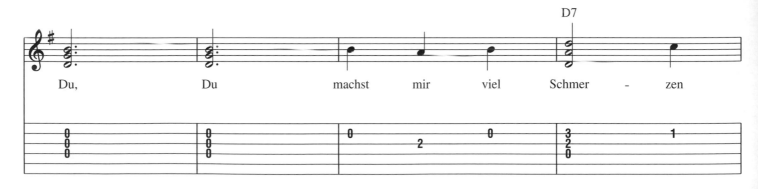

Du, Du machst mir viel Schmer - zen

Weisst nicht wie gut Ich Dir bin! _____

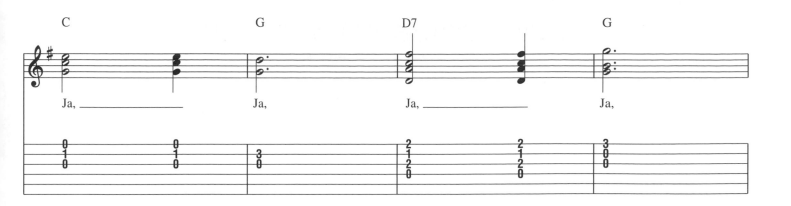

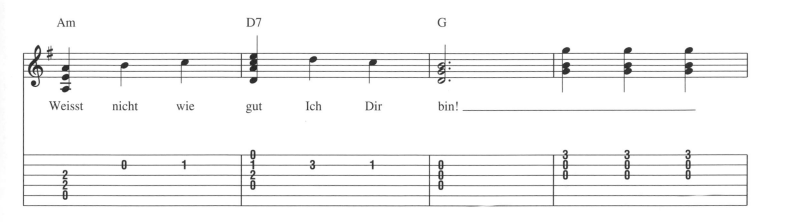

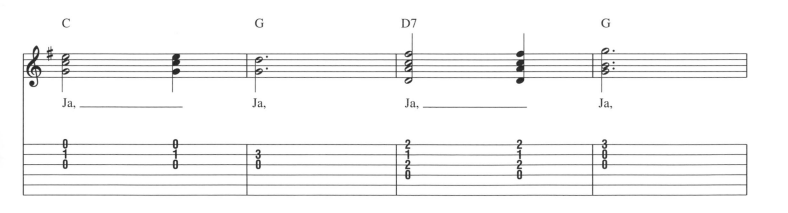

Eine Kleine Nachtmusik

Music by Wolfgang Amadeus Mozart

Strum Pattern: 4
Pick Pattern: 1

Far Above Cayuga's Waters

Lyrics by A.C. Weekes and W.M. Smith
Music by H.S. Thompson

Strum Pattern: 4
Pick Pattern: 3

Additional Lyrics

2. Far above the busy humming
Of the bustling town;
Reared against the arch of heaven
Looks she proudly down.

The Entertainer
By Scott Joplin

Fascination
(Valse Tzigane)

By F.D. Marchetti

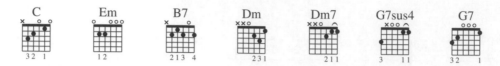

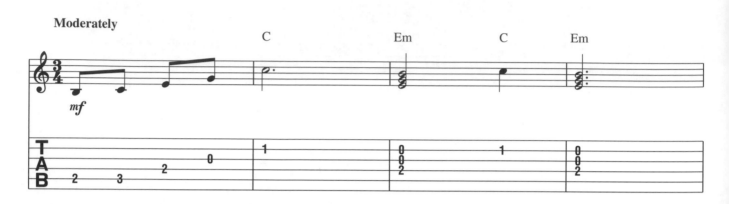

Strum Pattern: 7, 8
Pick Pattern: 8

Moderately

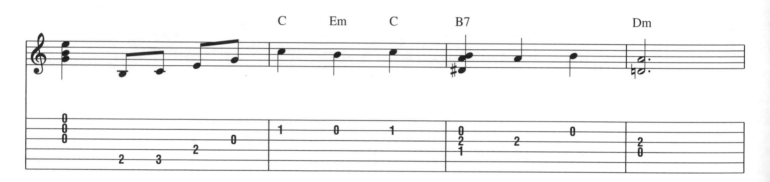

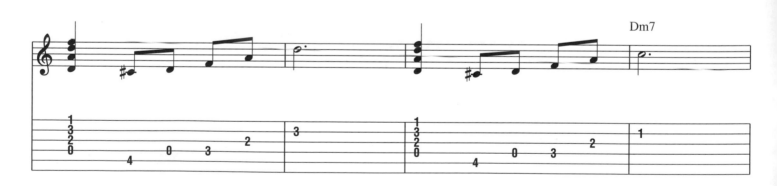

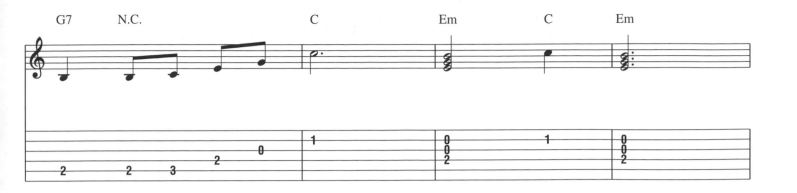

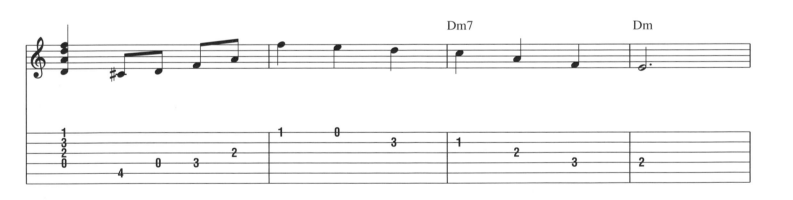

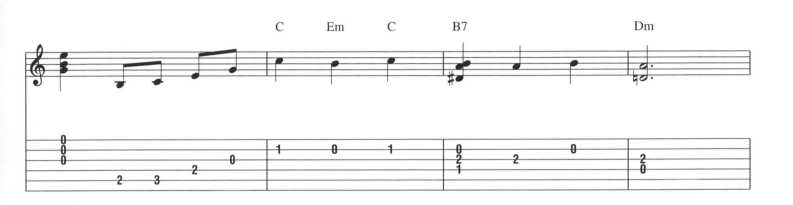

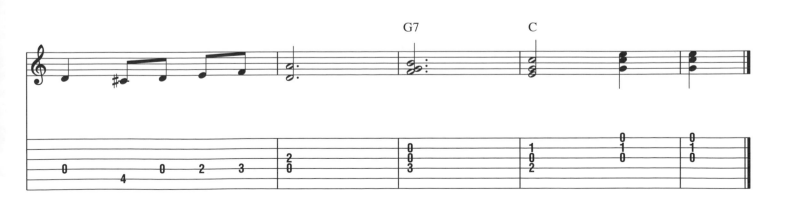

For He's a Jolly Good Fellow

Traditional

Strum Pattern: 7, 8
Pick Pattern: 8

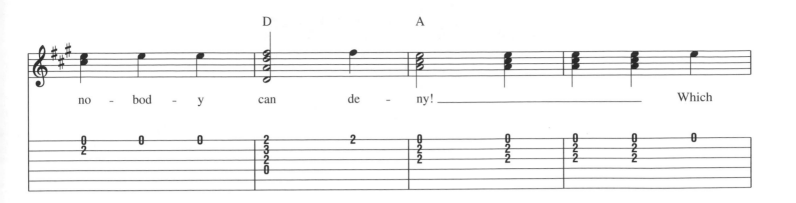

no - bod - y   can   de -   ny! _____ Which

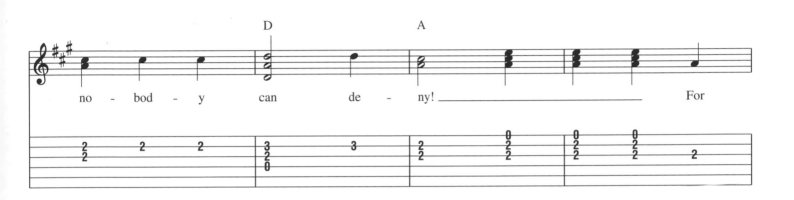

no - bod - y   can   de -   ny! _____ For

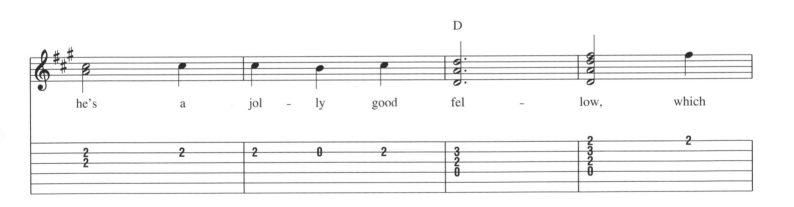

he's   a   jol - ly   good   fel -   low,   which

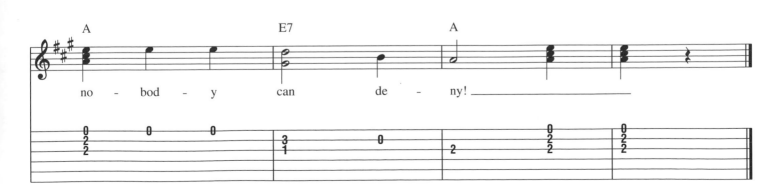

no - bod - y   can   de -   ny! _____

For Me and My Gal

Words by Edgar Leslie and E. Ray Goetz
Music by George W. Meyer

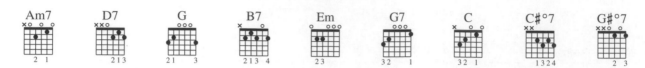

Strum Pattern: 3, 4
Pick Pattern: 1, 3

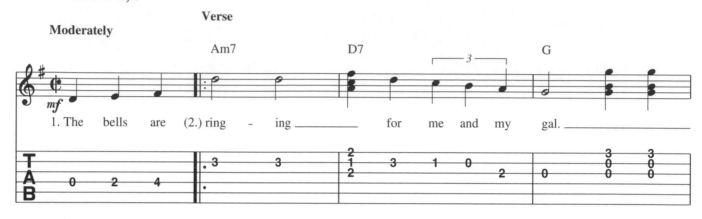

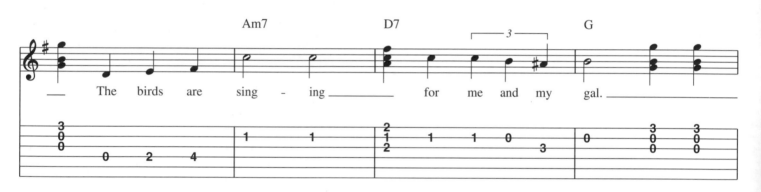

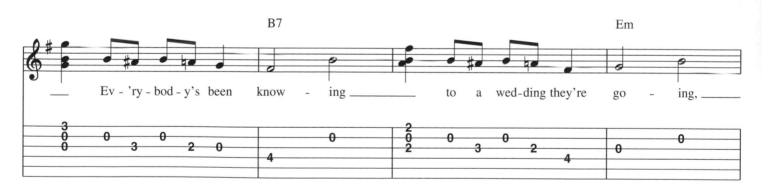

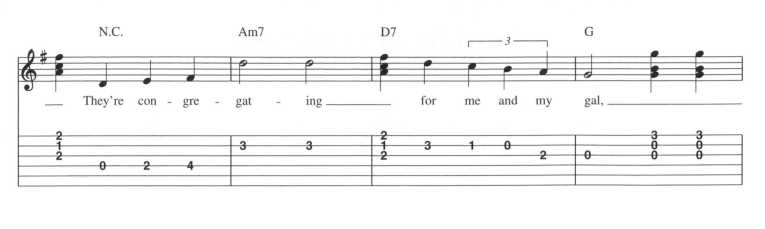

They're con - gre - gat - ing _____ for me and my gal, _____

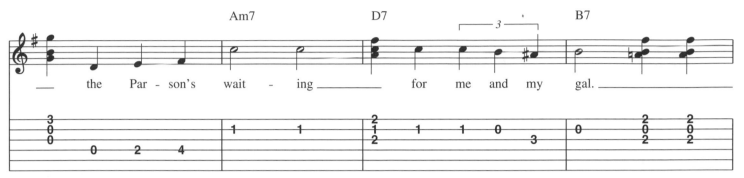

_____ the Par - son's wait - ing _____ for me and my gal. _____

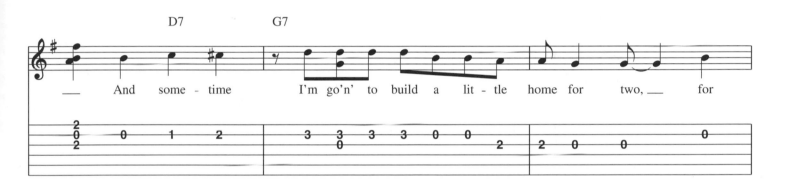

_____ And some - time I'm go'n' to build a lit - tle home for two, _____ for

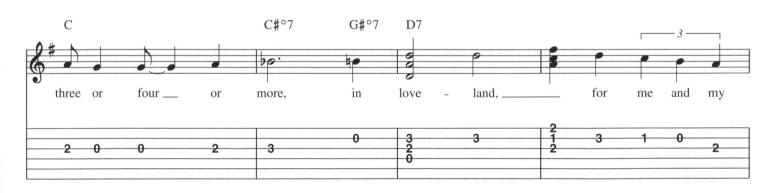

three or four _____ or more, in love - land, _____ for me and my

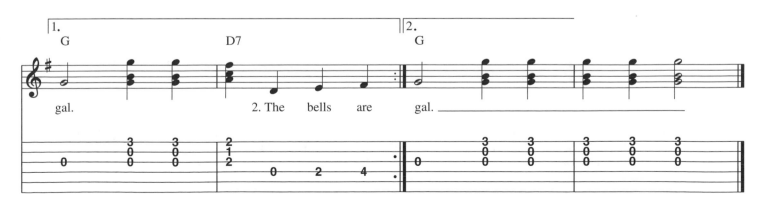

gal. | 2. The bells are gal. _____

Frankie and Johnny

Anonymous Blues Ballad

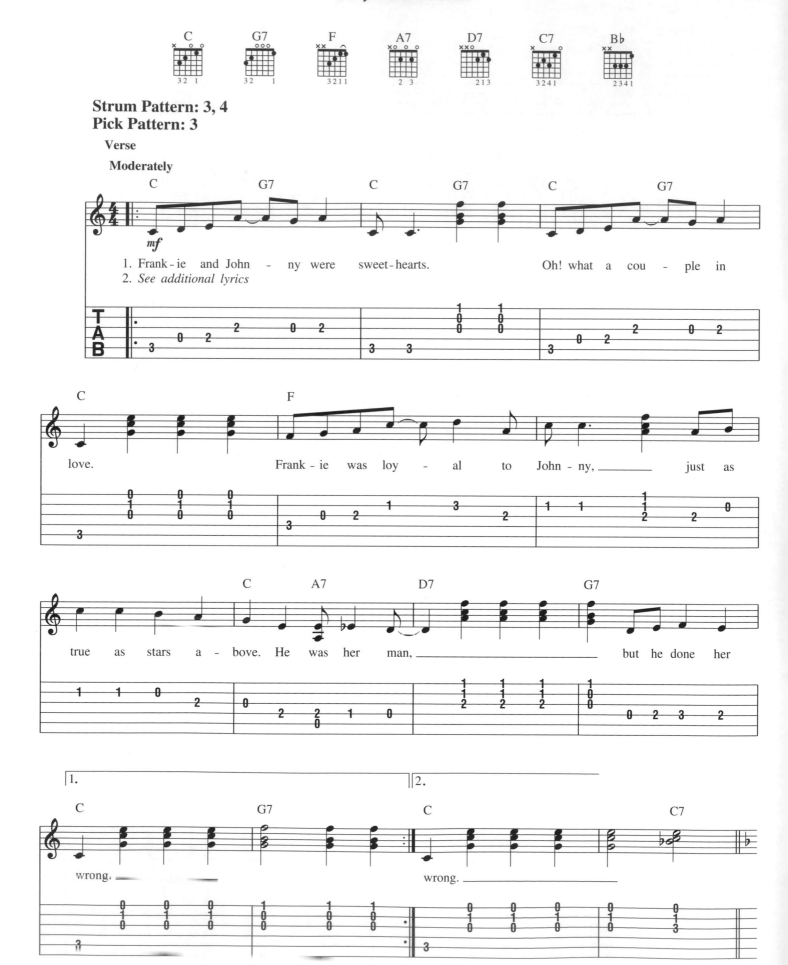

Strum Pattern: 3, 4
Pick Pattern: 3

Verse
Moderately

1. Frank - ie and John - ny were sweet-hearts. Oh! what a cou - ple in
2. *See additional lyrics*

love. Frank - ie was loy - al to John - ny, _____ just as

true as stars a - bove. He was her man, _____ but he done her

1. wrong. _____
2. wrong. _____

Outro

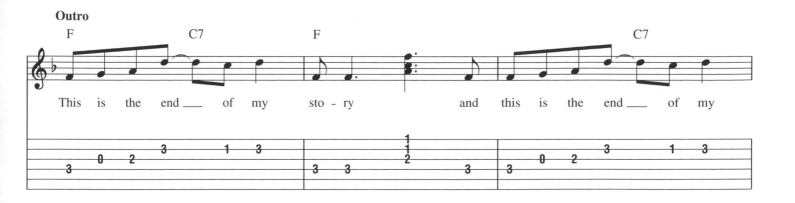

This is the end ___ of my sto-ry and this is the end ___ of my

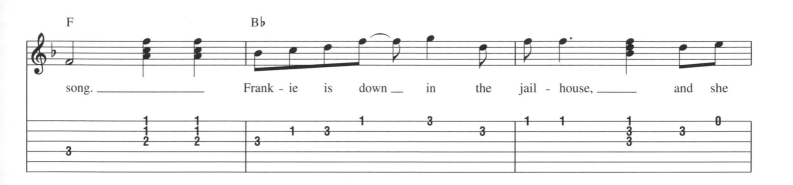

song. _____ Frank-ie is down ___ in the jail - house, _____ and she

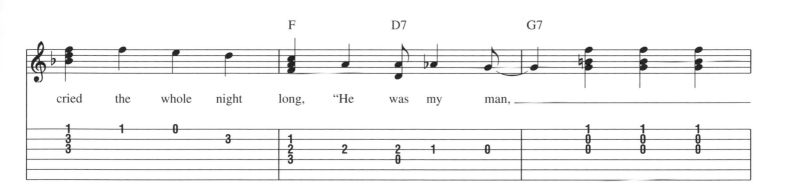

cried the whole night long, "He was my man, ___

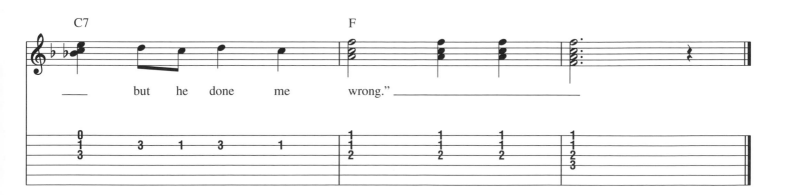

___ but he done me wrong." ___

Additional Lyrics

2. Johnnie saw Frankie a comin',
   Out the back door he did scoot.
   Frankie took aim with her pistol,
   And the gun went root toot - toot.
   He was her man, but he done her wrong.

Freight Train

Traditional

Strum Pattern: 3
Pick Pattern: 1

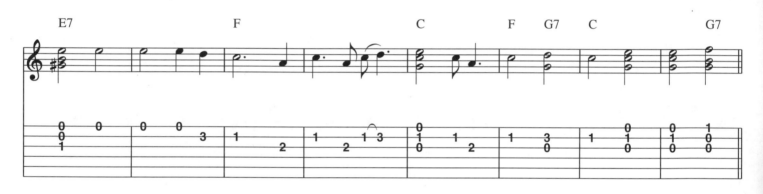

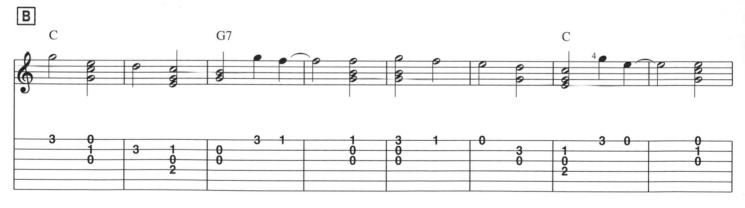

Für Elise

Music by Ludwig Van Beethoven

Strum Pattern: 7, 9
Pick Pattern: 7, 9

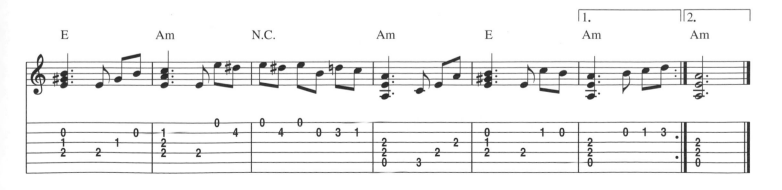

Funiculi, Funicula

Traditional

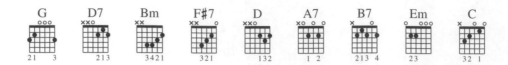

Strum Pattern: 7
Pick Pattern: 7

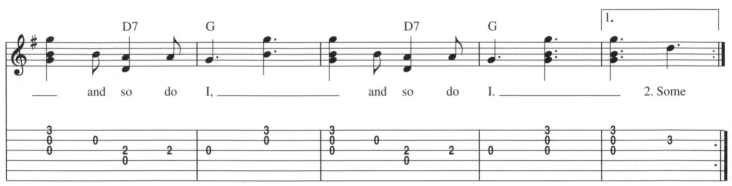

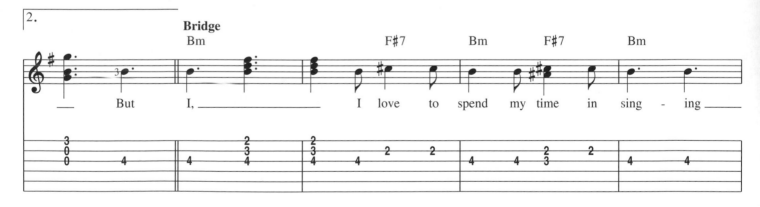

Additional Lyrics

2. Some think it well to be all melancholic,
   To pine and sigh, to pine and sigh.

Git Along, Little Dogies

Western American Cowboy Song

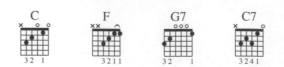

Strum Pattern: 7
Pick Pattern: 8

Verse

Moderately

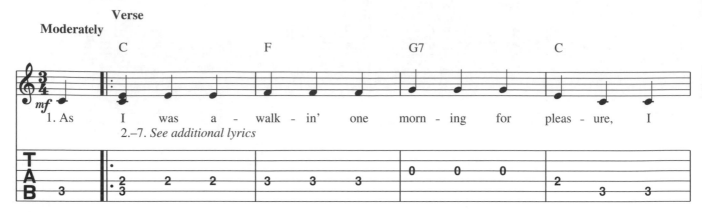

1. As I was a-walk-in' one morn-ing for pleas-ure, I
2.–7. *See additional lyrics*

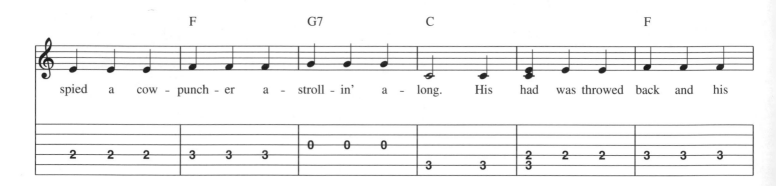

spied a cow-punch-er a-stroll-in' a-long. His had was thrown back and his

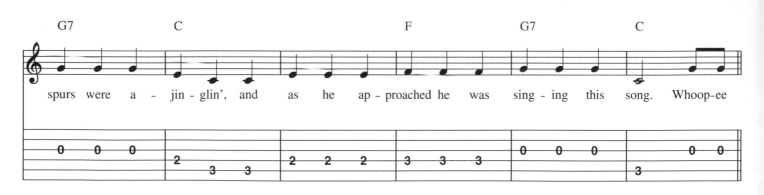

spurs were a-jin-glin', and as he ap-proached he was sing-ing this song. Whoop-ee

Chorus

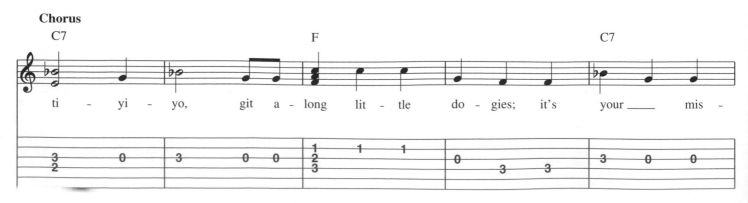

ti - yi - yo, git a - long lit - tle do - gies; it's your _____ mis -

for - tune, and none of my own. Whoop-ee ti - yi - yo, git a - long lit - tle

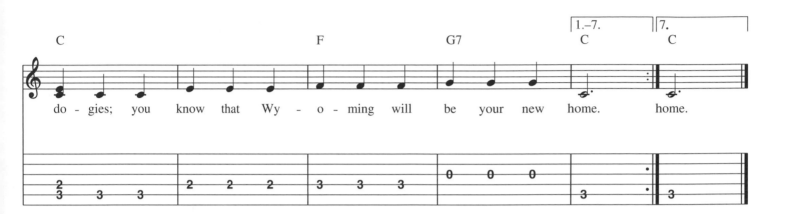

do - gies; you know that Wy - o - ming will be your new home. home.

Additional Lyrics

2. Early in the springtime we'll round up the dogies,
   Slap on their brands and bob off their tails;
   Round up our horses, load up the chuck wagon,
   Then throw those dogies upon the trail.

3. It's whooping and yelling and driving the dogies,
   Oh, how I wish you would go on.
   It's whooping and punching and go on, little dogies,
   For you know Wyoming will be your new home.

4. Some of the boys goes up the trails for pleasure,
   But that's where they git it most awfully wrong;
   For you haven't any idea the trouble they give us,
   When we go driving them dogies along.

5. When the night comes on and we hold them on the bed-ground,
   These little dogies that roll on so slow;
   Roll up the herd and cut out the strays,
   And roll the little dogies that never rolled before.

6. Your mother she was raised way down in Texas,
   Where the jimson weed and sandburs grow;
   Now we'll fill you up on prickly pear and cholla,
   Till you are ready for the trail to Idaho.

7. Oh, you'll be soup for Uncle Sam's Injuns,
   "It's beef, heap beef," I hear them cry.
   Git along, git along, git along, little dogies,
   You're going to be beef steers by and by.

Give Me That Old Time Religion

Traditional

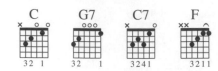

Strum Pattern: 3, 4
Pick Pattern: 1, 3

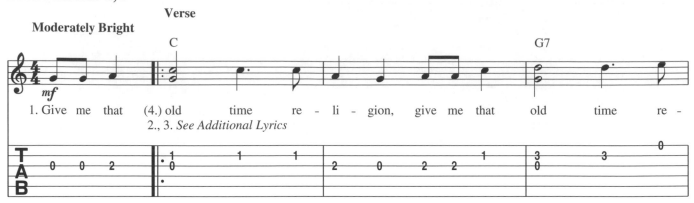

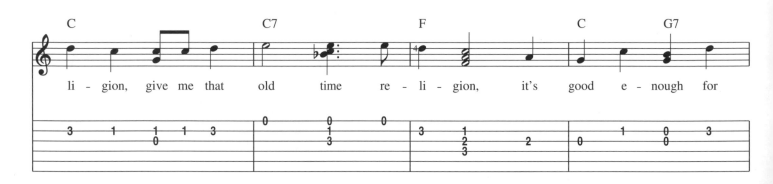

Additional Lyrics

2. It was good for our fathers,
   It was good for our fathers,
   It was good for our fathers,
   And it's good enough for me!

3. It was good for our mothers,
   It was good for our mothers,
   It was good for our mothers,
   And it's good enough for me!

Go Tell Aunt Rhody

Traditional

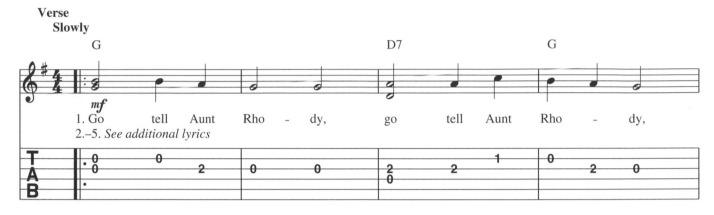

Strum Pattern: 3
Pick Pattern: 3

Verse
Slowly

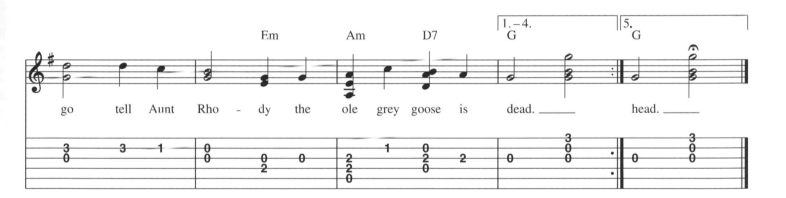

1. Go tell Aunt Rho - dy, go tell Aunt Rho - dy,
2.–5. *See additional lyrics*

go tell Aunt Rho - dy the ole grey goose is dead. _____ head. _____

Additional Lyrics

2. The one she was saving,
   The one she was saving,
   The one she was saving,
   To make a feather bed.

3. The gander is weeping,
   The gander is weeping,
   The gander is weeping,
   Because his wife is dead.

4. The goslings are crying,
   The goslings are crying,
   The goslings are crying,
   Because their mama's dead.

5. She died in the water,
   She died in the water,
   She died in the water,
   With her heels above her head.

Give My Regards to Broadway

from YANKEE DOODLE DANDY

Words and Music by George M. Cohan

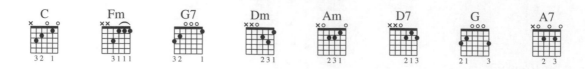

Strum Pattern: 3, 4
Pick Pattern: 1, 3

Moderately slow

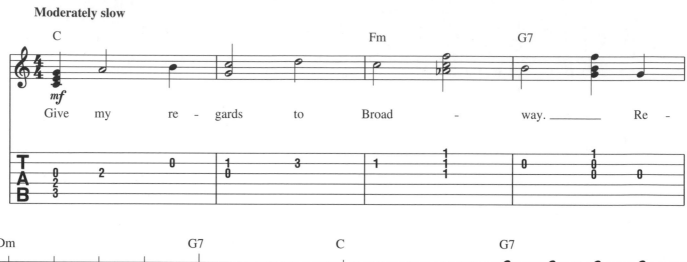

Give my re - gards to Broad - way. ____ Re -

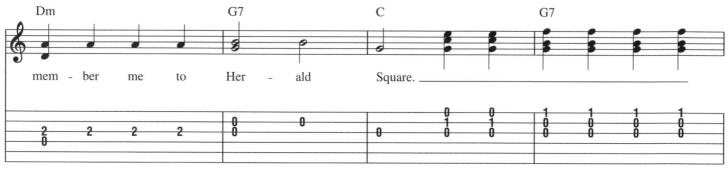

mem - ber me to Her - ald Square. ____

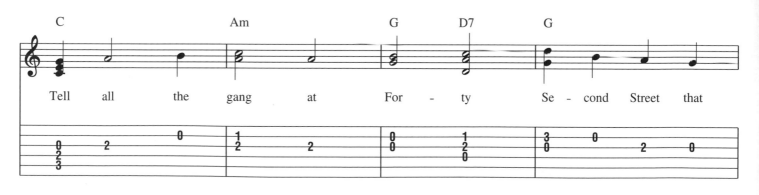

Tell all the gang at For - ty Se - cond Street that

I will soon be there. ____

Whis - per of how I'm yearn - ing _____ to

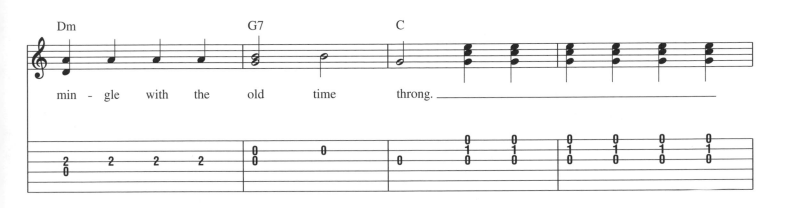

min - gle with the old time throng. _____

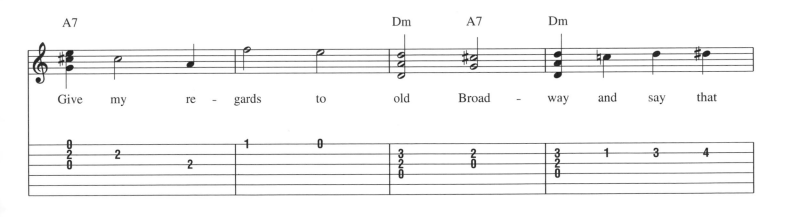

Give my re - gards to old Broad - way and say that

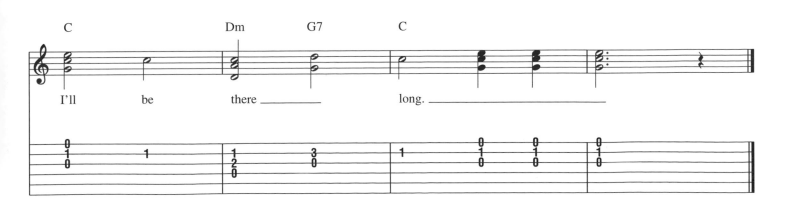

I'll be there _____ long. _____

The Glow Worm

English Words by Lilla Cayley Robinson
German Words and Music by Paul Lincke

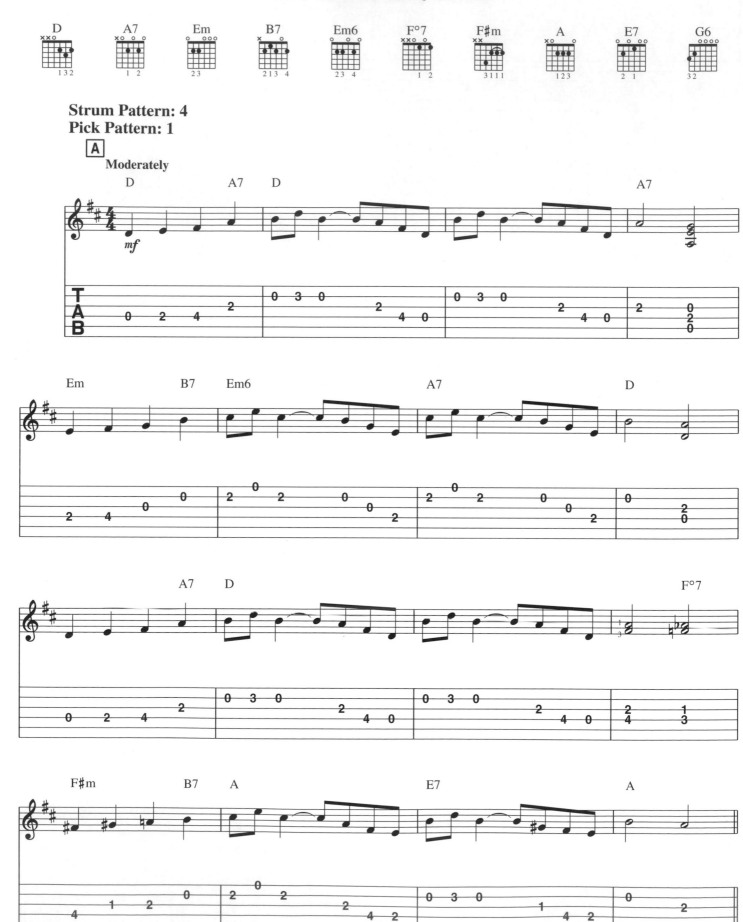

Strum Pattern: 4
Pick Pattern: 1

138

Go, Tell It on the Mountain

African-American Spiritual
Verses by John W. Work, Jr.

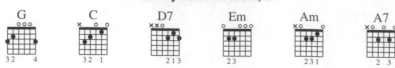

Strum Pattern: 3, 4
Pick Pattern: 1, 4

Chorus

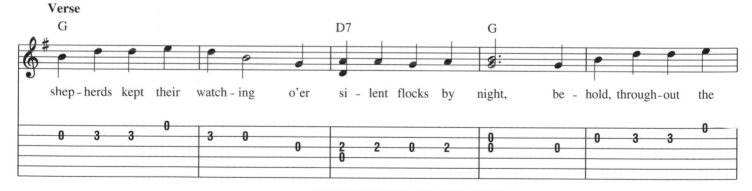

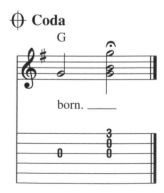

Additional Lyrics

2. The shepherds feared and trembled
   When lo! above the earth
   Rang out the angel chorus
   That hailed our Savior's birth.

3. Down in a lowly manger
   Our humble Christ was born.
   And God sent us salvation
   That blessed Christmas morn.

Good Night Ladies

Words by E.P. Christy
Traditional Music

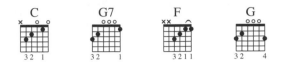

Strum Pattern: 3
Pick Pattern: 3

Chorus
Brightly

Good night la - dies, good night la - dies, good night la - dies, we're

going to leave you now. ____ Mer - ri - ly we roll a - long, roll a - long, roll a - long.

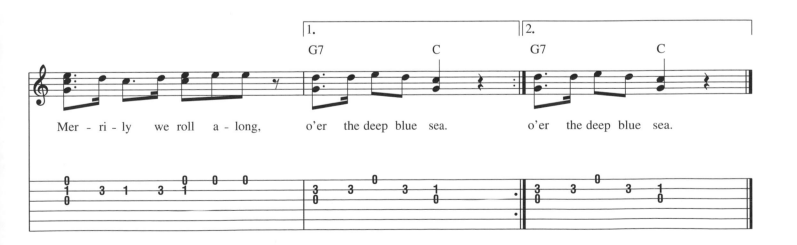

Mer - ri - ly we roll a - long, o'er the deep blue sea. o'er the deep blue sea.

Goober Peas

Words by P. Pindar
Music by P. Nutt

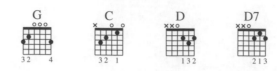

Strum Pattern: 4
Pick Pattern: 3

Verse
Moderately

1. Sit - ting by the road - side on a sum - mer day, _____
2., 3., 4. *See additional lyrics*

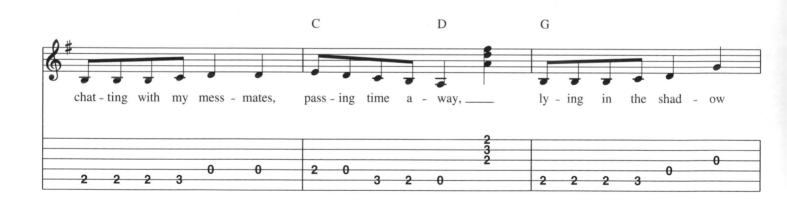

chat - ting with my mess - mates, pass - ing time a - way, _____ ly - ing in the shad - ow

un - der - neath the trees, _____ good - ness, how de - li - cious, eat - ing goo - ber peas! _____

Chorus

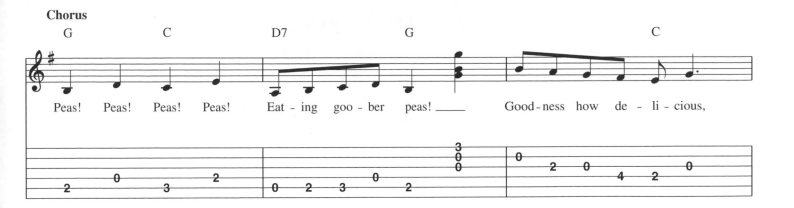

Peas! Peas! Peas! Peas! Eat - ing goo - ber peas! ____ Good - ness how de - li - cious,

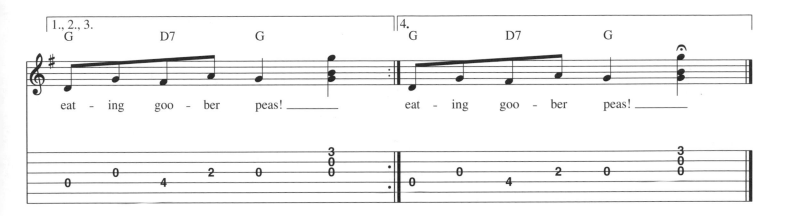

eat - ing goo - ber peas! _____ eat - ing goo - ber peas! ____

Additional Lyrics

2. When a horseman passes, the soldiers have a rule,
To cry out at their loudest, "Mister, here's your mule!"
But another pleasure enchantinger than these,
Is wearing out your grinders, eating goober peas!

3. Just before the battle the Gen'ral hears a row,
He says, "The Yanks are coming, I hear their rifles now."
He turns around in wonder, and what do you think he sees?
The Georgia Militia—eating goober peas!

4. I think my song has lasted almost long enough,
The subject's interesting, but rhymes are mighty rough,
I wish this war was over, when free from rags and fleas,
We'd kiss our wives and sweethearts and gobble goober peas!

Greensleeves

Sixteenth Century Traditional English

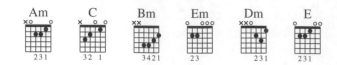

Strum Pattern: 7
Pick Pattern: 7

Verse
Slowly

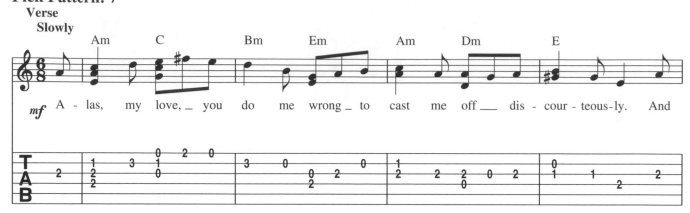

mf A - las, my love, __ you do me wrong __ to cast me off __ dis - cour - teous-ly. And

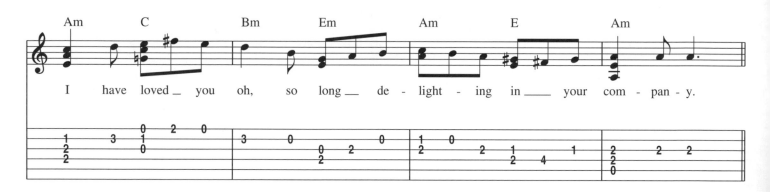

I have loved __ you oh, so long __ de - light - ing in ___ your com - pan - y.

Chorus

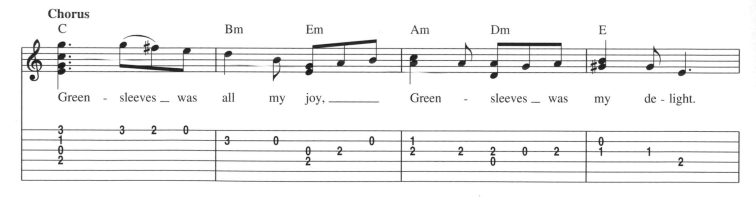

Green - sleeves __ was all my joy, _____ Green - sleeves __ was my de - light.

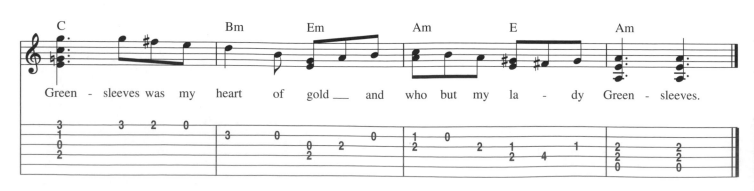

Green - sleeves was my heart of gold __ and who but my la - dy Green - sleeves.

Hail, Hail, the Gang's All Here

Traditional

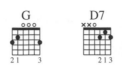

Strum Pattern: 7, 8
Pick Pattern: 7, 8

Moderately

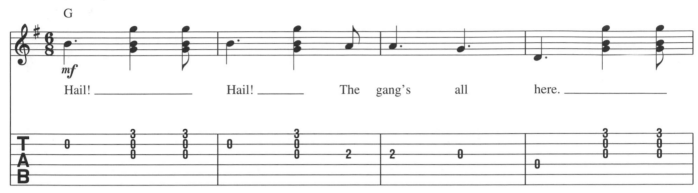

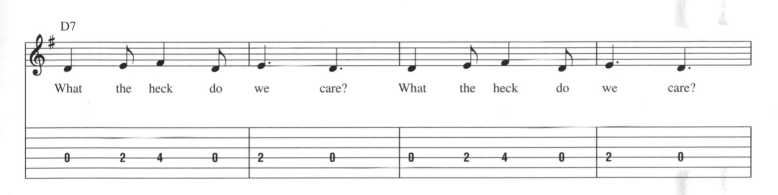

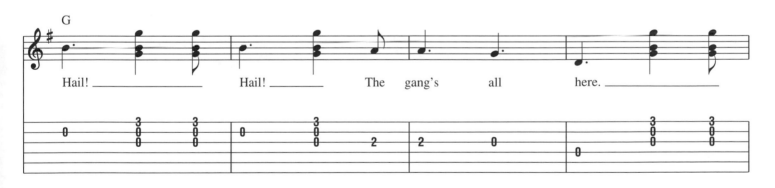

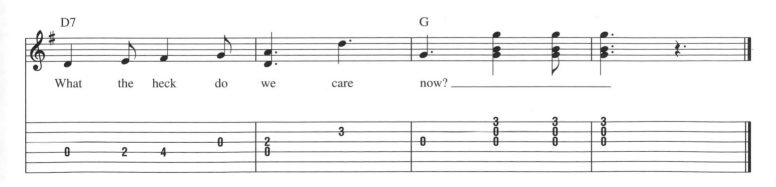

Hail to the Chief

By James Sanderson

Strum Pattern: 4
Pick Pattern: 1

B

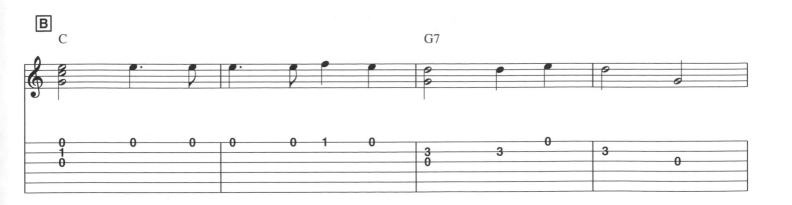

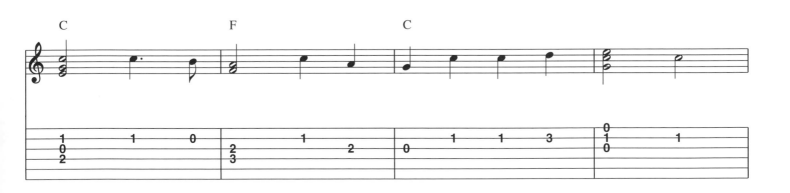

Halleljah!

from MESSIAH

By George Frideric Handel

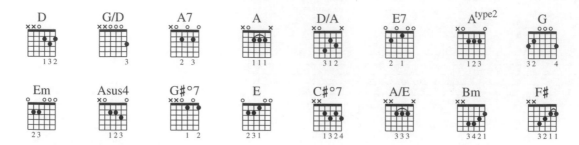

Strum Pattern: 4
Pick Pattern: 4

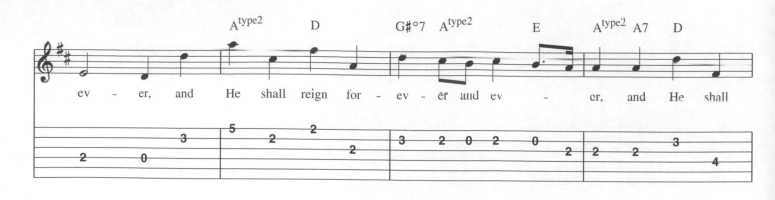

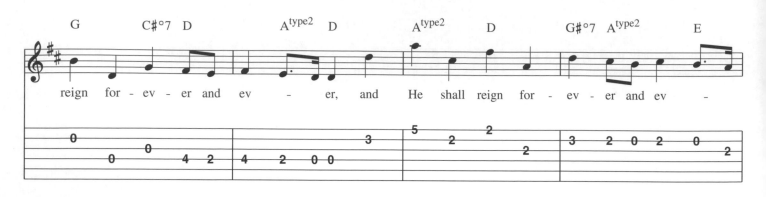

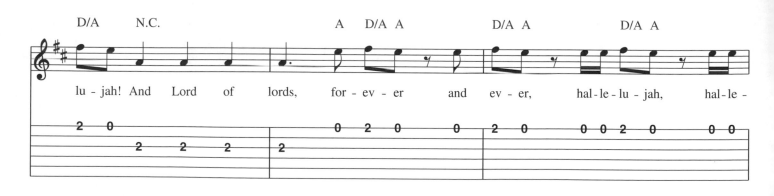

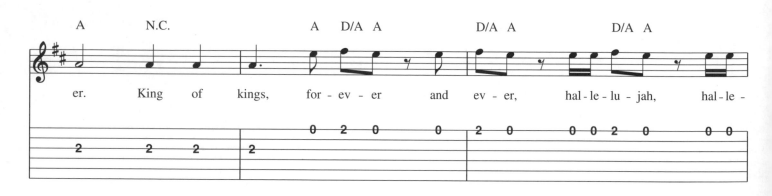

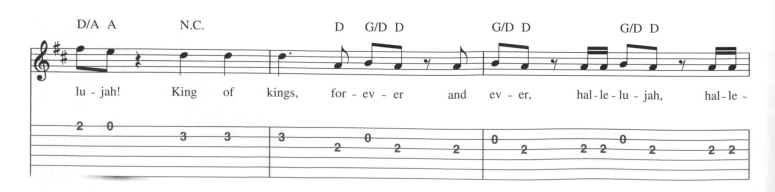

Hava Nagilah
(Let's Be Happy)

Lyrics by Moshe Nathanson
Music by Abraham Z. Idelsohn

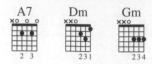

Strum Pattern: 4
Pick Pattern: 4

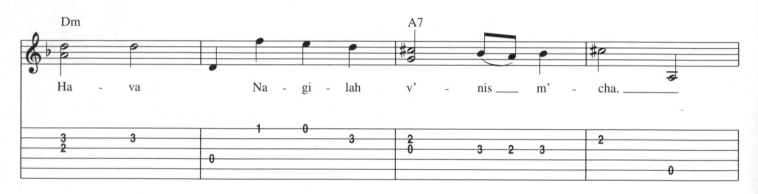

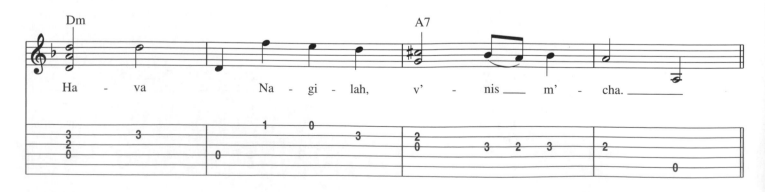

He's Got the Whole World in His Hands

African-American Folksong

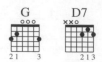

Strum Pattern: 3, 4
Pick Pattern: 1, 3

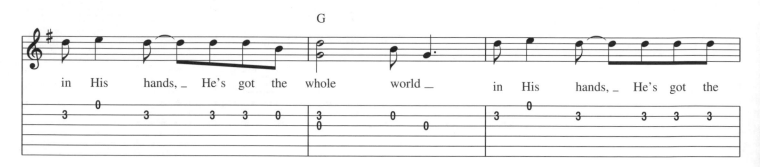

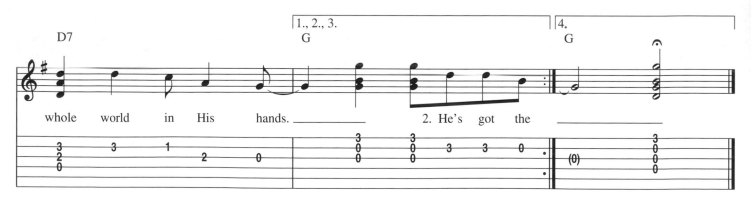

Additional Lyrics

2. He's got the wind and the rain in His hands,
   He's got the wind and the rain in His hands,
   He's got the wind and the rain in His hands,
   He's got the whole world in His hands.

3. He's got the tiny little baby in His hands,
   He's got the tiny little baby in His hands,
   He's got the tiny little baby in His hands,
   He's got the whole world in His hands.

4. He's got you and me, brother, in his hands,
   He's got you and me, sister, in his hands,
   He's got you and me, brother, in his hands,
   He's got the whole world in his hands.

Hearts and Flowers

Words by Mary D. Brine
Music by Theodore Moses Tobani

Strum Pattern: 5
Pick Pattern: 2

Hello! Ma Baby

Words by Ida Emerson
Music by Joseph E. Howard

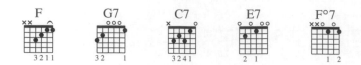

Strum Pattern: 3
Pick Pattern: 1

Verse
Brightly

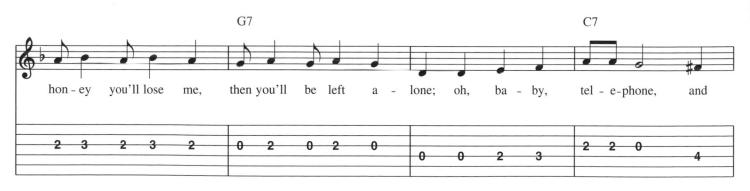

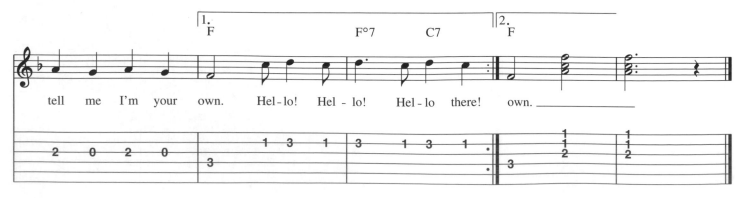

Hindustan

Words and Music by Oliver Wallace and Harold Weeks

Strum Pattern: 2
Pick Pattern: 4

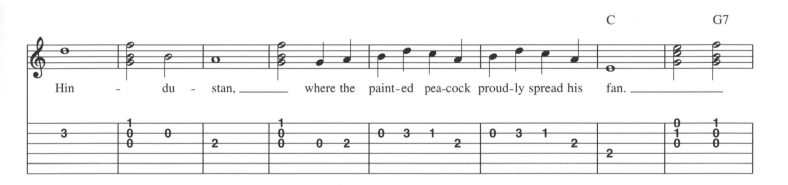

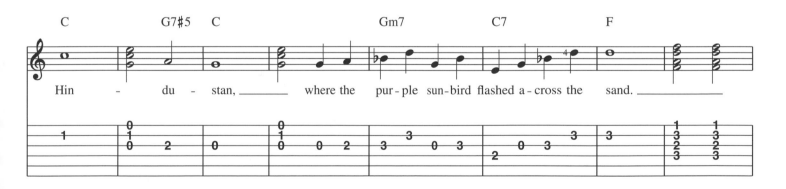

Home on the Range

Lyrics by Dr. Brewster Higley
Music by Dan Kelly

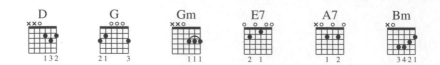

Strum Pattern: 7
Pick Pattern: 9

Verse

Slowly

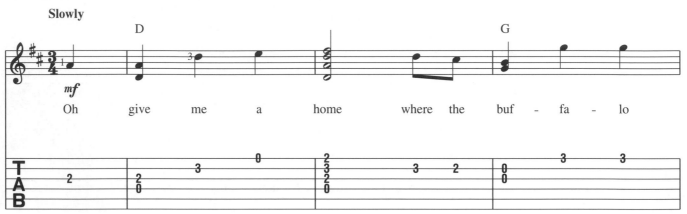

Oh give me a home where the buf - fa - lo

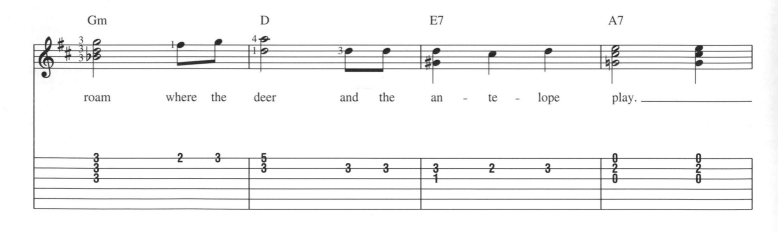

roam where the deer and the an - te - lope play. _____

Where sel - dom is heard a dis - cour - ag - ing

Home Sweet Home

Words by John Howard Payne
Music by Henry R. Bishop

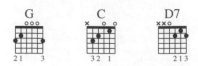

Strum Pattern: 4
Pick Pattern: 3

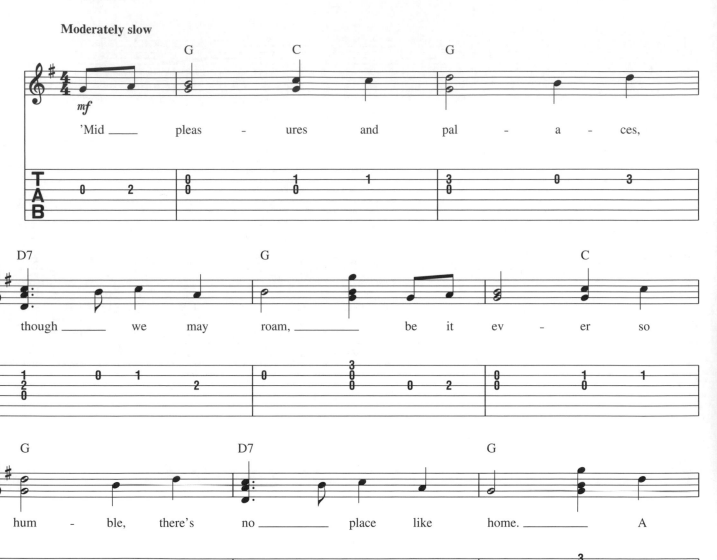

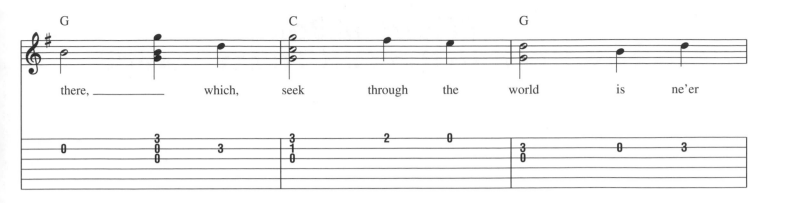

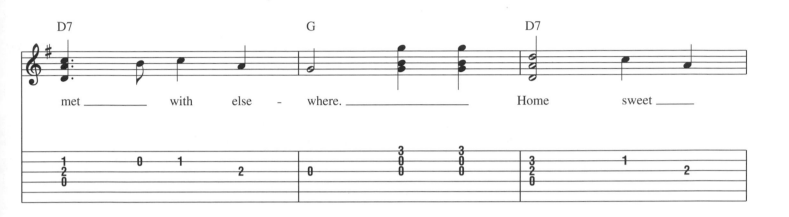

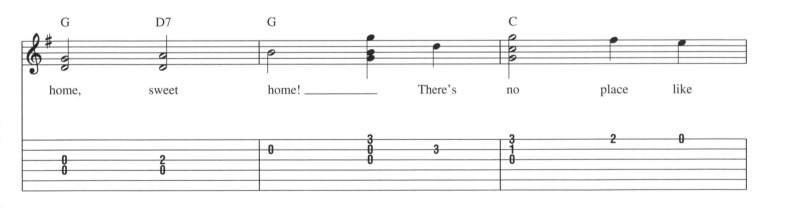

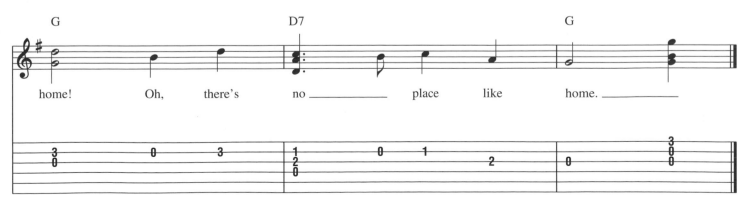

(There'll Be)
A Hot Time in the Old Town Tonight

Words by Joe Hayden
Music by Theodore M. Metz

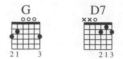

Strum Pattern: 3, 4
Pick Pattern: 1, 3

Moderately slow

When you hear ___ the ___ bells go ding - ling - ling,

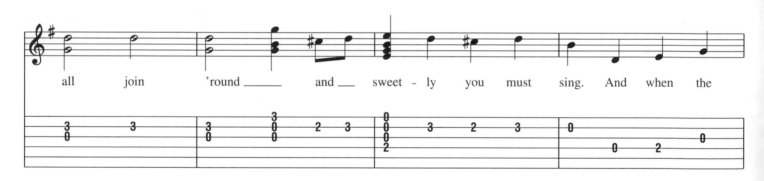

all join 'round ___ and ___ sweet - ly you must sing. And when the

verse is through, ___ in the cho - rus all join in, there'll be a

hot time in the old town to - night.

House of the Rising Sun

Southern American Folksong

Strum Pattern: 8
Pick Pattern: 8

Verse

Moderately

1. There is a ____ house in ____ New Or - leans they call the
2. *See additional lyrics*

Ris - ing ____ Sun. ____ It has been the ru - in of man - y a poor

girl, and I, oh Lord, was ____ one. ____ 2. Go Sun. ____

Additional Lyrics

2. Go speak to my baby sister and say,
"Don't do as I have done."
Stay away from places like this one in New Orleans
They call the Rising Sun.

Humoresque

By Antonin Dvorak

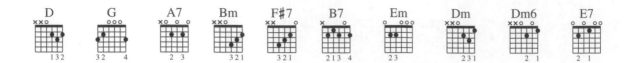

Strum Pattern: 4
Pick Pattern: 4

Moderately

To Coda ⊕

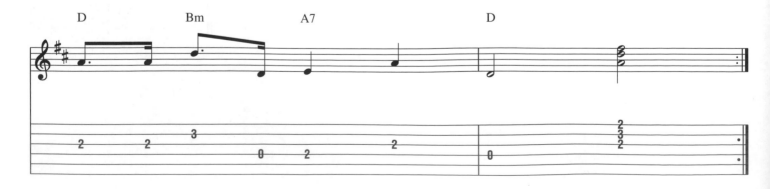

D.C. al Coda

$\bigoplus$ **Coda**

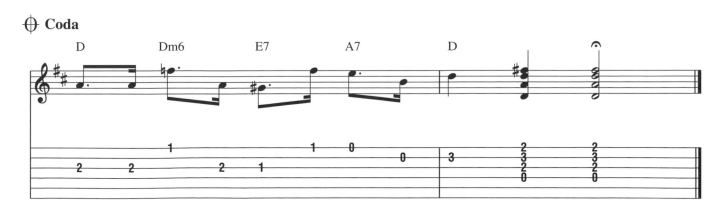

I Ain't Got Nobody
(And Nobody Cares for Me)

Words by Roger Graham
Music by Spencer Williams and Dave Peyton

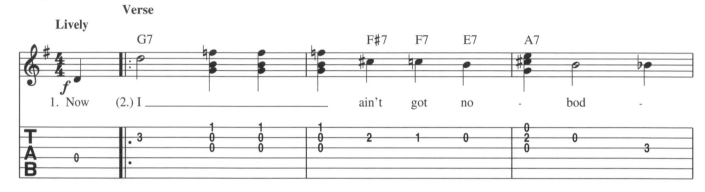

Strum Pattern: 4
Pick Pattern: 3

Verse

Lively

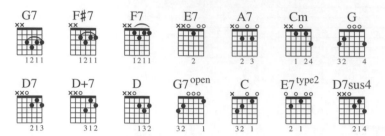

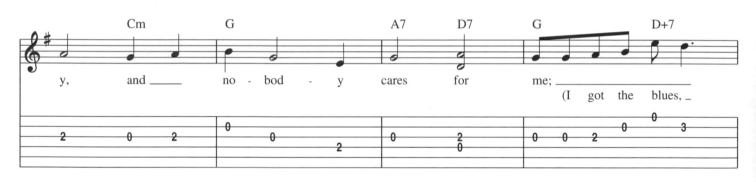

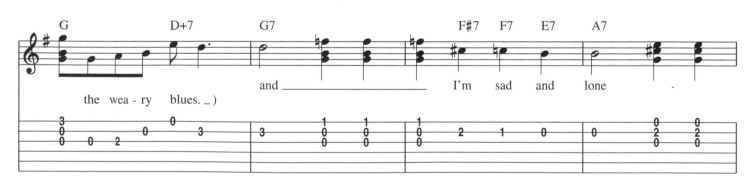

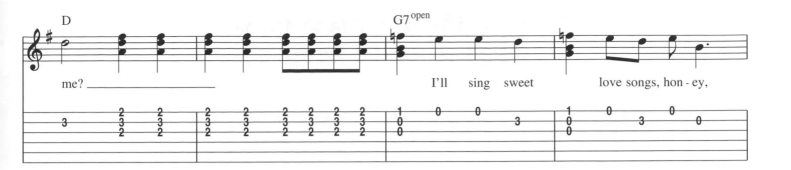

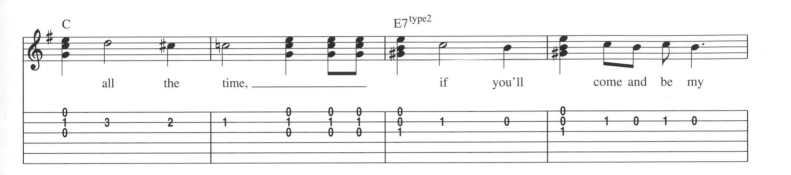

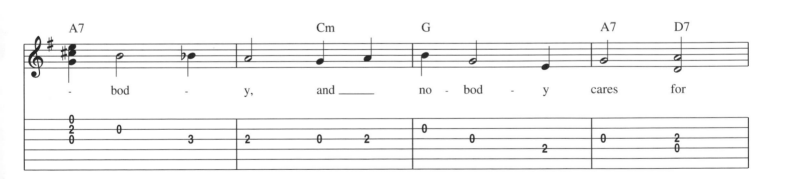

I Gave My Love a Cherry
(The Riddle Song)
Traditional

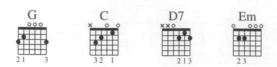

Strum Pattern: 2
Pick Pattern: 2

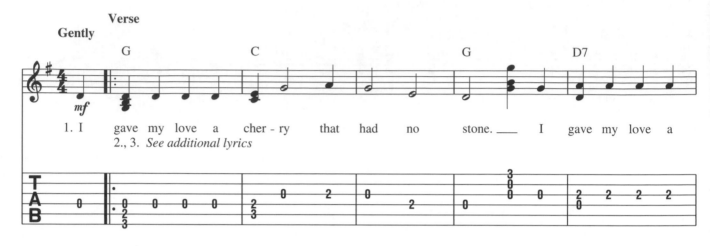

Verse
Gently

1. I gave my love a cher-ry that had no stone. ___ I gave my love a
2., 3. *See additional lyrics*

chick-en that had no bone. ___ I told my love a sto-ry that had no

end, ___ I gave my love a ba-by with no cry-in'. ___ 2. How in'.

Additional Lyrics

2. How can there be a cherry that has no stone?
How can there be a chicken that has no bone?
How can there be a story that has no end?
How can there be a baby with no cryin'?

3. A cherry, when it's blooming, it has no stone.
A chicken, when it's pipping, it has no bone.
The story that I love, it has no end.
A baby, when it's sleeping, has no cryin'.

I Want a Girl
(Just Like the Girl that Married Dear Old Dad)

Words by William Dillon
Music by Harry von Tilzer

Strum Pattern: 3
Pick Pattern: 3

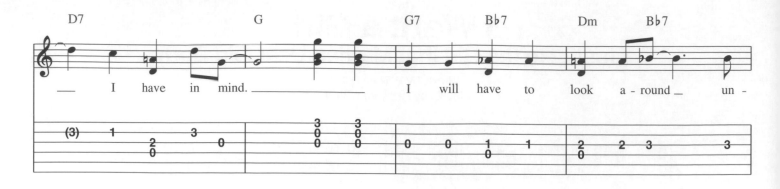

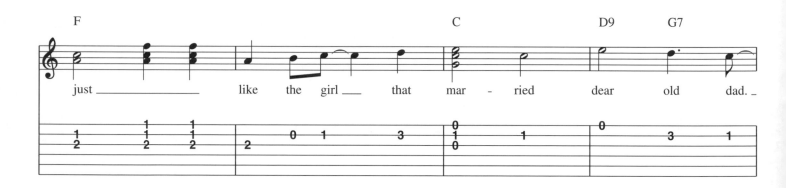

Chorus

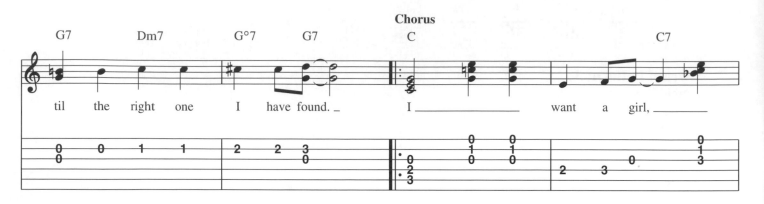

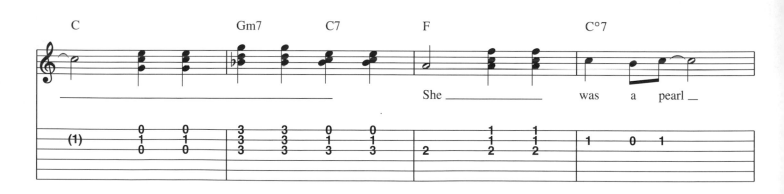

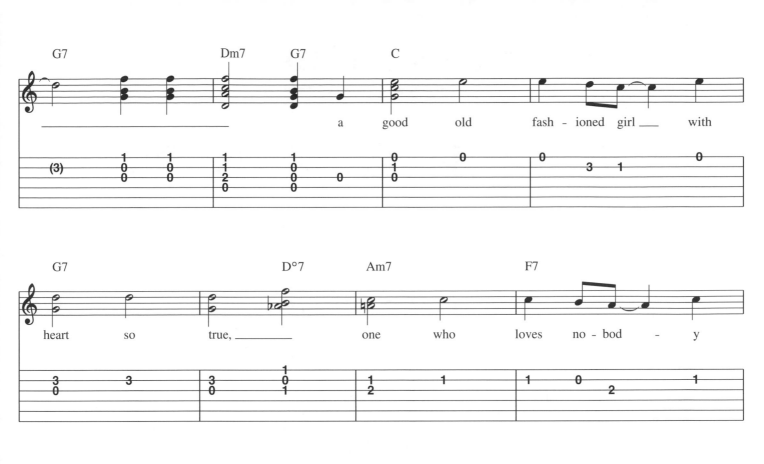

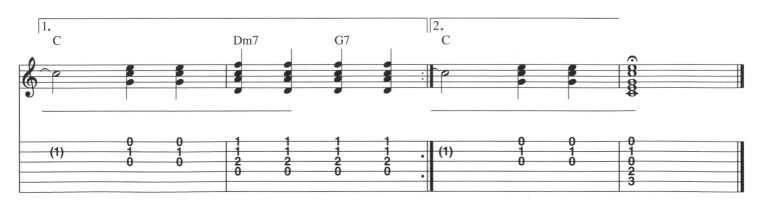

I Love You Truly

Words and Music by Carrie Jacobs-Bond

Strum Pattern: 7, 8
Pick Pattern: 7, 8

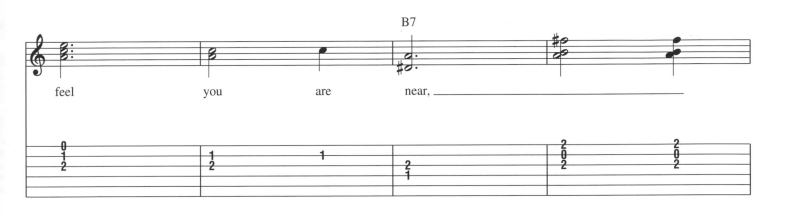

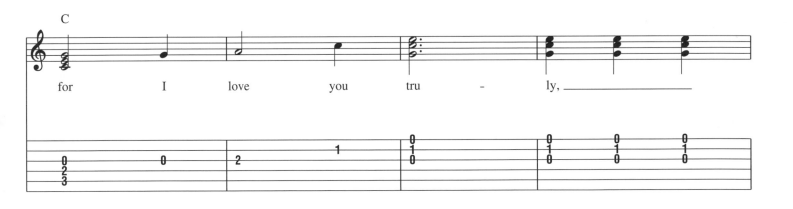

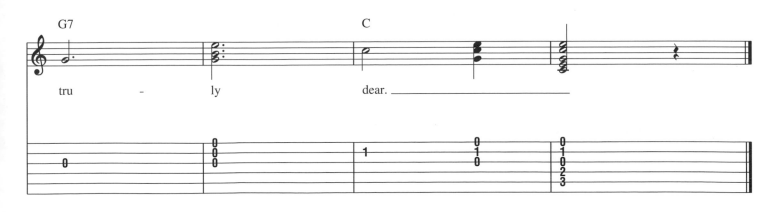

I Wish I Were Single Again

Words and Music by J.C. Beckel

Strum Pattern: 7
Pick Pattern: 8

Verse
Moderate Waltz

1. I wish I __ were sin - gle a - gain, _____ I wish I __ were sin - gle a - gain!
3., 4. *See additional lyrics*

__ Oh, when I was sin - gle my pock - ets would jin - gle I wish I __ were sin - gle a - gain! _____ 2. I

Verse

mar - ried __ a wife, _ oh then, _____ I mar - ried _ a wife, _ oh then. _____ I mar - ried a

wife; _ she ru - ined my life. Oh, I wish I __ were sin - gle a - gain! _____ 3. She gain! _____

Additional Lyrics

3. She binged me, she banged me, oh then,
   She binged me, she banged me, o then.
   She binged me, she banged me;
   She thought she would hang me.
   I wish I were single again!

4. She went for the rope, oh then,
   She went for the rope, oh then.
   She went for the rope,
   But then it was broke.
   I wish I were single again!

Just a Closer Walk With Thee

Traditional
Arranged by Kenneth Morris

Strum Pattern: 3, 4
Pick Pattern: 3, 4

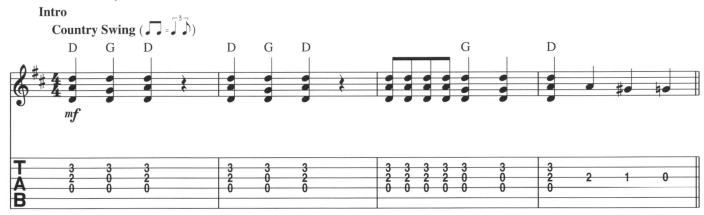

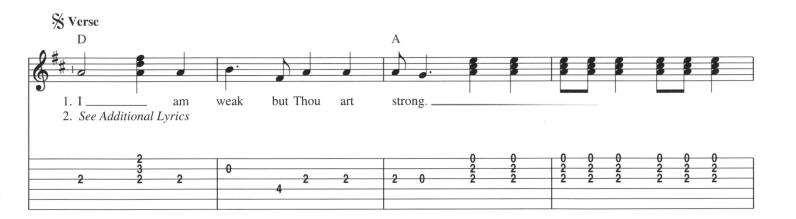

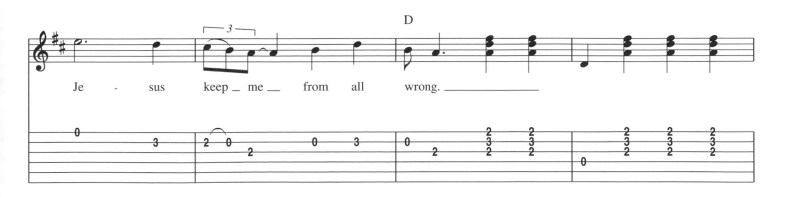

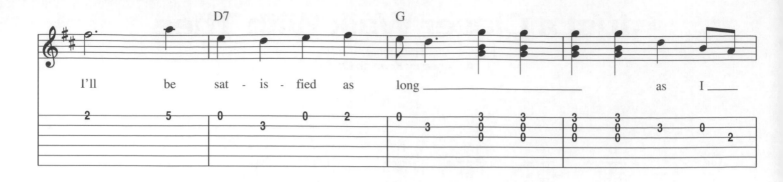

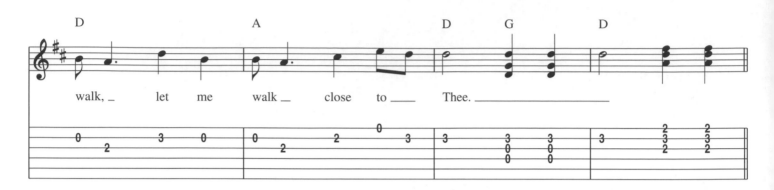

Chorus

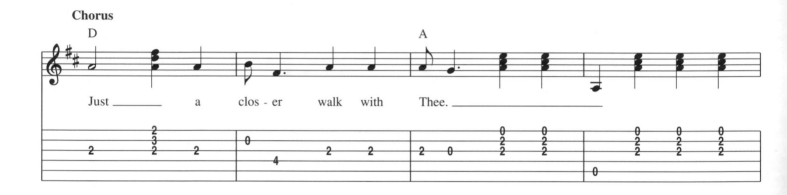

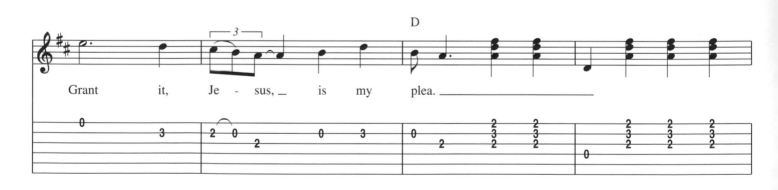

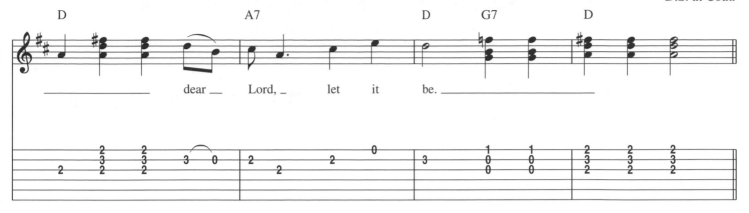

dear ___ Lord, ___ let it be. ___

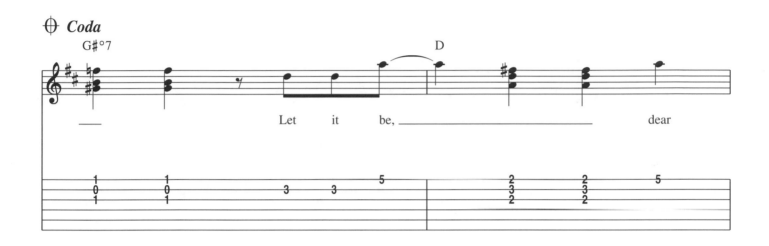

⊕ *Coda*

Let it be, ___ dear

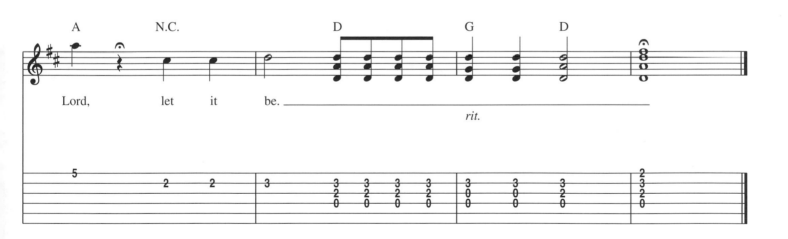

Lord, let it be. ___

rit.

Additional Lyrics

2. When my feeble life is o'er,
   Time for me will be no more.
   Guide me gently safely o'er
   To Thy Kingdom shore to Thy shore.

I Wonder Who's Kissing Her Now

Lyrics by Will M. Hough and Frank R. Adams
Music by Joseph E. Howard and Harold Orlob

Strum Pattern: 8
Pick Pattern: 8

Verse
Moderate Waltz

1. You have loved lots of girls in the sweet long a - go, and each one has meant heav-en to you,
2. *See additional lyrics*

you have vow'd your af - fec-tion to each one in turn and have sworn to them all you'd be true.

You have kissed 'neath the moon while the world seemed the tune, then you've left her to hunt a new game.

Does it ev - er oc - cur to you la - ter, my boy, _ that she's prob-ably do-ing the same? _ I

Chorus

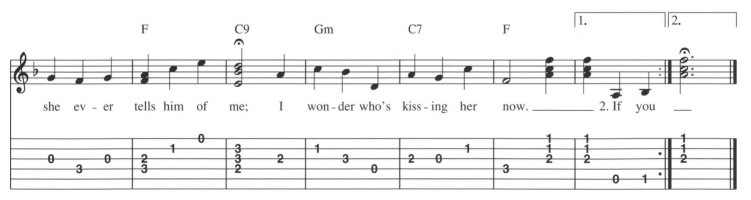

Additional Lyrics

2. If you want to feel wretched and lonely and blue,
   Just imagine the girl you love best
   In the arms of some fellow who's stealing a kiss
   From the lips that you once fondly pressed.
   But the world moves apace and the loves of today
   Flit away with a smile and a tear,
   So you never can tell who is kissing her now,
   Or just whom you'll be kissing next year.

I'll Be With You in Apple Blossom Time

Words by Neville Fleeson
Music by Albert von Tilzer

Strum Pattern: 7, 8
Pick Pattern: 7, 8

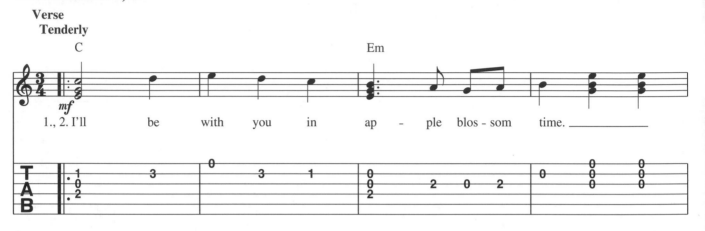

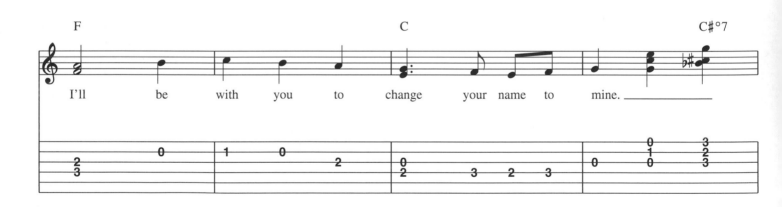

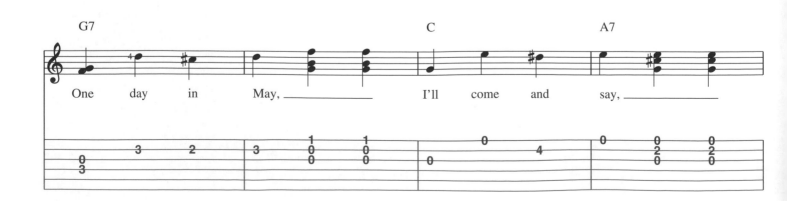

"Hap - py the bride the sun shines on to - day." _____

What a won - der - ful wed - ding there will be. _____

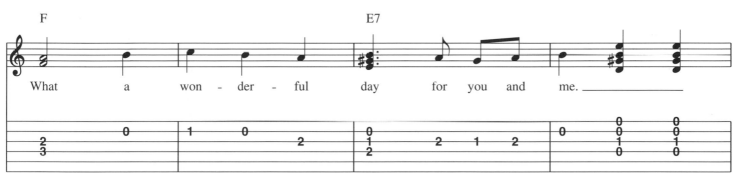

What a won - der - ful day for you and me. _____

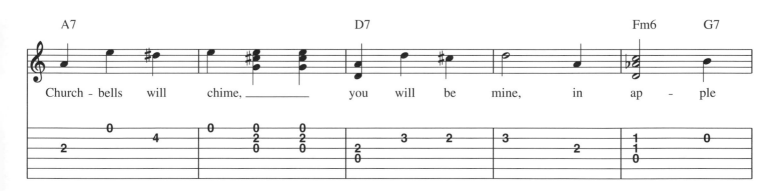

Church - bells will chime, _____ you will be mine, in ap - ple

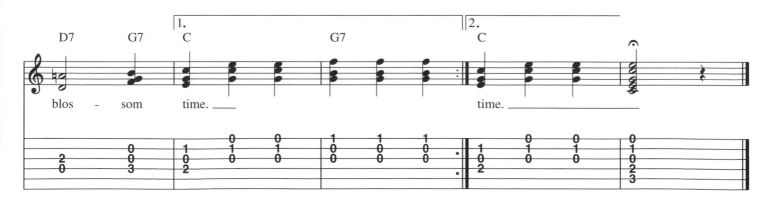

blos - som time. _____ time. _____

I'm Always Chasing Rainbows

Words by Joseph McCarthy
Music by Harry Carroll

Strum Pattern: 3, 4
Pick Pattern: 1, 3

183

I've Been Working on the Railroad

American Folksong

If You Were the Only Girl in the World

Words by Clifford Grey
Music by Nat D. Ayer

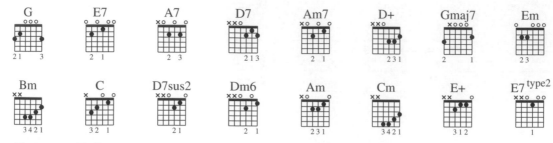

Strum Pattern: 7, 8
Pick Pattern: 7, 8

Verse

Slowly

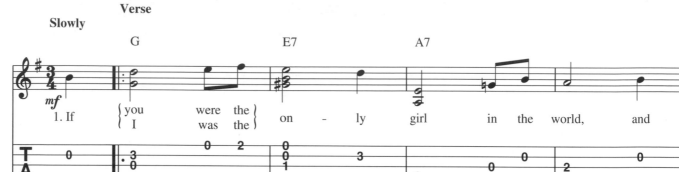

1. If {you were the / I was the} on - ly girl in the world, and

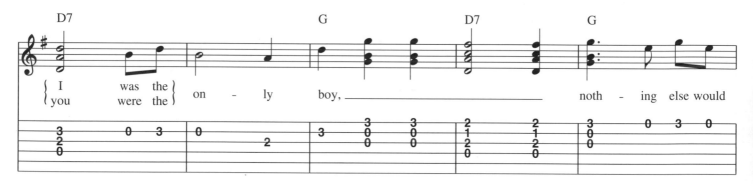

{I was the / you were the} on - ly boy, _____ noth - ing else would

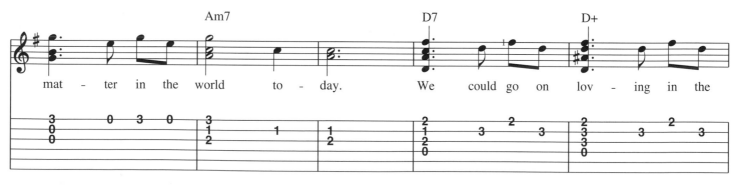

mat - ter in the world to - day. We could go on lov - ing in the

same old way. A Gar - den of E - den just made for

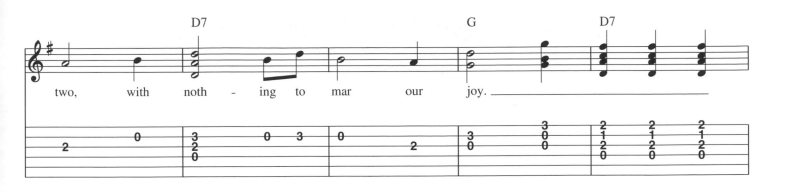

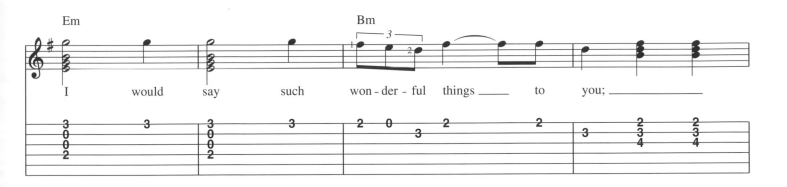

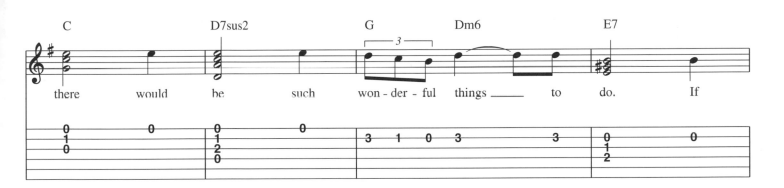

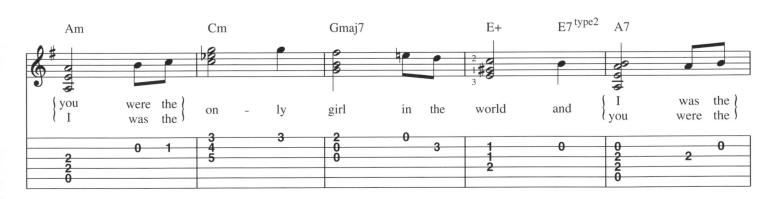

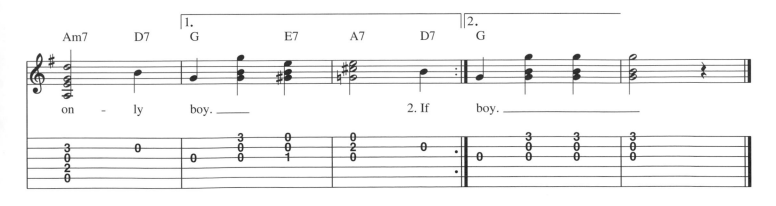

In the Good Old Summertime

from THE DEFENDER

Words by Ren Shields
Music by George Evans

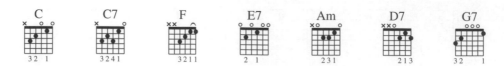

Strum Pattern: 7, 8
Pick Pattern: 7, 8

Moderately

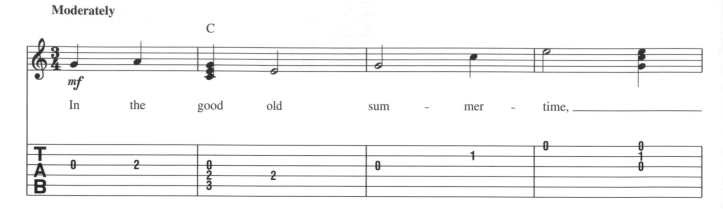

In the good old sum - mer - time, _____

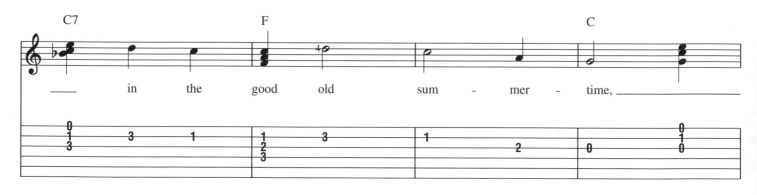

_____ in the good old sum - mer - time, _____

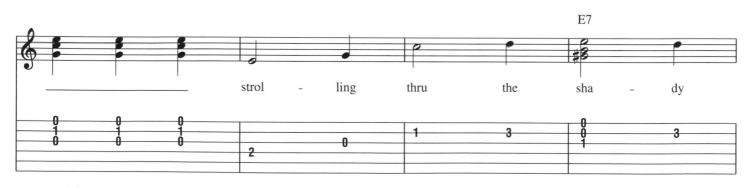

strol - ling thru the sha - dy

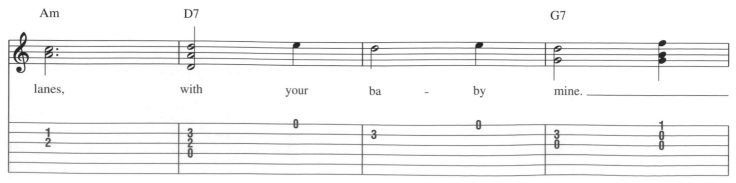

lanes, with your ba - by mine. _____

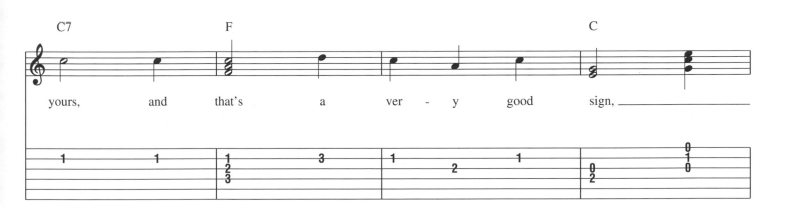

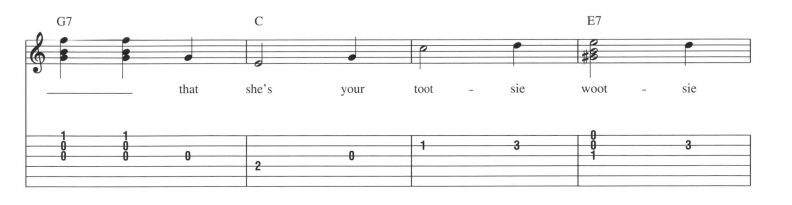

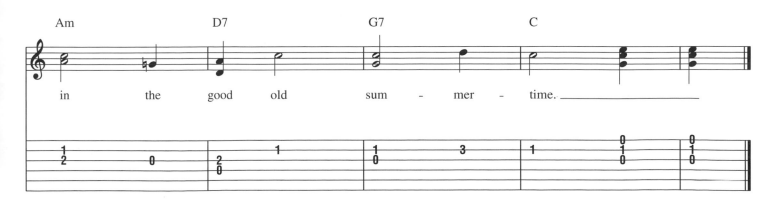

In the Shade of the Old Apple Tree

Words by Harry H. Williams
Music by Egbert Van Alstyne

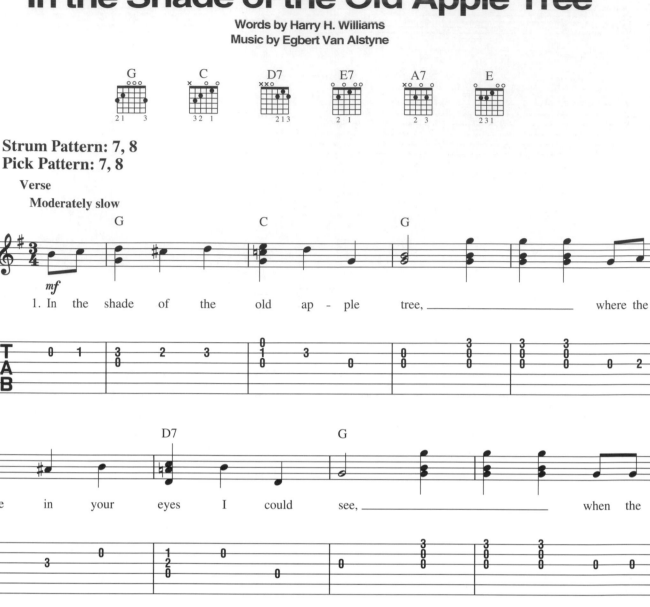

Strum Pattern: 7, 8
Pick Pattern: 7, 8

Verse
Moderately slow

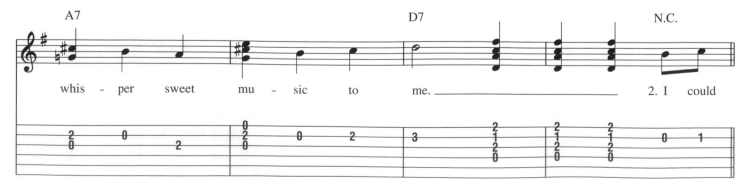

Verse

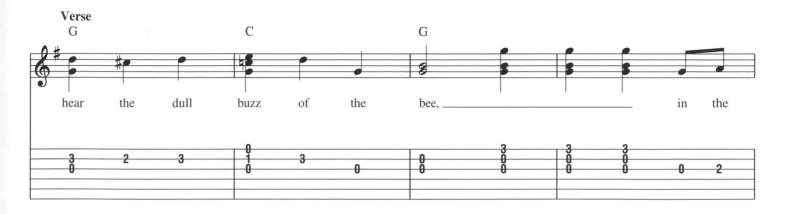

hear the dull buzz of the bee, _____ in the

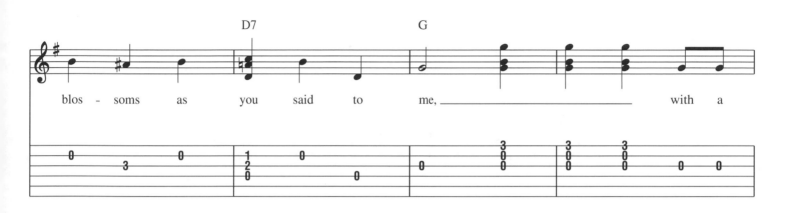

blos - soms as you said to me, _____ with a

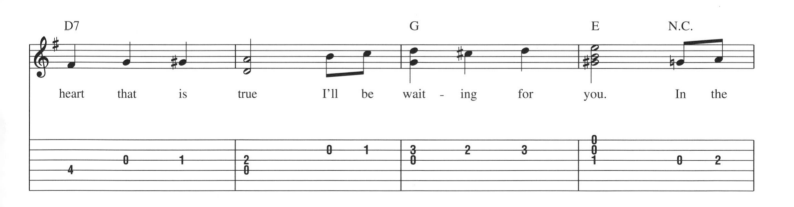

heart that is true I'll be wait - ing for you. In the

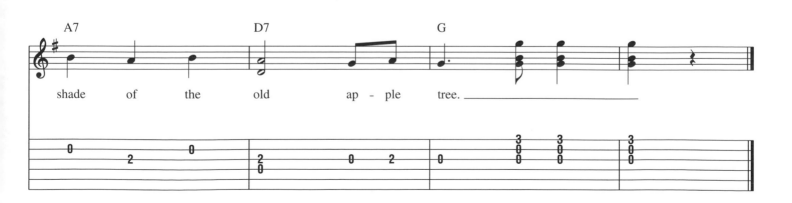

shade of the old ap - ple tree. _____

Indiana
(Back Home Again in Indiana)

Words by Ballard MacDonald
Music by James F. Hanley

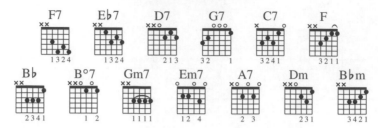

Strum Pattern: 4
Pick Pattern: 5

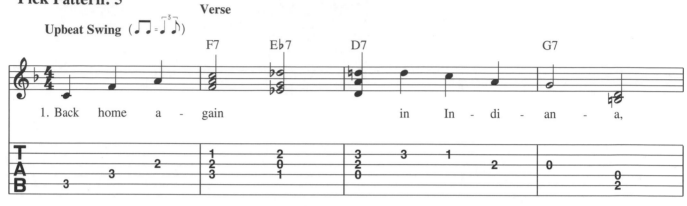

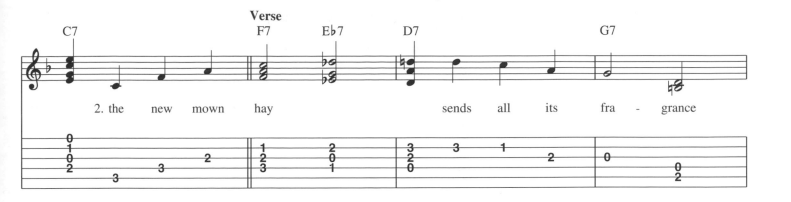

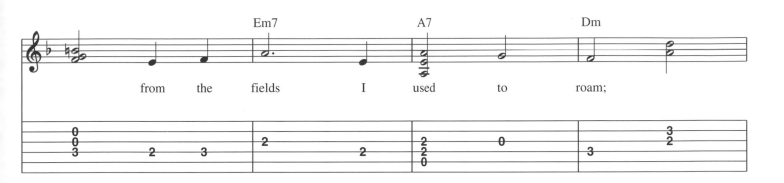

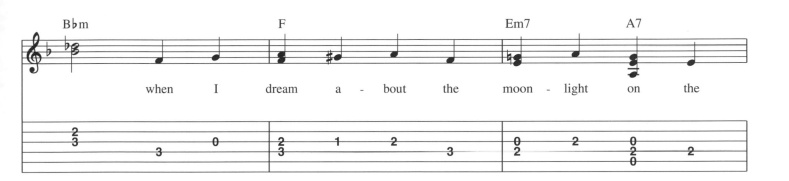

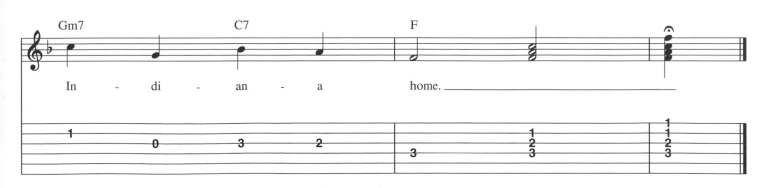

Jesu, Joy of Man's Desiring

By Johann Sebastian Bach

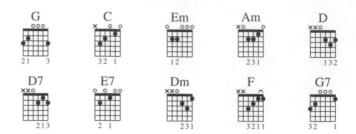

Strum Pattern: 8
Pick Pattern: 8

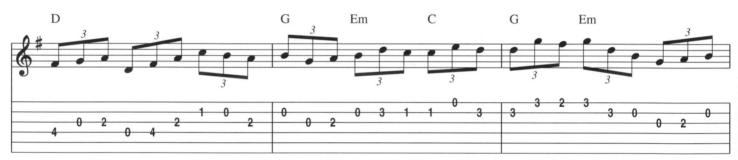

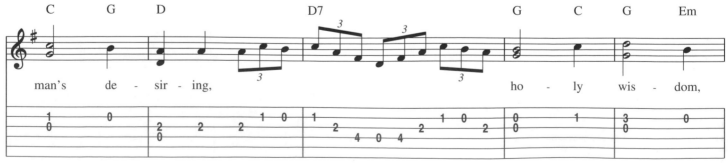

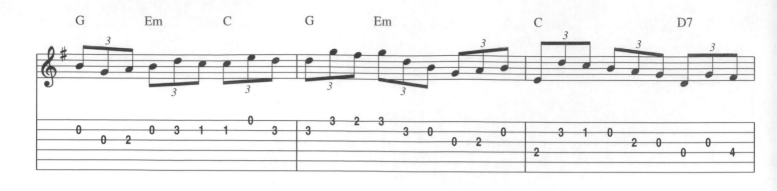

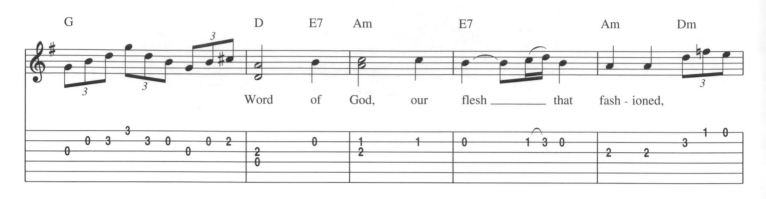

Word of God, our flesh _____ that fash - ioned,

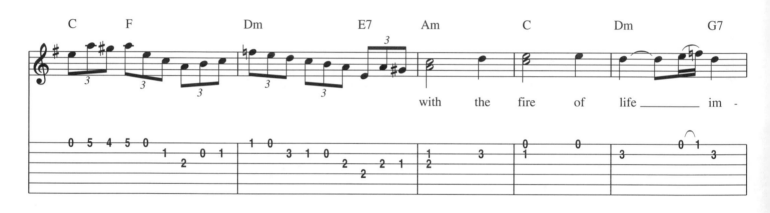

with the fire of life _____ im -

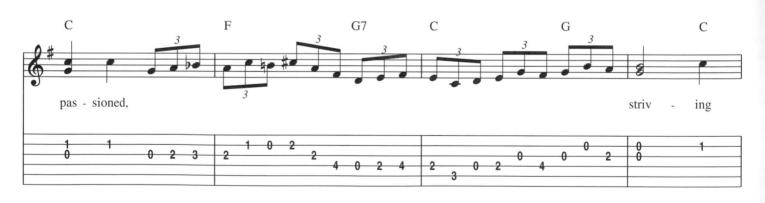

pas - sioned,   striv - ing,

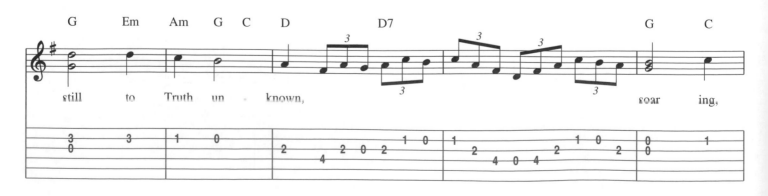

still to Truth un known,   soar ing,

dy - ing round ____ Thy _____ throne.

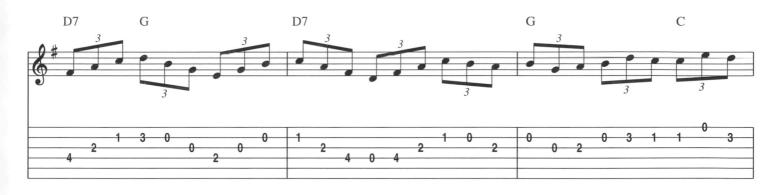

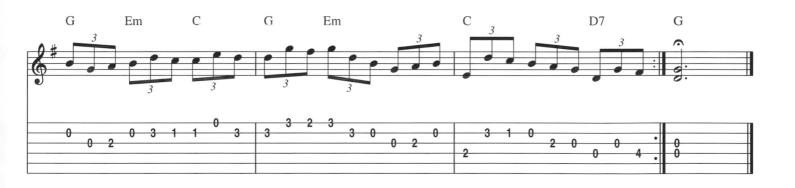

Additional Lyrics

2. Through the way where hope is guiding,
Hark, what peaceful music rings!
Where the flock in Thee confiding,
Drink of joy from deathless springs.
Their's is beauty's fairest pleasure,
Their's is wisdom's holiest treasure.
Thou dost ever lead Thine own,
In the love of joys unknown.

Joshua
(Fit the Battle of Jericho)

African-American Spiritual

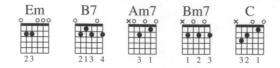

Strum Pattern: 4
Pick Pattern: 1

Chorus
Moderately slow

Gid - e - on, you may talk a - bout your men of Saul; but there's

D.C. al Coda

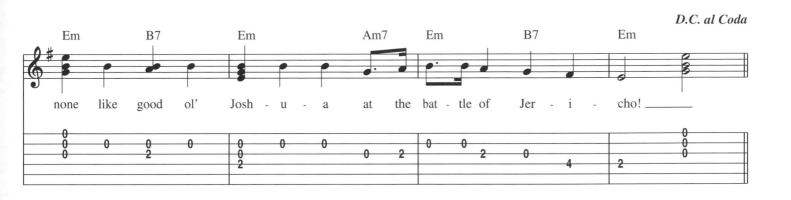

none like good ol' Josh - u - a at the bat - tle of Jer - i - cho! _____

Coda

Outro

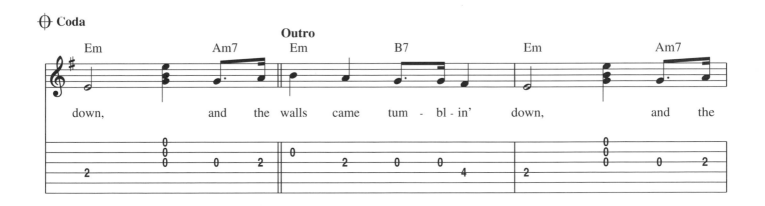

down, and the walls came tum - bl - in' down, and the

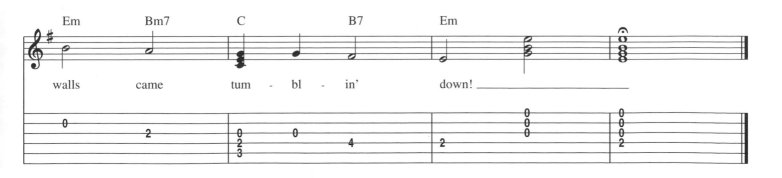

walls came tum - bl - in' down! _____

Kum Ba Yah

Traditional

Strum Pattern: 4
Pick Pattern: 1, 2

Additional Lyrics

2. Hear me crying, Lord, Kum ba ya!
   Hear me crying, Lord, Kum ba ya!
   Hear me crying, Lord, Kum ba ya!
   Oh Lord! Kum ba ya!

3. Hear me praying, Lord, Kum ba ya!
   Hear me praying, Lord, Kum ba ya!
   Hear me praying, Lord, Kum ba ya!
   O Lord! Kum ba ya!

4. Oh I need you, Lord, Kum ba ya!
   Oh I need you, Lord, Kum ba ya!
   Oh I need you, Lord, Kum ba ya!
   Oh Lord! Kum ba ya!

Lavender's Blue

Traditional

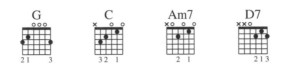

Strum Pattern: 8
Pick Pattern: 8

Verse
Moderately

1. Lav - en - der's blue, did-dle, did-dle, Lav - en - der's green, _____ when I am
3. *See additional lyrics*

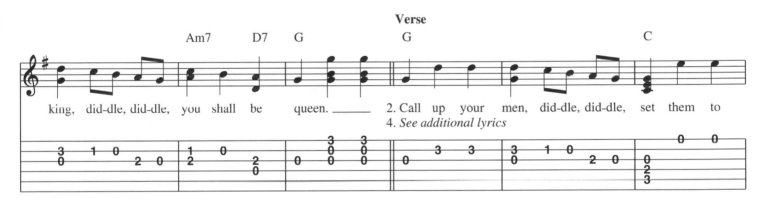

king, did-dle, did-dle, you shall be queen. _____ 2. Call up your men, did-dle, did-dle, set them to
4. *See additional lyrics*

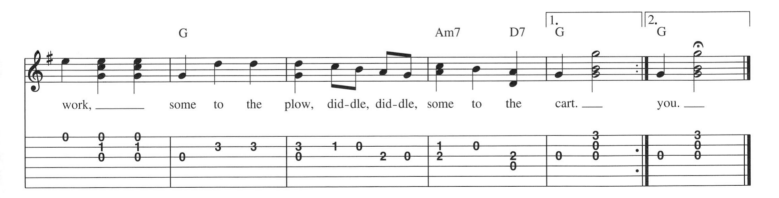

work, _____ some to the plow, did-dle, did-dle, some to the cart. ___ you. ___

Additional Lyrics

3. Some to make hay, diddle, diddle,
   Some to cut corn,
   While you and I, diddle, diddle,
   Keep ourselves warm.

4. Lavender's green, diddle, diddle,
   Lavender's blue,
   If you love me, diddle, diddle,
   I will love you.

La Cucaracha

Traditional

Strum Pattern: 3
Pick Pattern: 4

Verse
Brightly

mf 1. When a fel - low loves a maid - en, and that maid - en does - n't
2. - 7. *See Additional Lyrics*

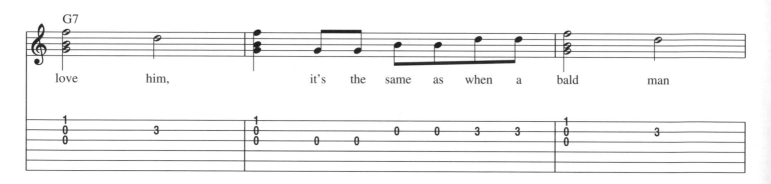

love him, it's the same as when a bald man

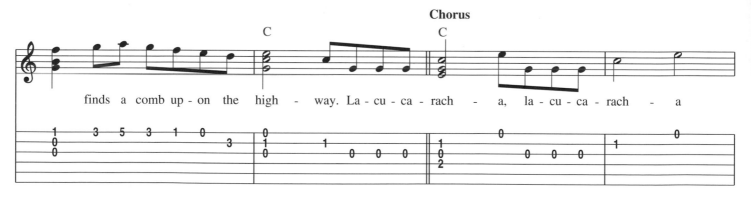

finds a comb up - on the high - way. La - cu - ca - rach - a, la - cu - ca - rach - a

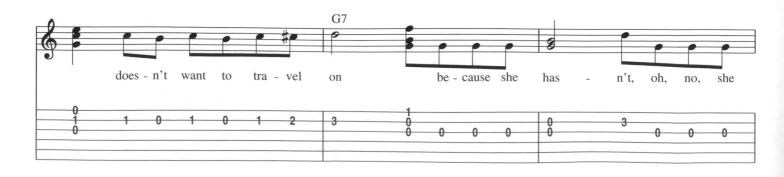

does - n't want to tra - vel on be - cause she has - n't, oh, no, she

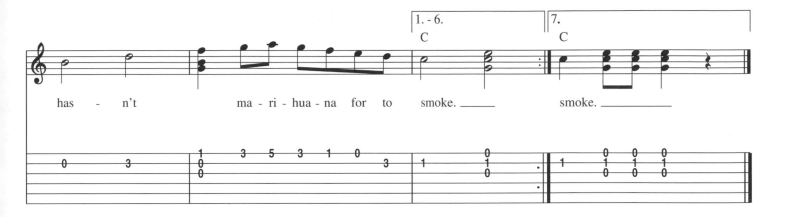

has - n't   ma - ri - hua - na   for   to   smoke. _____   smoke. _____

Additional Lyrics

2. All the maidens are of pure gold;
   All the married girls are silver;
   All the widows are of copper,
   And old women merely tin.

3. My neighbor across the highway
   Used to be called Dona Clara,
   And if she has not expired
   Likely that's her name tomorrow.

4. All the girls up at Las Vegas
   Are most awful tall and skinny,
   But they're worse for plaintive pleading
   Than the souls of Purgatory.

5. All the girls here in the city
   Don't know how to give you kisses,
   While the ones from Albuquerque
   Stretch their necks to avoid misses.

6. All the girls from Mexico
   Are as pretty as a flower
   And they talk so very sweetly,
   Fill your heart quite up with love.

7. One thing makes me laugh most hearty
   Pancho Villa with no shirt on
   Now the Carranzistas beat it
   Because Villa's men are coming.

Spanish Lyrics

1. Cuando uno quiera a una,
   Yesta una nolo quiera,
   Es lo mismo que si un calvo
   En la calle encuen trún peine.

   Chorus:
   La cucaracha, la cucaracha
   Ya no quieras cominar,
   Porque no tienes, porque la falta
   Marihuana que fumar.

2. Las muchachas son de orro;
   Las casadas son de plata;
   Las viudas son de cobre,
   Y las viejas oja de lata.

3. Mi vecina de enfrente
   Se llamaba Dona Clara
   Y si no habia muerto
   Es probable se llamara.

4. Las muchachas de La Vegas
   Son muy altas y delgaditas
   Pero son mas pediguenas
   Que las animas benditas.

5. Las muchachas de la villa
   No saben ni dar un beso.
   Cuando las de Albuquerque
   Hasta estiran el pescuezo.

6. Las muchachas Mexicanas
   Son lindas como un flor,
   Y hablan tan dulcemente
   Que encantan de amor.

7. Una cosa me da risa
   Pancho Villa sin vamisa.
   Ya se van los Carranzistas
   Porque vienen los Villistas.

La Golondrina

By N. Serradell

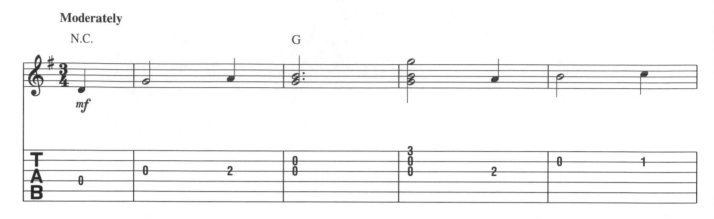

Strum Pattern: 7, 8
Pick Pattern: 7, 8

Moderately

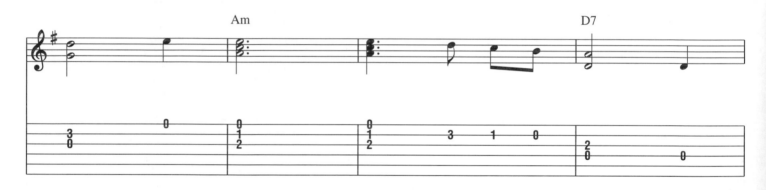

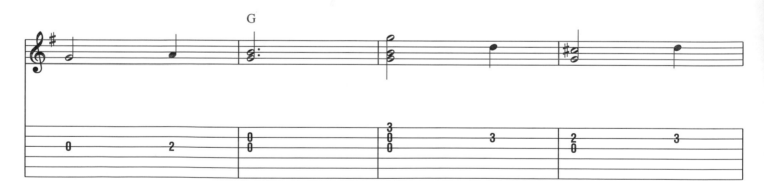

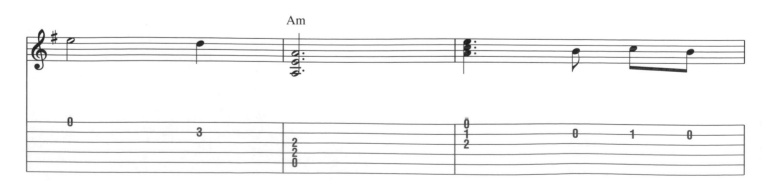

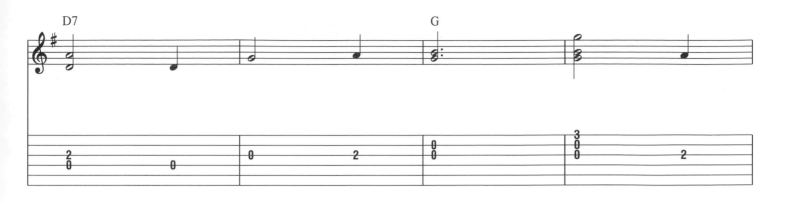

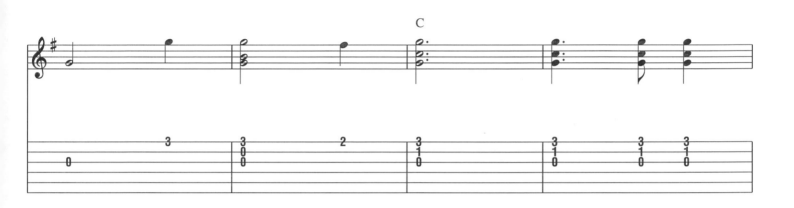

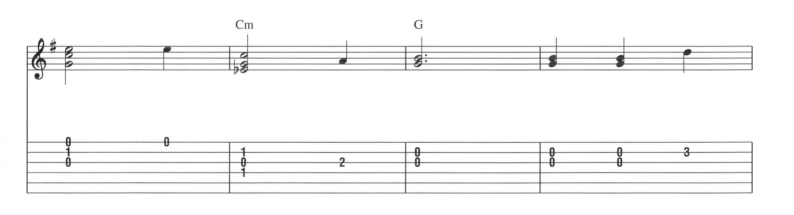

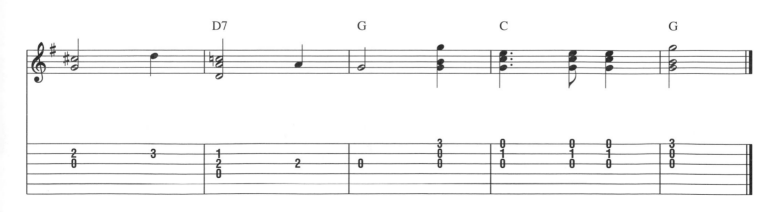

La Paloma
(The Dove)
By S. Yradier

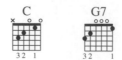

Strum Pattern: 2, 4
Pick Pattern: 1, 3

Moderately

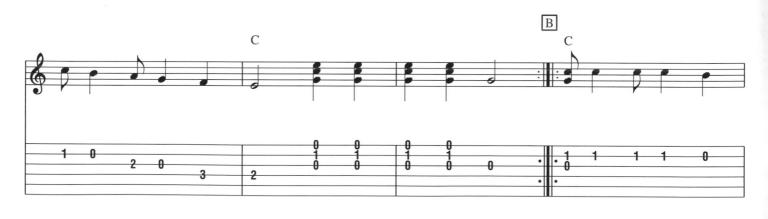

Let Me Call You Sweetheart

Words by Beth Slater Whitson
Music by Leo Friedman

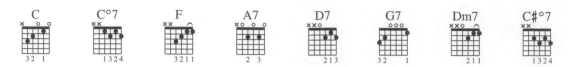

Strum Pattern: 7
Pick Pattern: 8

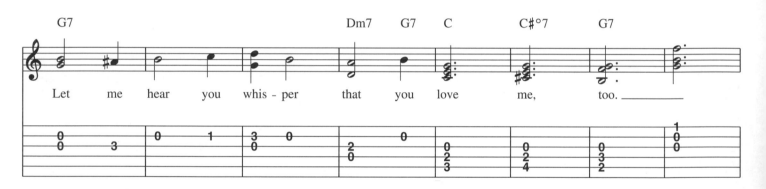

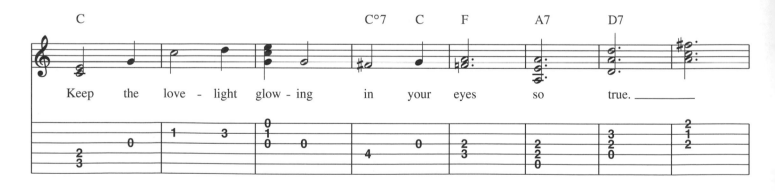

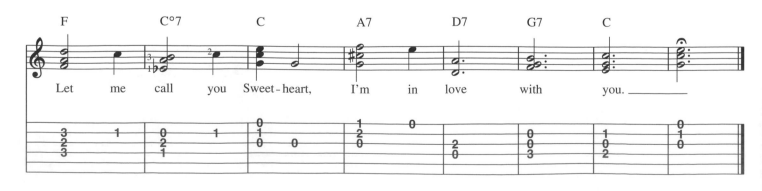

The Liberty Bell

By John Philip Sousa

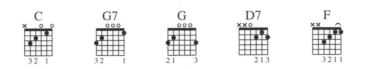

Strum Pattern: 7, 8
Pick Pattern: 7, 8

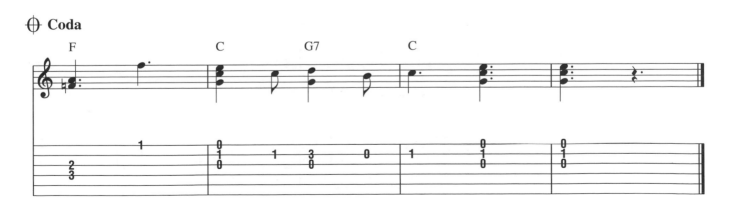

Limehouse Blues

from ZIEGFELD FOLLIES

Words by Douglas Furber
Music by Philip Braham

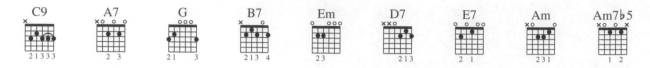

Strum Pattern: 10
Pick Pattern: 10

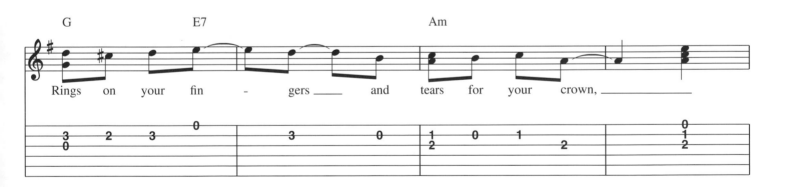

Listen to the Mocking Bird

Words by Alice Hawthorne
Music by Richard Milburn

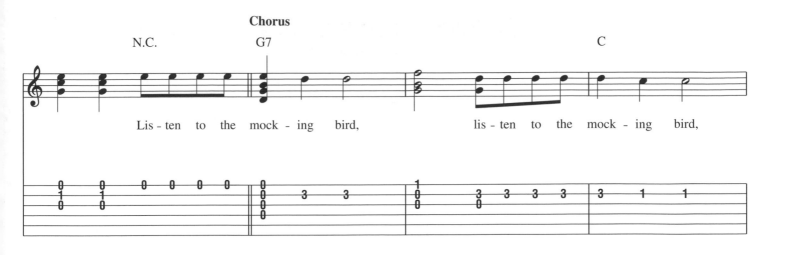

Listen to the mock-ing bird, listen to the mock-ing bird,

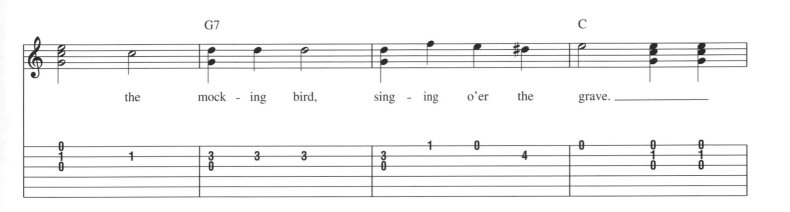

the mock-ing bird, sing-ing o'er the grave.

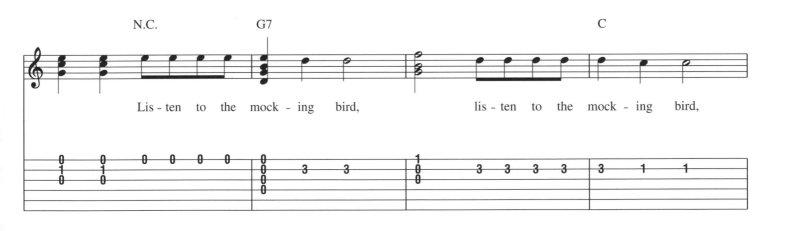

Listen to the mock-ing bird, listen to the mock-ing bird,

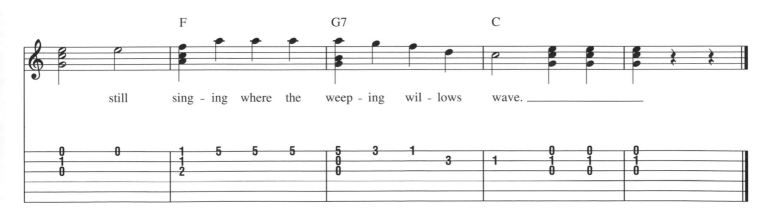

still sing-ing where the weep-ing wil-lows wave.

Little Brown Jug

Words and Music by Joseph E. Winner

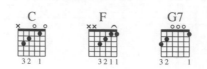

Strum Pattern: 10
Pick Pattern: 10

Verse

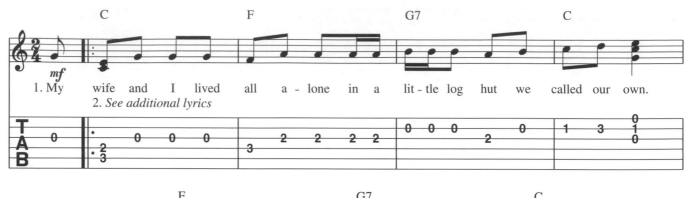

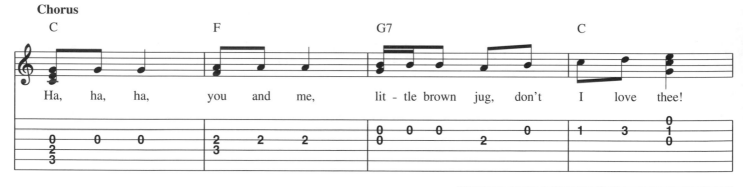

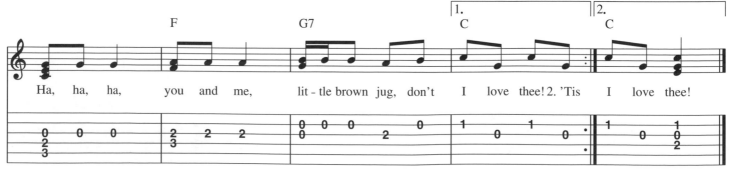

Additional Lyrics

2. 'Tis you who makes my friend my foes,
   'Tis you who makes me wear old clothes;
   Here you are so near my nose,
   So tip her up and down she goes!

The Lonesome Road

African-American Spiritual

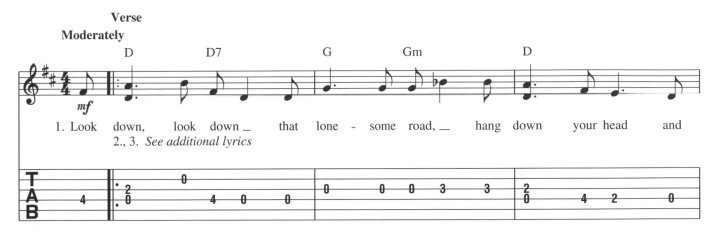

Strum Pattern: 3
Pick Pattern: 4

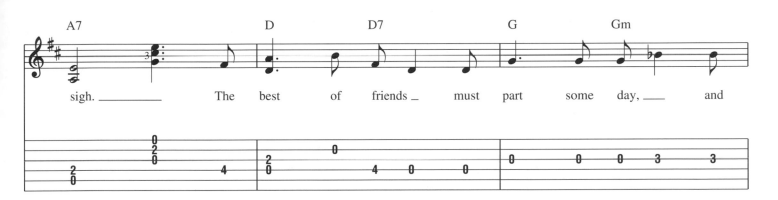

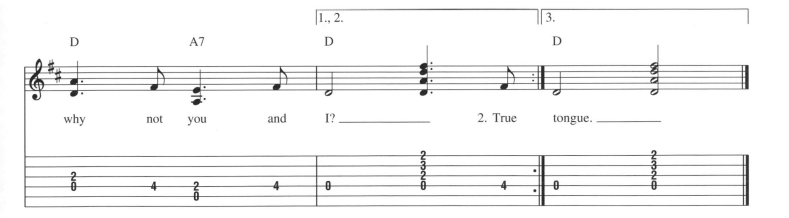

Additional Lyrics

2. True love, true love, what have I done?
   That you should treat me so?
   You caused me to talk and to walk with you
   Like I never done before.

3. I wish to God that I had died,
   Had died 'fore I was born.
   Before I seen your smilin' face,
   And heard your lyin' tongue.

Loch Lomand

Traditional

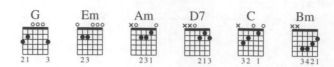

Strum Pattern: 3
Pick Pattern: 4

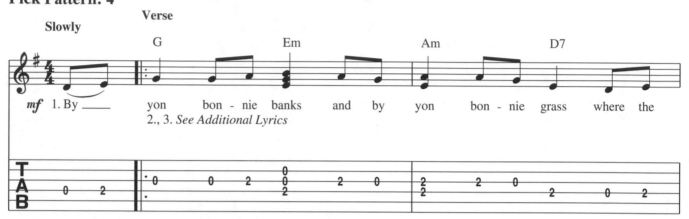

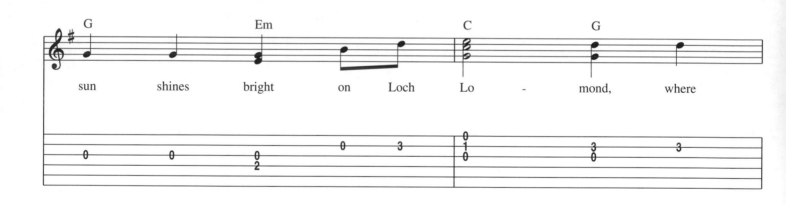

Additional Lyrics

2. 'Twas then that we parted in yon shady glen,
   On the steep, steep side of Ben Lomond.
   Where in purple hue, the Highland hills we view
   And the moon coming out in the gloaming.

3. The wee birdies sing, and the wildflowers spring,
   And in sunshine, the waters are sleeping.
   But the broken heart, it kens, nae second spring again,
   Tho' the woeful may cease their greeting.

Look for the Silver Lining

from SALLY

Words by Buddy DeSylva
Music by Jerome Kern

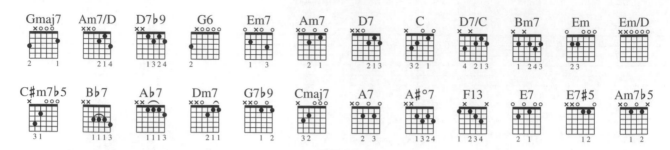

Strum Pattern: 3, 4
Pick Pattern: 2, 3

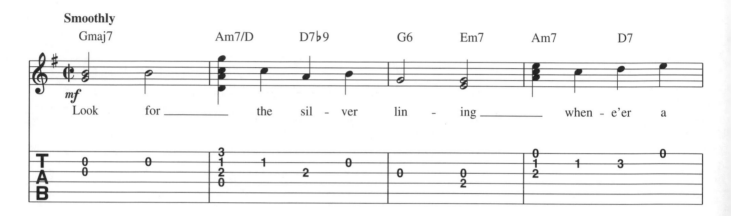

Look for ___ the sil - ver lin - ing ___ when - e'er a

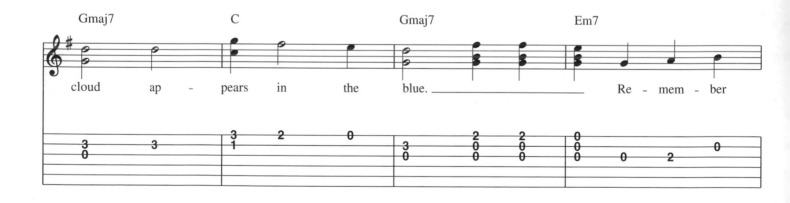

cloud ap - pears in the blue. ___ Re - mem - ber

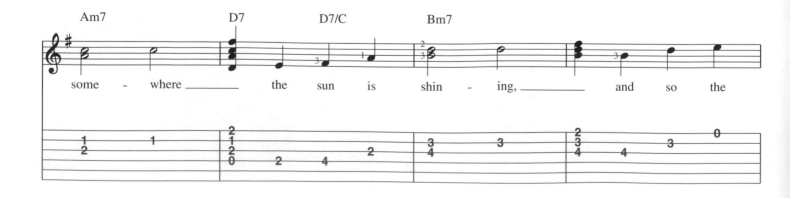

some - where ___ the sun is shin - ing, ___ and so the

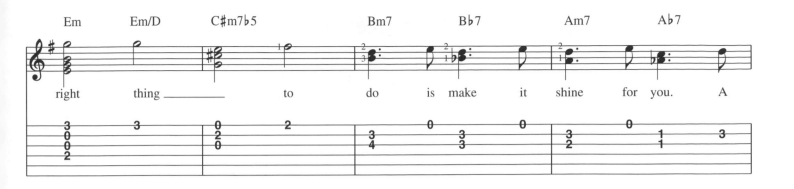

right thing _____ to do is make it shine for you. A

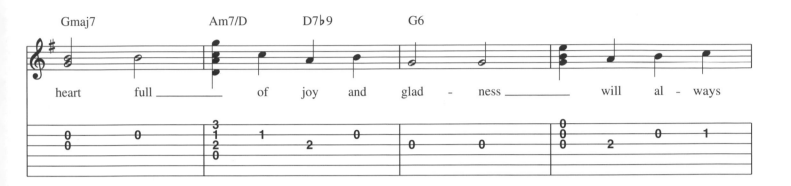

heart full _____ of joy and glad - ness _____ will al - ways

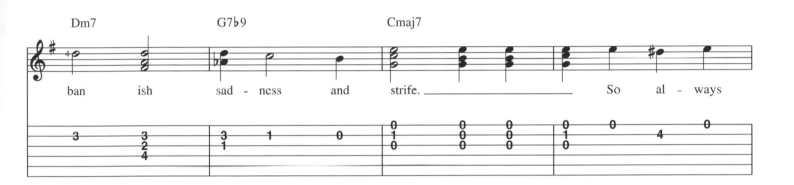

ban - ish sad - ness and strife. _____ So al - ways

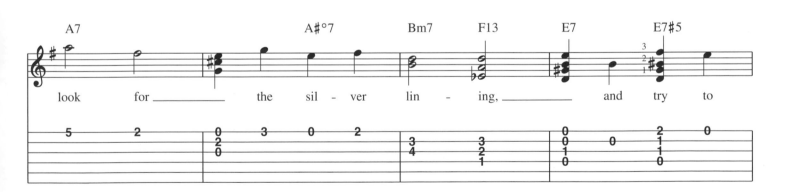

look for _____ the sil - ver lin - ing, _____ and try to

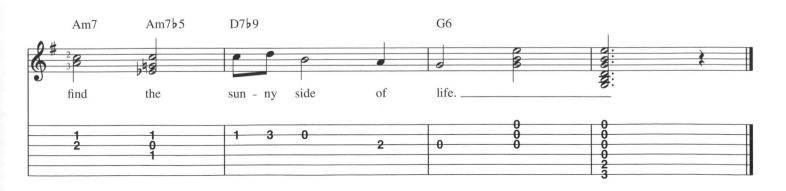

find the sun - ny side of life. _____

Lullaby
(Cradle Song)
By Johannes Brahms

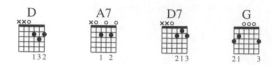

Strum Pattern: 7
Pick Pattern: 7

Tenderly

Gu - ten a - bend, gut' Nacht, mit __ Ro - sen __ be - dacht, __ mit __

Näg' - lein be - steckt, schlupf' __ un - ter die Deck': Mor - gen

früh, __ wenn Gott will, __ wirst du wie - der ge - weckt, __ mor - gen

früh, __ wenn Gott will, __ wirst du wie - der ge - weckt.

Marianne

Traditional

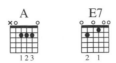

Strum Pattern: 4
Pick Pattern: 3

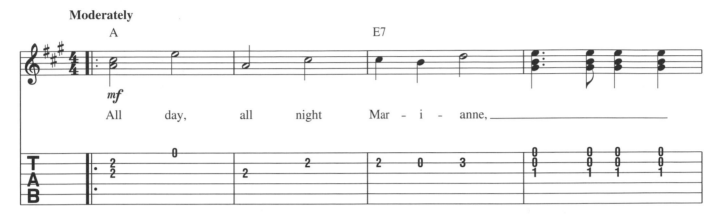

Moderately

All day, all night Mar - i - anne,

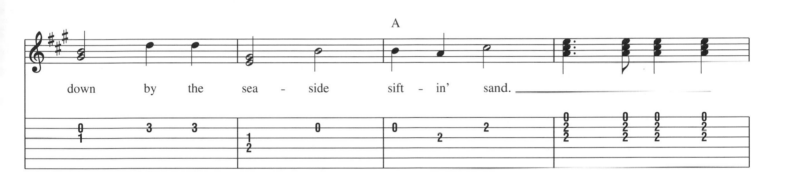

down by the sea - side sift - in' sand.

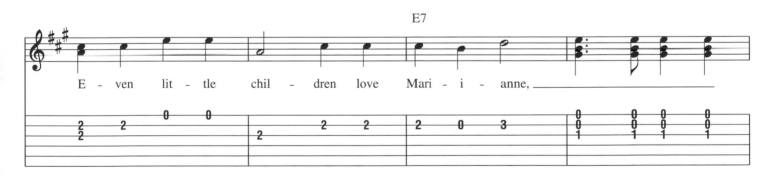

E - ven lit - tle chil - dren love Mari - i - anne,

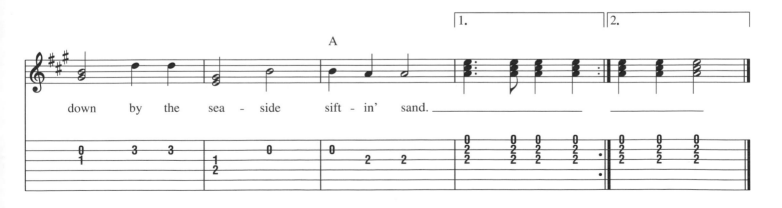

down by the sea - side sift - in' sand.

1.   2.

Maori Farewell Song

Traditional Hawaiian Folksong

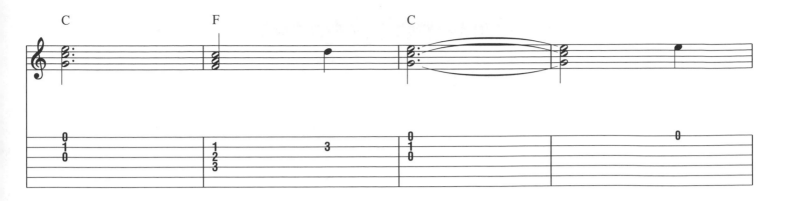

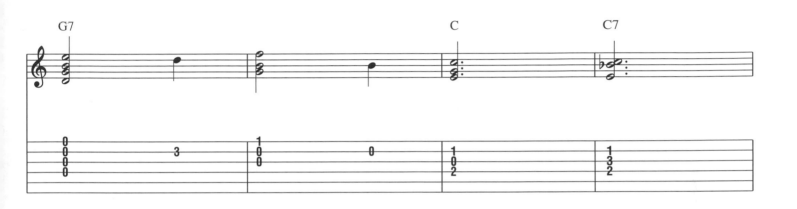

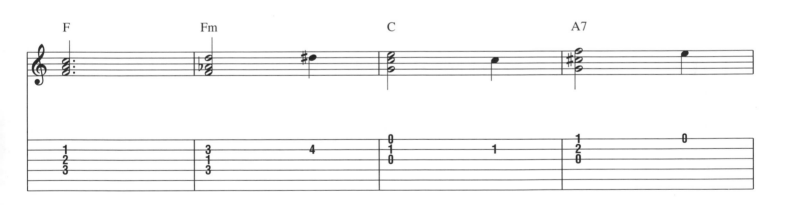

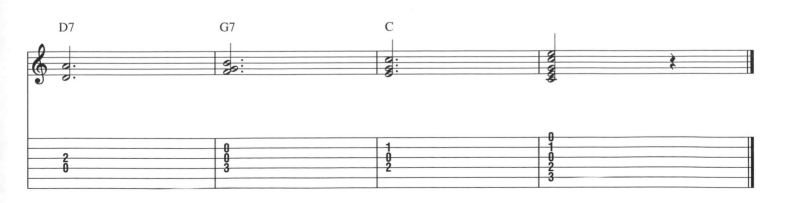

Marine's Hymn

Words by Henry C. Davis
Melody based on a theme by Jacques Offenbach

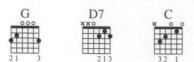

Strum Pattern: 4
Pick Pattern: 3

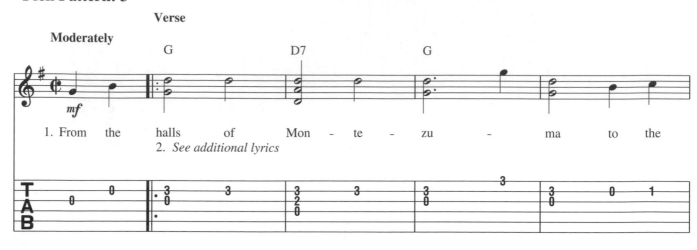

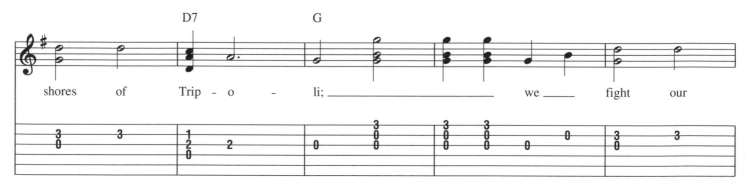

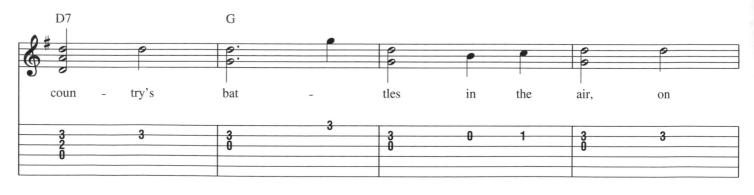

Additional Lyrics

2. From the flags unfurled to ev'ry breeze
   From dawn to setting sun;
   We have fought in ev'ry *clime and place
   Where we could take a gun.
   In the snow of far off Northern lands
   And in sunny tropic scenes;
   You will always find us on the job
   The United States Marine.

*climate

Mary's a Grand Old Name

from FORTY-FIVE MINUTES FROM BROADWAY

Words and Music by George M. Cohan

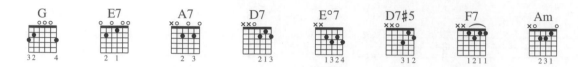

Strum Pattern: 4
Pick Pattern: 1

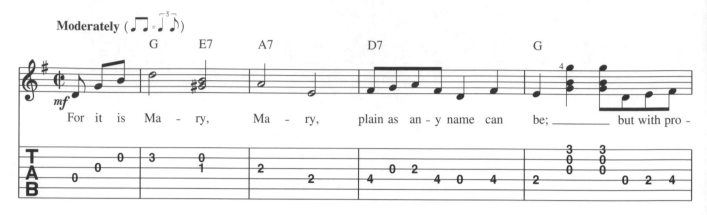

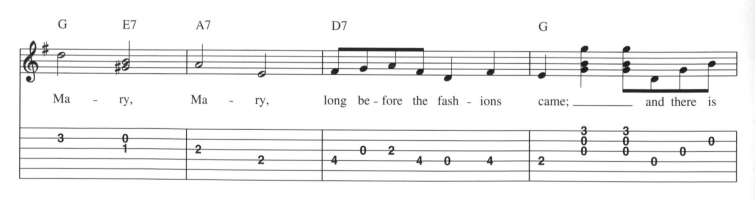

Meet Me in St. Louis, Louis

from MEET ME IN ST. LOUIS
Words by Andrew B. Sterling
Music by Kerry Mills

Strum Pattern: 7
Pick Pattern: 8

Verse
Moderately

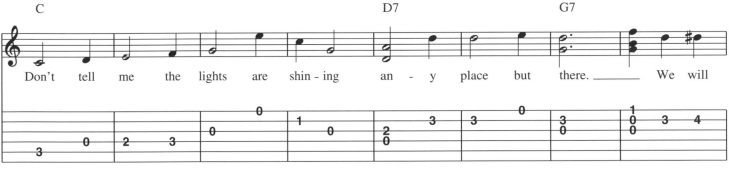

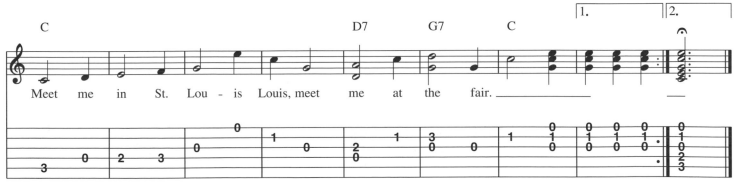

Meet Me Tonight in Dreamland

Words by Beth Slater Whitson
Music by Leo Friedman

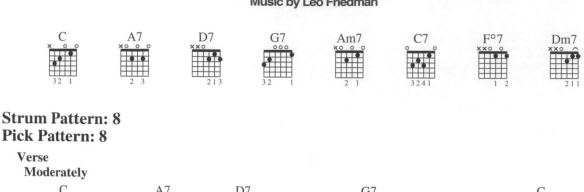

Strum Pattern: 8
Pick Pattern: 8

Verse
Moderately

1., 2. Meet me to-night in dream-land un-der the sil-v'ry moon. ____

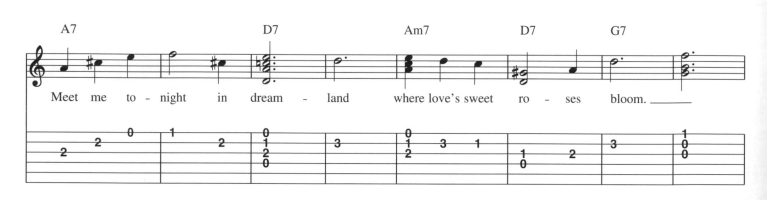

Meet me to-night in dream-land where love's sweet ro-ses bloom. ____

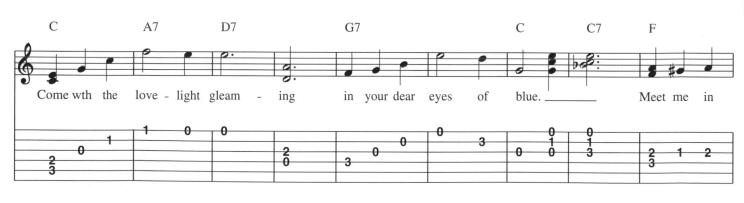

Come wth the love-light gleam-ing in your dear eyes of blue. ____ Meet me in

dream-land, sweet dream-y dream-land; there let my dreams come true. ____ true. ____

Memories

Words by Gus Kahn
Music by Egbert Van Alstyne

Strum Pattern: 7, 8
Pick Pattern: 7, 8

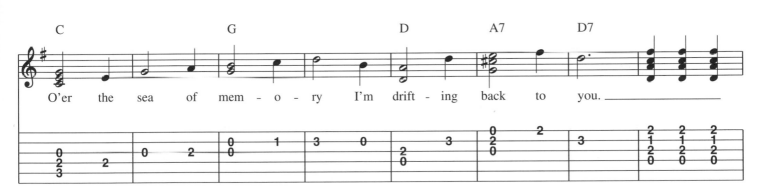

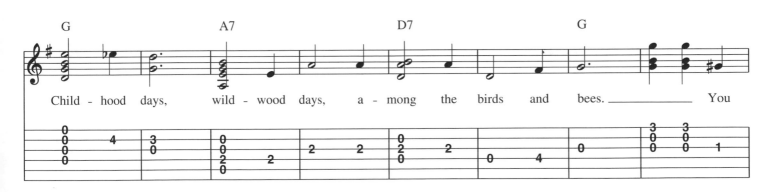

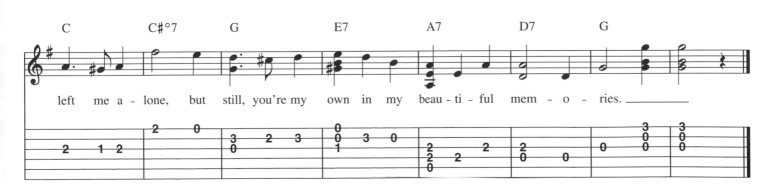

Melody of Love

By H. Engelmann

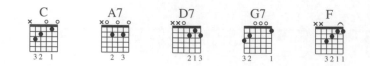

Strum Pattern: 7, 8
Pick Pattern: 7, 8

Moderately slow

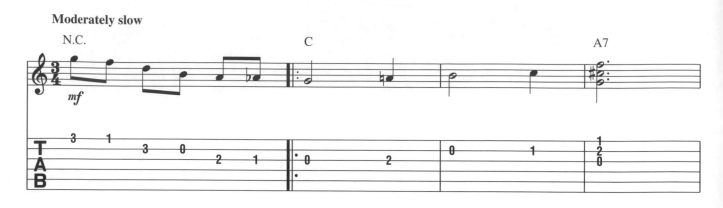

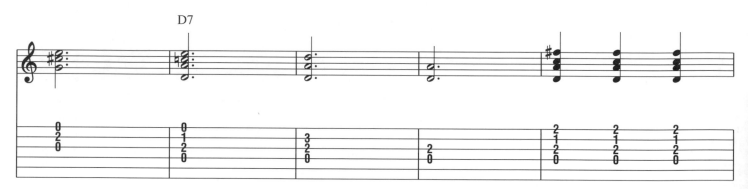

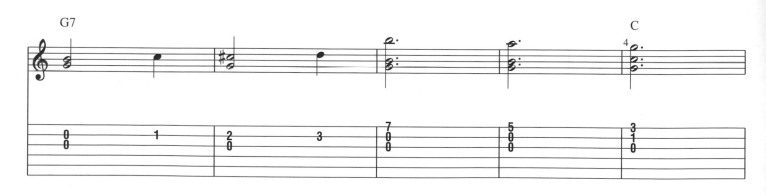

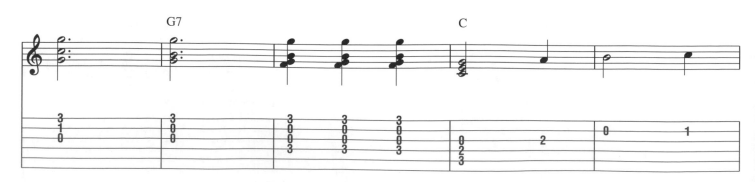

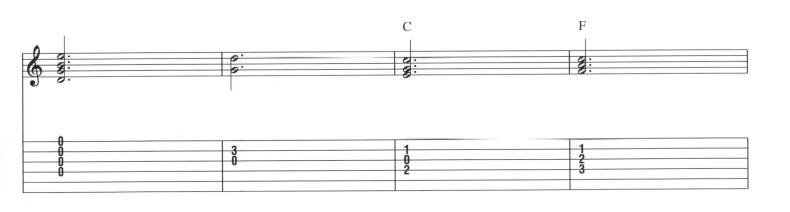

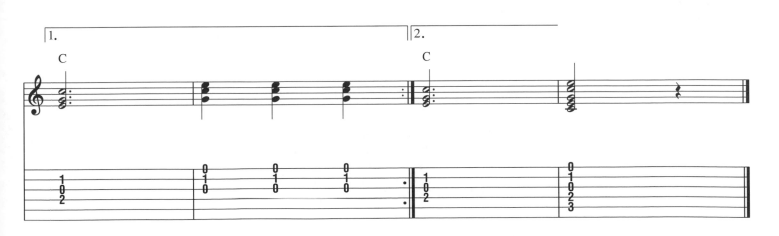

Michael Row the Boat Ashore

Traditional Folksong

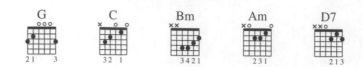

Strum Pattern: 3
Pick Pattern: 3

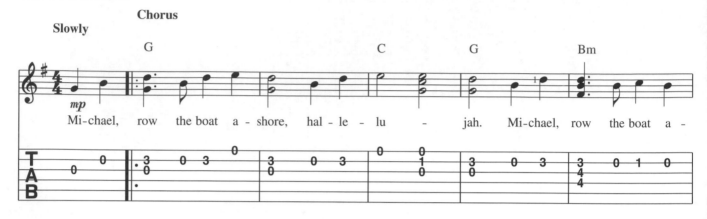

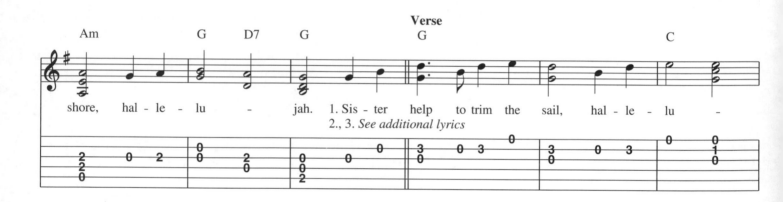

Additional Lyrics

2. Jordan River is chilly and cold, hallelujah.
   Kills the body but not the soul, halleljah.

3. Jordan River is deep and wide, hallelujah.
   Milk and honey on the other side, hallelujah.

Moonlight Bay

Words by Edward Madden
Music by Percy Wenrich

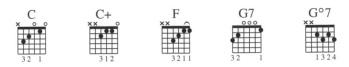

Strum Pattern: 3
Pick Pattern: 3

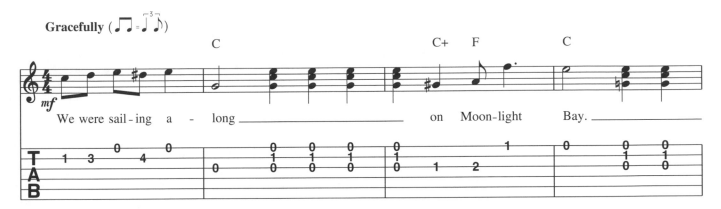

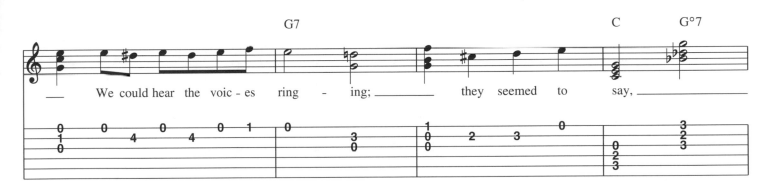

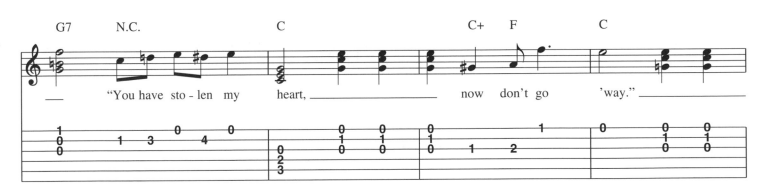

233

Midnight Special

Railroad Song

Strum Pattern: 2, 3
Pick Pattern: 3, 4

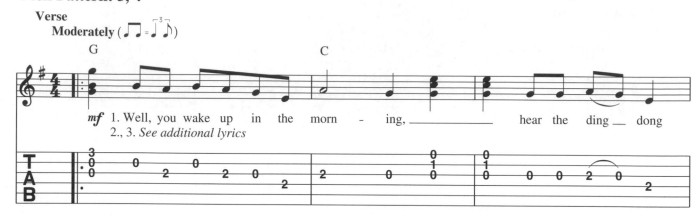

Verse
Moderately

1. Well, you wake up in the morn - ing, _____ hear the ding _ dong
2., 3. *See additional lyrics*

ring, _____ you go march - ing to the ta - ble, _____

_ see the same _ damn _ thing. _____ Well, it's on - ly one _ ta - ble, _____

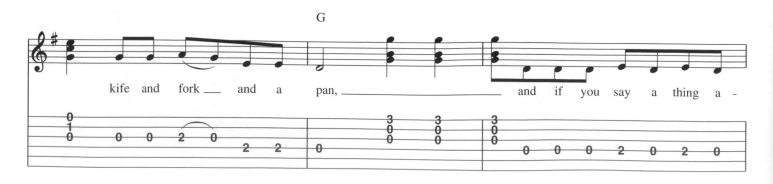

kife and fork _ and a pan, _____ and if you say a thing a -

234

Chorus

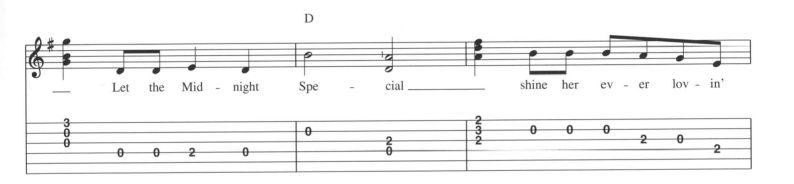

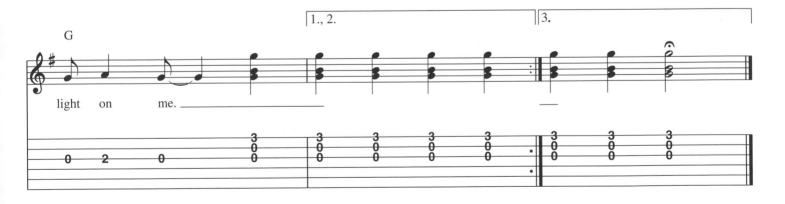

Additional Lyrics

2. If you ever go to Houston, you'd better walk right,
   And you better not stagger, and you better not fight.
   'Cause the Sheriff will arrest you, and he'll carry you down,
   And you can bet your bottm dollar, you're for Sugarland bound.

3. Lord, Thelma said she loved me, but I believe she told a lie,
   'Cause she hasn't been to see me since last July.
   She brought me little coffee, she brought me little tea,
   She brought me nearly ev'rything but the jailhouse key.

Molly Malone (Cockles & Mussels)

Traditional

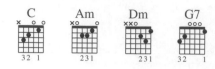

Strum Pattern: 7, 8
Pick Pattern: 9

Verse
Moderately

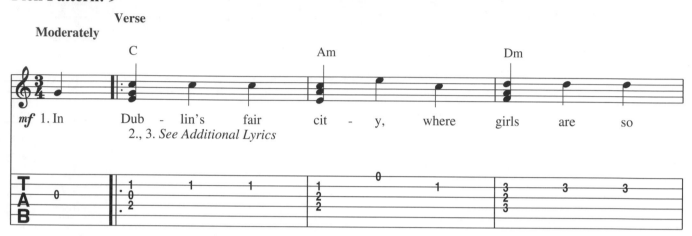

mf 1. In Dub - lin's fair cit - y, where girls are so
2., 3. *See Additional Lyrics*

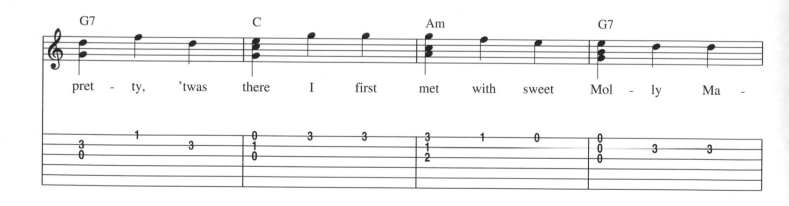

pret - ty, 'twas there I first met with sweet Mol - ly Ma -

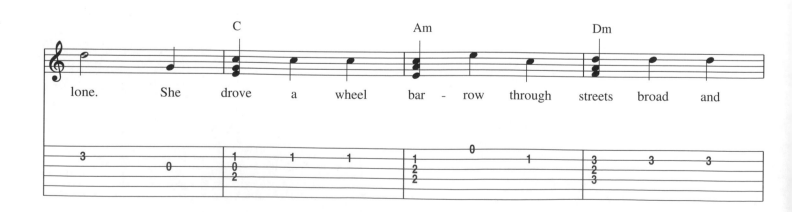

lone. She drove a wheel bar - row through streets broad and

Additional Lyrics

2. She was a fish monger, but sure was no wonder,
   For so were her mother and father before.
   They drove their wheel barrows
   Through streets broad and narrow
   Crying, "Cockles and mussels, alive, alive-o.
   Alive, alive-o, alive, alive-o,"
   Crying, "Cockles and mussels, alive, alive-o."

3. She died of a fever, and nothing could save her,
   And that was the end of sweet Molly Malone.
   Her ghost wheels a barrow
   Through streets broad and narrow,
   Crying, "Cockles and mussels, alive, alive-o.
   Alive, alive-o, alive, alive-o,"
   Crying, "Cockles and mussels, alive, alive-o."

M-O-T-H-E-R
(A Word That Means the World to Me)

Words by Howard Johnson
Music by Theodore Morse

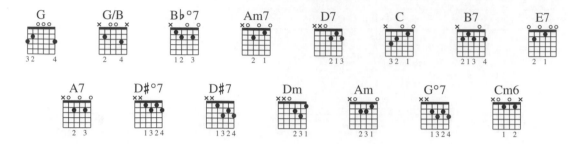

Strum Pattern: 3, 4
Pick Pattern: 1, 3

Verse
Moderately

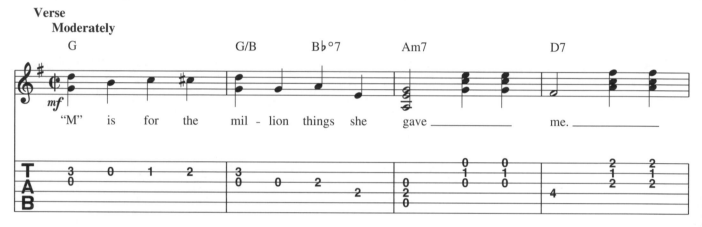

"M" is for the mil - lion things she gave _____ me. _____

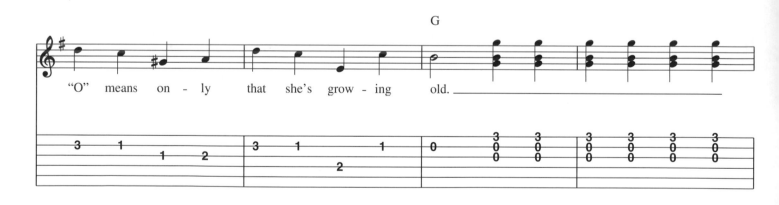

"O" means on - ly that she's grow - ing old. _____

"T" is for the tears were shed to save _____ me,

My Bonnie Lies Over the Ocean

Traditional

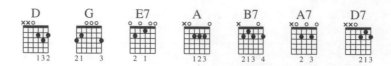

Strum Pattern: 7, 8
Pick Pattern: 8, 9

Verse
Moderately

My Bon - nie lies o - ver the o - cean.

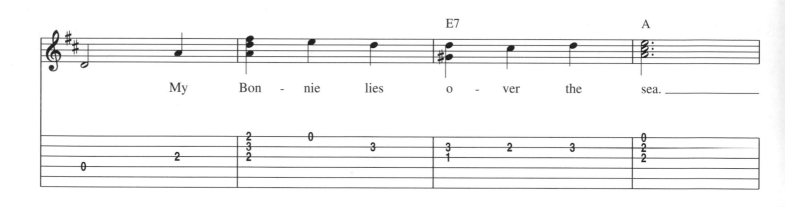

My Bon - nie lies o - ver the sea._____

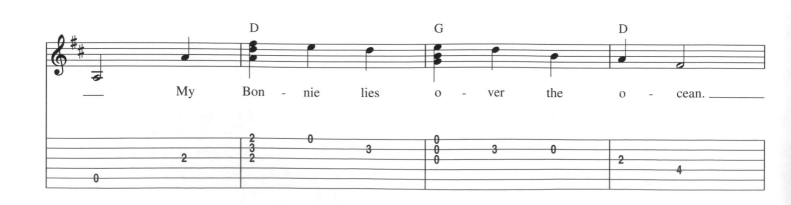

_____ My Bon - nie lies o - ver the o - cean._____

My Buddy

Lyrics by Gus Kahn
Music by Walter Donaldson

Strum Pattern: 7, 8
Pick Pattern: 7, 8

Verse
Slowly

1. Nights are long since you went a - way, I think a - bout you
2. *See additional lyrics*

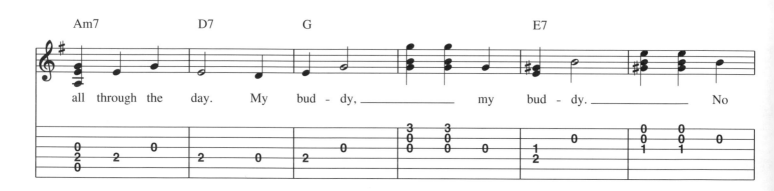

all through the day. My bud - dy, _____ my bud - dy. _____ No

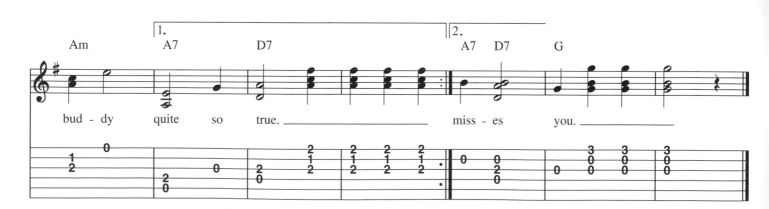

bud - dy quite so true. _____ miss - es you. _____

Additional Lyrics

2. Miss your voice, the touch of your hand,
   Just long to know that you understand.
   My buddy, my buddy.
   Your buddy misses you.

My Gal Sal

Words and Music by Paul Dresser

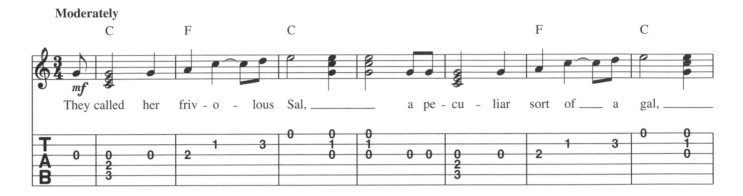

Strum Pattern: 8
Pick Pattern: 8

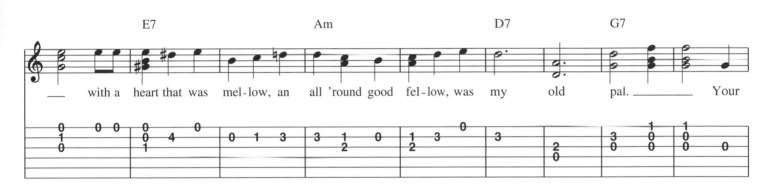

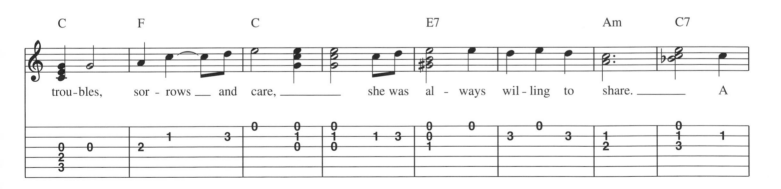

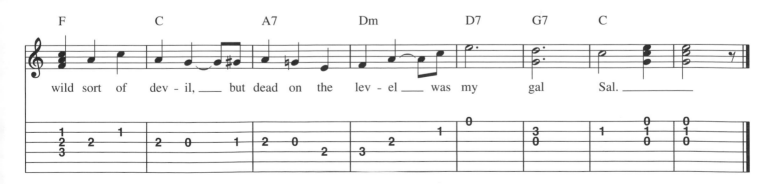

My Little Girl

Words by Sam M. Lewis and William Dillon
Music by Albert von Tilzer

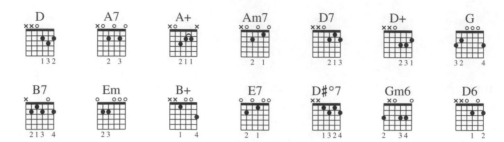

Strum Pattern: 3, 4
Pick Pattern: 1, 3

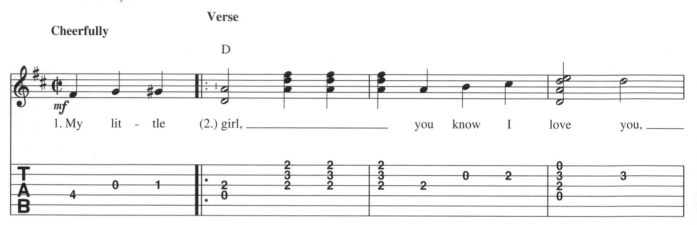

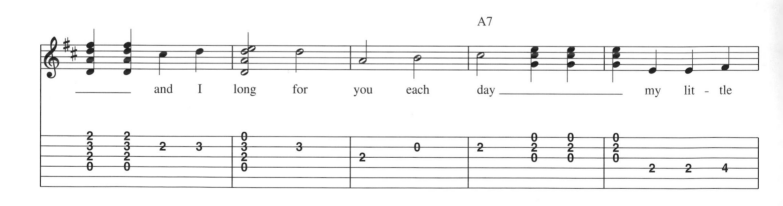

My Melancholy Baby

Words by George Norton
Music by Ernie Burnett

Strum Pattern: 3, 4
Pick Pattern: 3, 4

Chorus

Additional Lyrics

2. Birds in the trees, whispering breeze,
   Should not fail to lull you into peaceful dreams.
   So tell me why sadly you sigh,
   Sitting at the window where the pale moon beams.
   You shouldn't grieve, try and believe.
   Life is always sunshine when the heart beats true.
   Be of good cheer, smile through your tears,
   When you're sad it makes me feel the same as you.

My Wild Irish Rose

Words and Music by Chauncey Olcott

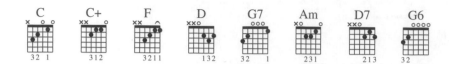

Strum Pattern: 7, 9
Pick Pattern: 8

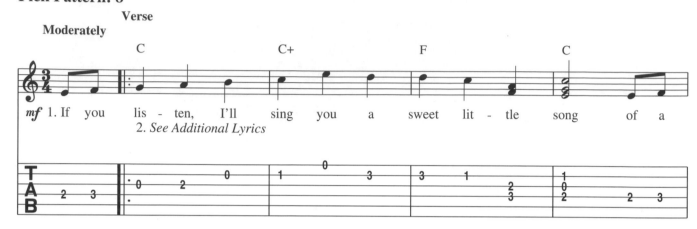

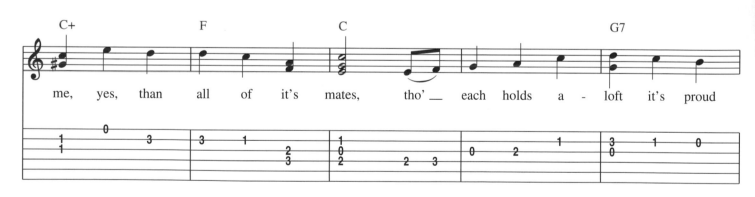

Additional Lyrics

2. They may sing of their roses, which by other names,
   Would smell just as sweetly, they say,
   But I know that my rose would never consent
   To have that sweet name taken away.
   Her glances are shy when e'er I pass by
   The bower where my true love grows.

'O Sole Mio

Words by Giovanni Capurro
Music by Eduardo di Capua

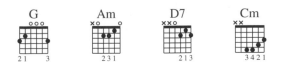

Strum Pattern: 6
Pick Pattern: 4

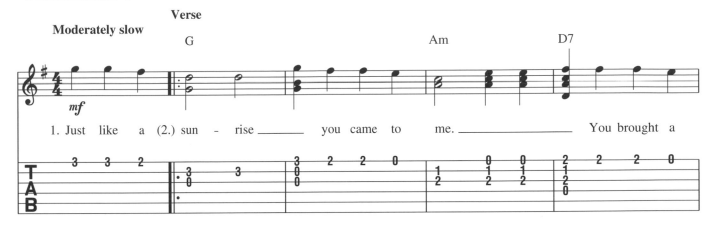

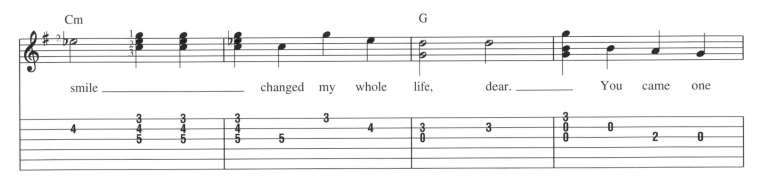

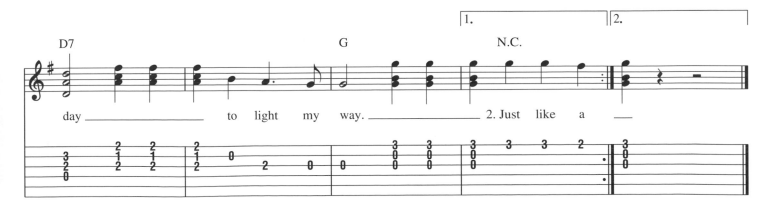

O Canada!

By Calixa Lavallee, l'Hon. Judge Routhier and Justice R.S. Weir

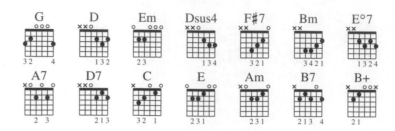

Strum Pattern: 4
Pick Pattern: 5

Verse

With Dignity

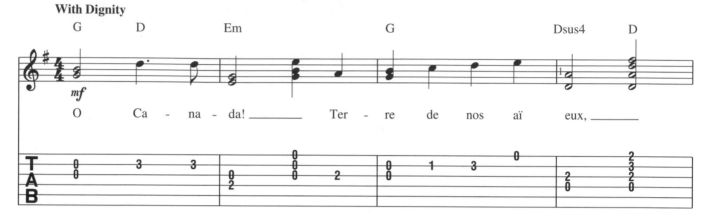

O Ca - na - da! _____ Ter - re de nos aï - eux, _____

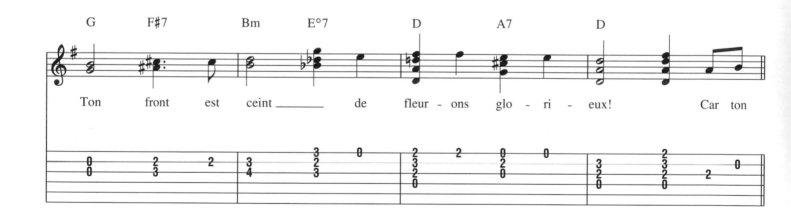

Ton front est ceint _____ de fleur - ons glo - ri - eux! Car ton

Bridge

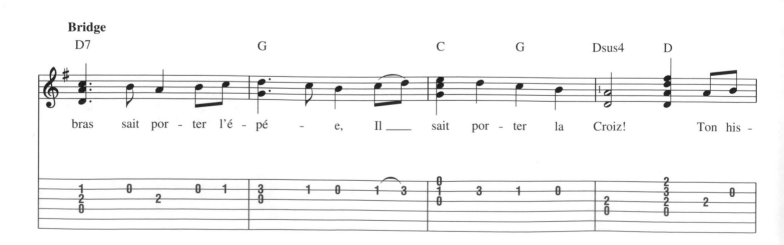

bras sait por - ter l'é - pé - e, Il _____ sait por - ter la Croiz! Ton his -

Outro

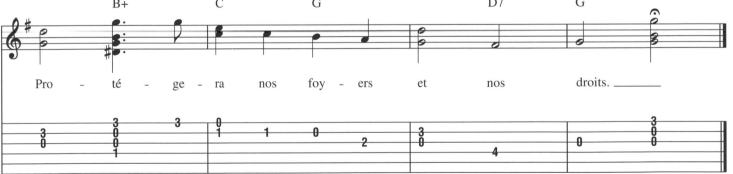

English Translation

Verse   O Canada!
Our home and native land!
True patriot love
In all thy sons command.

Bridge   With glowing hearts we see thee rise,
The true north strong and free!
From far and wide, O Canada!
We stand on guard for thee.

Outro   God keep our land
Glorious and free!
O Canada! We stand on guard for thee.
O Canada! We stand on guard for thee.

Ode to Joy

(Fourth Movement Theme, Symphony No. 9)

By Ludwig van Beethoven

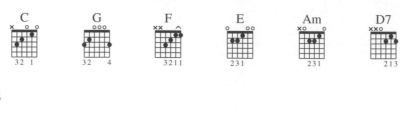

Strum Pattern: 3
Pick Pattern: 3

Moderately

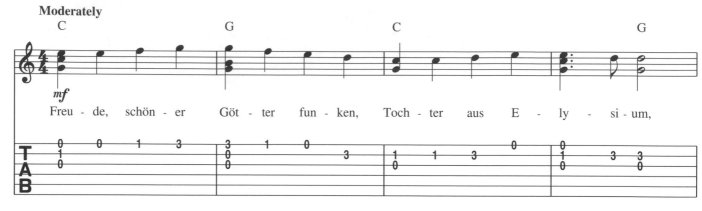

Freu - de, schön - er Göt - ter fun - ken, Toch - ter aus E - ly - si - um,

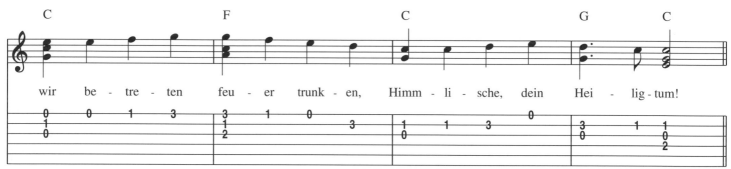

wir be - tre - ten feu - er trunk - en, Himm - li - sche, dein Hei - lig - tum!

Dei - ne Zau - ber bin - den __ wie - der, was die __ Mo - de stren ge - teilt; al -

- le Men - schen wer - den Brü - der, __ wo dein sanf - ter Flü - gel weilt. Flü - gel weilt.

Oh Marie

Words and Music by Eduardo di Capua

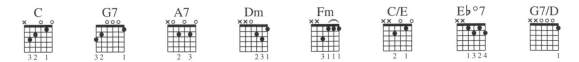

Strum Pattern: 7
Pick Pattern: 7

Moderately

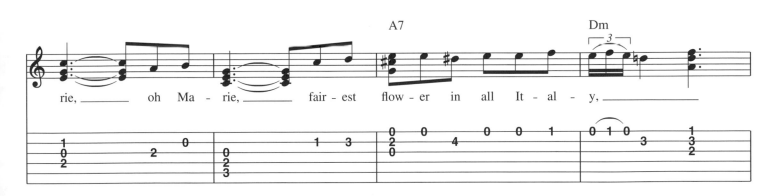

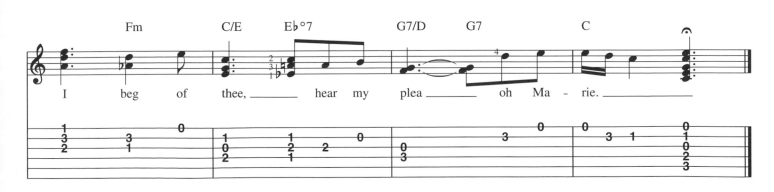

Oh! Susanna

Words and Music by Stephen C. Foster

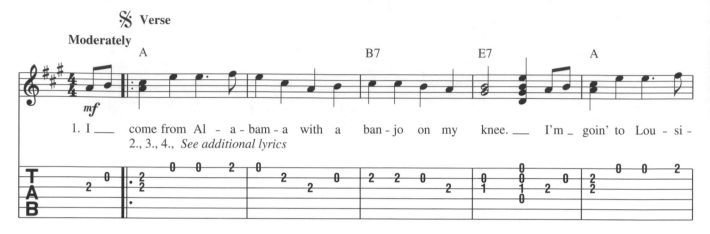

Strum Pattern: 3
Pick Pattern: 4

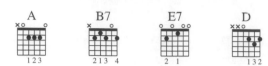

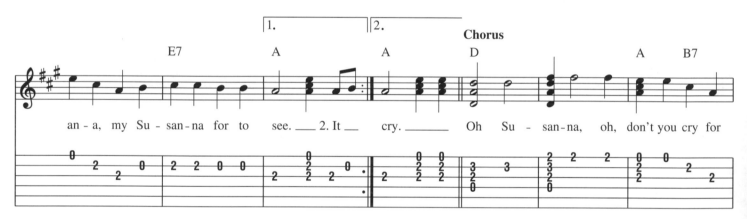

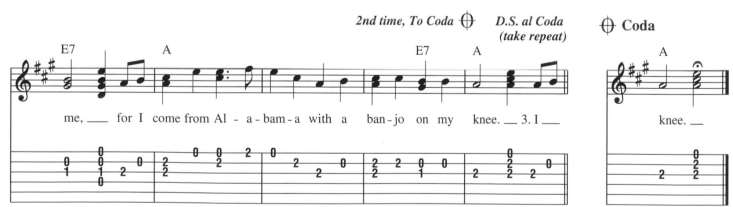

Additional Lyrics

2. It rained all night the day I left,
The weather it was dry,
The sun so hot I froze to death,
Susanna don't you cry.

3. I had a dream the other night
When everything was still,
I thought I saw Susanna
A-coming down the hill.

4. The buckwheat cake was in her mouth
The tear was in her eye.
Says I, "I'm coming from the South,
Susanna, don't you cry."

Old MacDonald

Traditional Children's Song

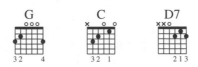

Strum Pattern: 2
Pick Pattern: 4

Verse
Lively

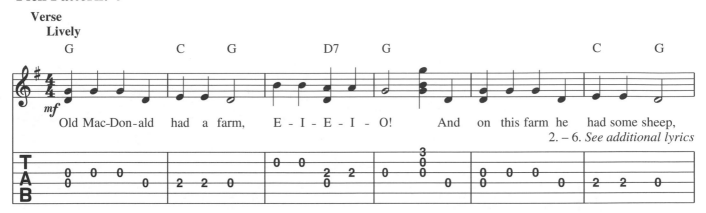

Old Mac-Don-ald had a farm, E - I - E - I - O! And on this farm he had some sheep,

2. – 6. *See additional lyrics*

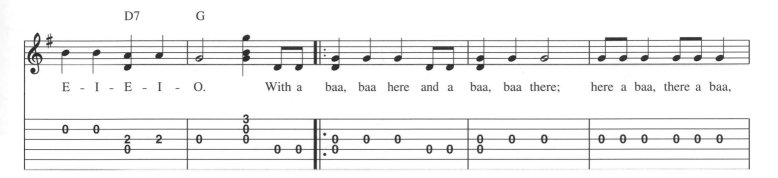

E - I - E - I - O. With a baa, baa here and a baa, baa there; here a baa, there a baa,

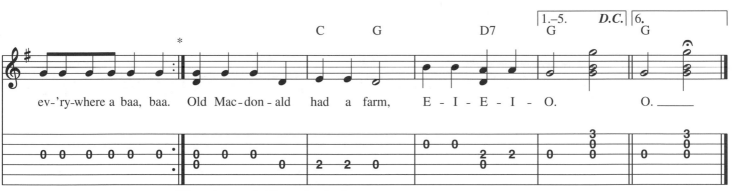

ev'-ry-where a baa, baa. Old Mac-don-ald had a farm, E - I - E - I - O. O. _____

*Repeat as needed for each animal.

Additional Lyrics

2. Cows… moo, moo.

3. Pigs… oink, oink.

4. Ducks… quack, quack.

5. Chickens… cluck, cluck.

6. Turkeys… gobble, gobble.

Oh! You Beautiful Doll

Words by A. Seymour Brown
Music by Nat D. Ayer

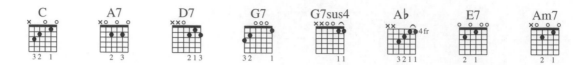

Strum Pattern: 3
Pick Pattern: 3

Verse
Moderately

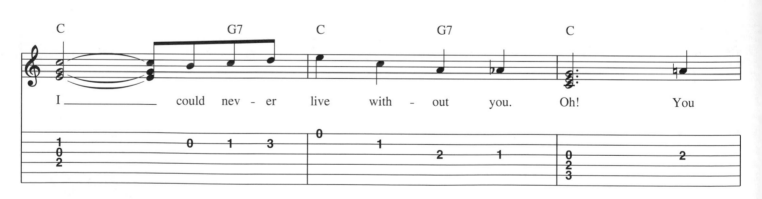

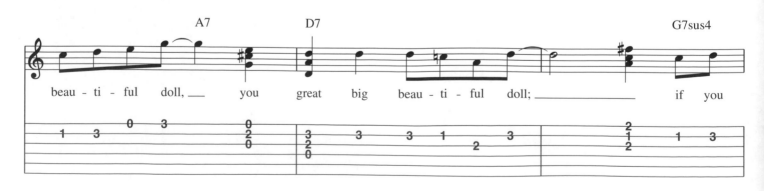

258

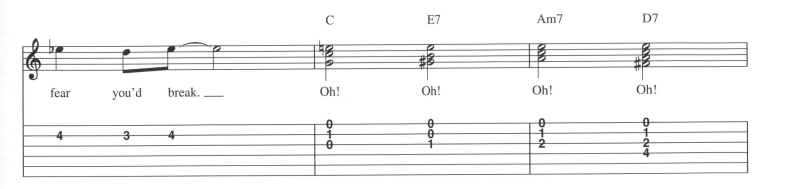

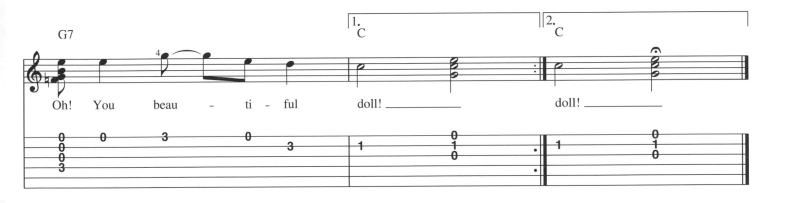

Old Folks at Home
(Swanee River)

Words and Music by Stephen C. Foster

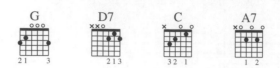

Strum Pattern: 2
Pick Pattern: 4

1. Way down up-on the Swa-nee Riv-er, far, far a-
2. - 6. *See additional lyrics*

way. _____ There's where my heart is turn-ing ev-er,

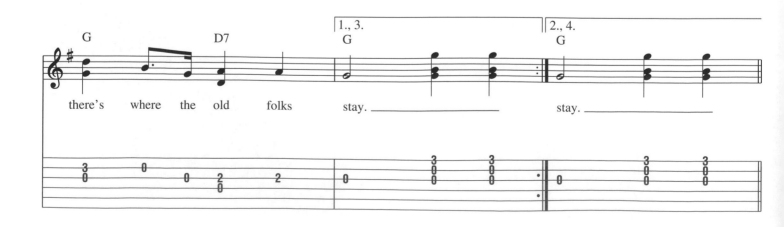

there's where the old folks stay. _____ stay. _____

Chorus

All the world is sad and drear-y ev-'ry-where I

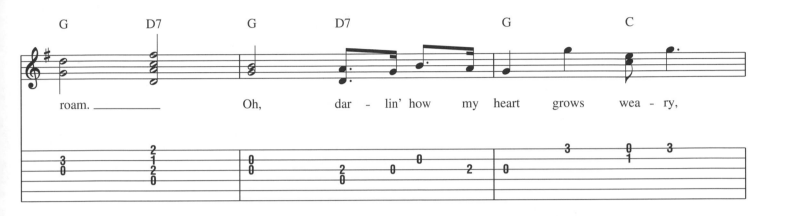

roam. _____ Oh, dar-lin' how my heart grows wea-ry,

3rd time, To Coda ⊕   *1st time, D.C.*
                        2nd time, D.C. al Coda   ⊕ **Coda**

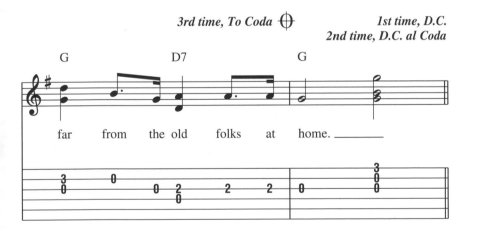

far from the old folks at home. _____

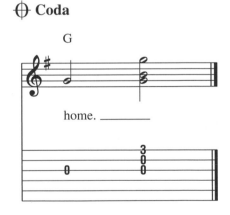

home. _____

Additional Lyrics

2. All up and down the whole creation,
   Sadly I roam.
   Still longing for the old plantation,
   And for the old folks at home.

3. All 'round the little farm I wandered
   When I was young.
   Then many happy days I squandered,
   Many the songs I sung.

4. When I was playing with my brother,
   Happy was I.
   Oh, take me to my kind old mother,
   There let me live and die.

5. One little nut among the bushes,
   Happy was I.
   Still sadly to my mem'ry rushes.
   No matter where I rove.

6. When will I see the bees a-humming,
   All 'roun' the comb?
   When will I hear the banjo strumming,
   Down in my good old home?

On a Sunday Afternoon

Words by Andrew B. Sterling
Music by Harry von Tilzer

Strum Pattern: 8
Pick Pattern: 8

Moderately

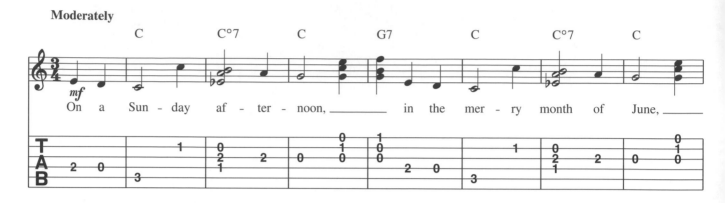

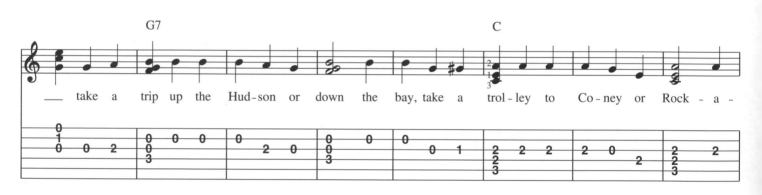

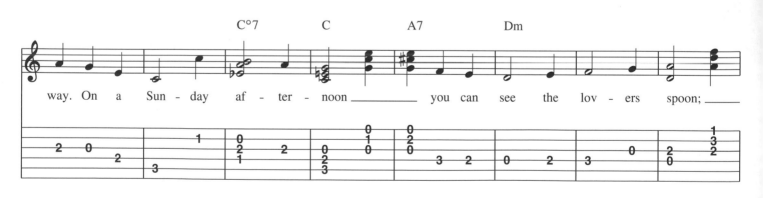

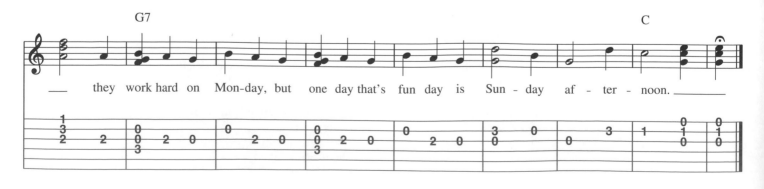

On Top of Old Smoky

Kentucky Mountain Folksong

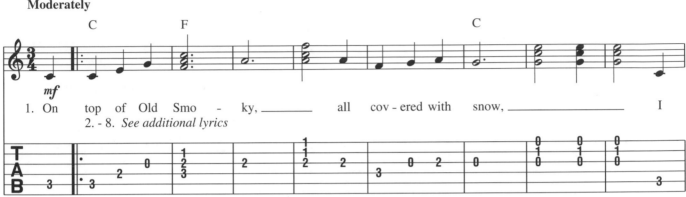

Strum Pattern: 8
Pick Pattern: 8

Verse
Moderately

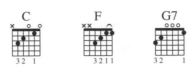

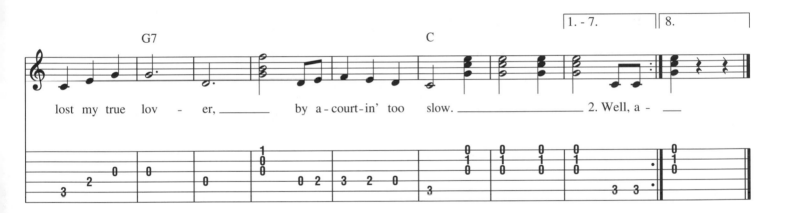

1. On top of Old Smo - ky, _____ all cov - ered with snow, _____
2. - 8. *See additional lyrics*

lost my true lov - er, _____ by a - court-in' too slow. _____ 2. Well, a -

Additional Lyrics

2. Well, a-courting's a pleasure,
And parting is grief.
But a false-hearted lover
Is worse than a thief.

3. A thief he will rob you
And take all you have,
But a false-hearted lover
Will send you to your grave.

4. And the grave will decay you
And turn you to dust.
And where is the young man
A poor girl can trust?

5. They'll hug you and kiss you
And tell you more lies
Than the cross-ties on the railroad,
Or the stars in the skies.

6. They'll tell you they love you,
Just to give your heart ease.
But the minute your back's turned,
They'll court whom they please.

7. So come all you young maidens
And listen to me,
Never place your affection
On a green willow tree.

8. For the leaves they will wither
And the roots they will die.
And your true love will leave you,
And you'll never know why.

Over the River and Through the Woods

Traditional

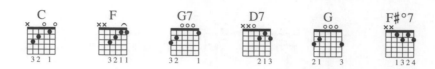

Strum Pattern: 8
Pick Pattern: 8

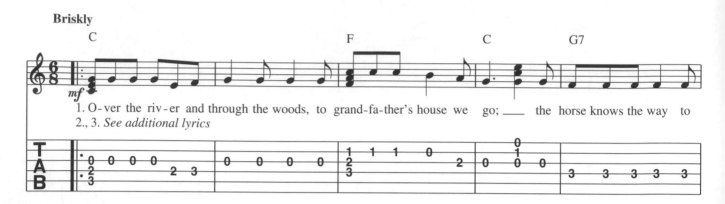

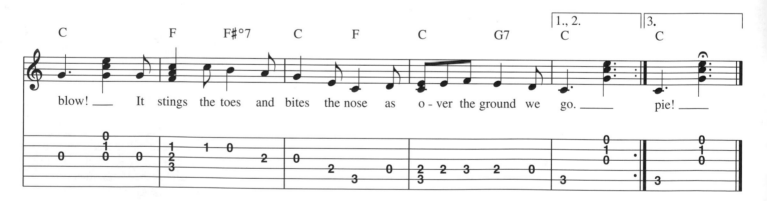

Additional Lyrics

2. Over the river and through the woods,
   To have a first-rate play;
   Oh hear the bells ring, "Ting-a-ling-ling!"
   Hurrah for Thanksgiving Day!
   Over the river and through the woods,
   Trot fast my dapple gray!
   Spring over the gound like a hunting hound!
   For this is Thanksgiving Day.

3. Over the river and through the woods,
   And straight through the barnyard gate,
   We seem to go extremely slow;
   It is so hard to wait!
   Over the river and through the woods,
   Now grandmother's cap I spy!
   Hurrah for the fun! Is the pudding done?
   Hurrah for the pumpkin pie!

Over There

Words and Music by George M. Cohan

Strum Pattern: 10
Pick Pattern: 10

Paper Doll

Words and Music by Johnny S. Black

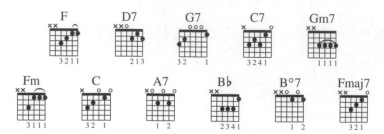

Strum Pattern: 4
Pick Pattern: 5

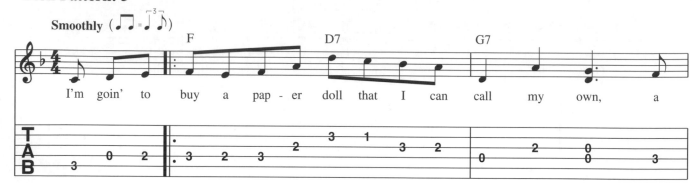

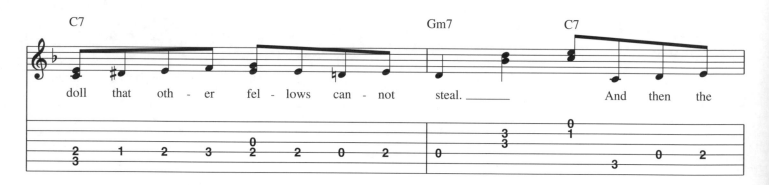

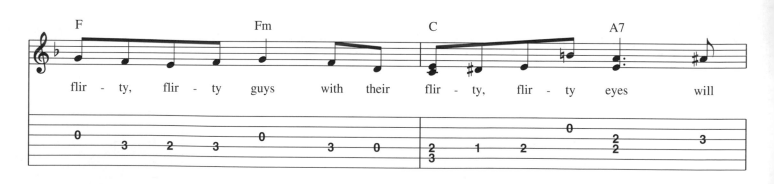

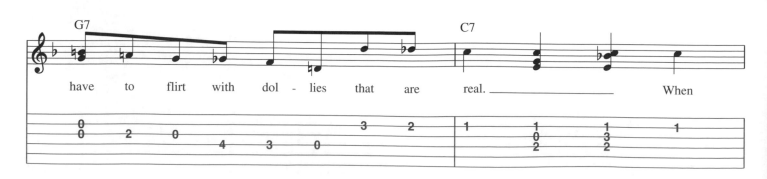

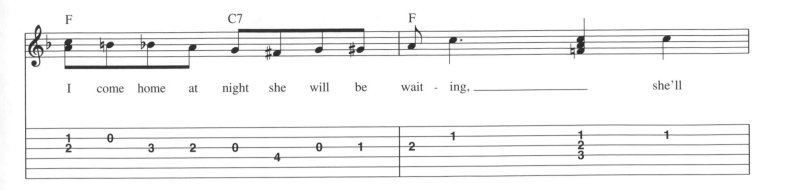

I come home at night she will be wait - ing, _____ she'll

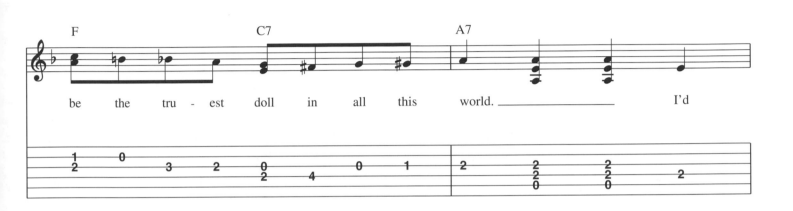

be the tru - est doll in all this world. _____ I'd

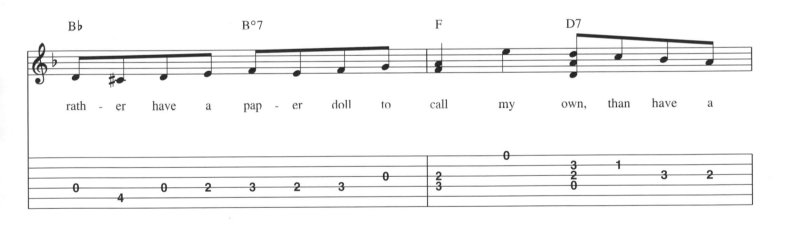

rath - er have a pap - er doll to call my own, than have a

fick - le - mind - ed real live girl. _____ I'm goin' to girl. _____

Peg o' My Heart

Words by Alfred Bryan
Music by Fred Fisher

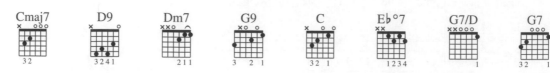

Strum Pattern: 3
Pick Pattern: 3

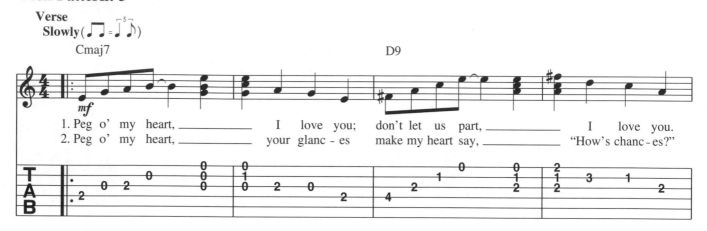

1. Peg o' my heart, _____ I love you; don't let us part, _____ I love you.
2. Peg o' my heart, _____ your glanc - es make my heart say, _____ "How's chanc - es?"

I al - ways knew, _____ it would be you, _____ since I heard your lilt - ing laugh - ter,
Come, be my own, _____

it's your I - rish heart I'm af - ter. come, make your home ___ in my heart. _____

Polly Wolly Doodle
Traditional American Minstrel Song

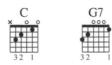

Strum Pattern: 2
Pick Pattern: 4

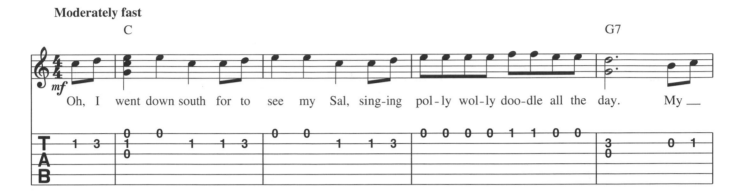

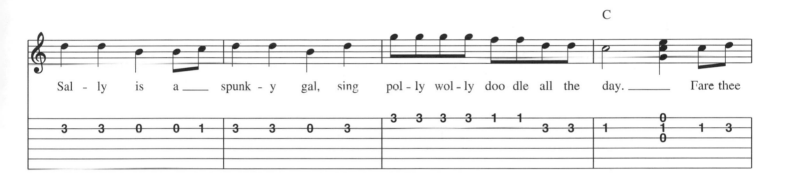

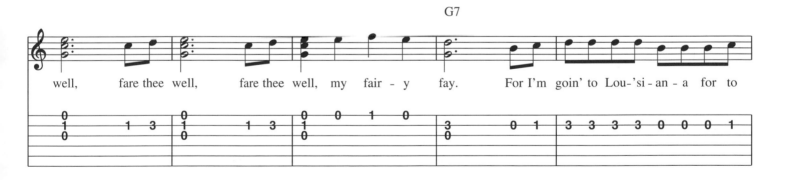

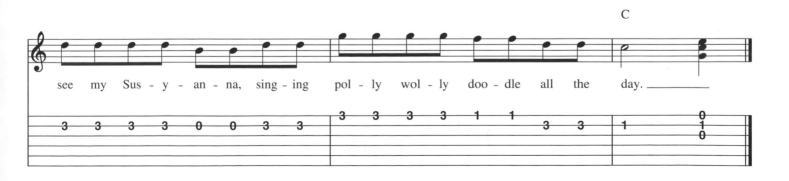

Pomp and Circumstance

Words by Arthur Benson
Music by Edward Elgar

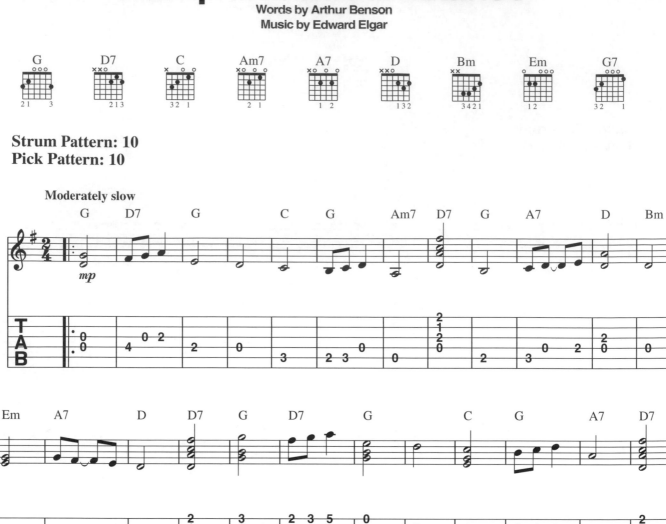

Strum Pattern: 10
Pick Pattern: 10

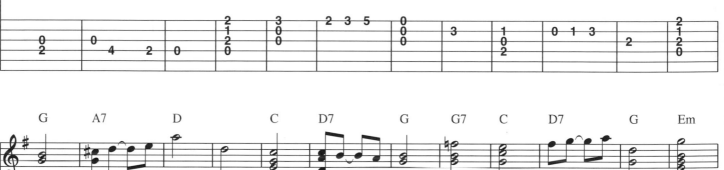

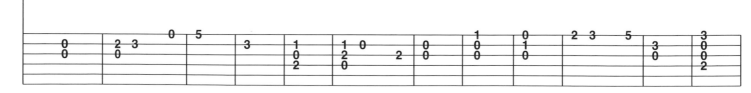

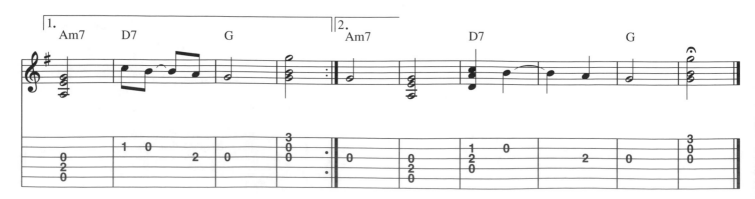

Pop Goes the Weasel

Traditional

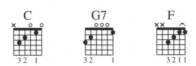

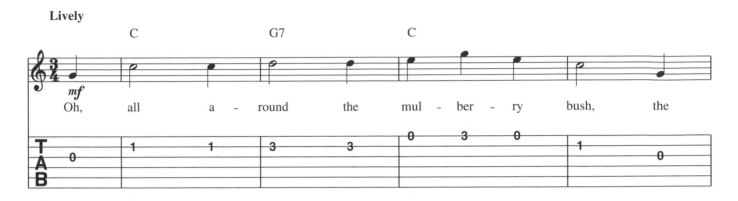

Strum Pattern: 9
Pick Pattern: 7

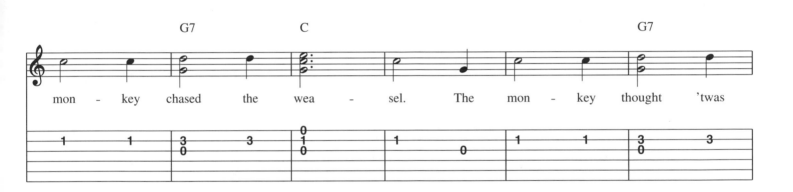

Oh, all a - round the mul - ber - ry bush, the

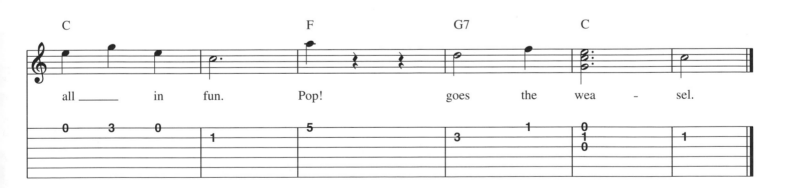

mon - key chased the wea - sel. The mon - key thought 'twas

all _____ in fun. Pop! goes the wea - sel.

Poor Butterfly

Words by John L. Golden
Music by Raymond Hubbell

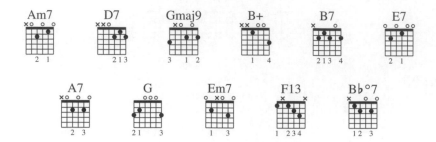

Strum Pattern: 2
Pick Pattern: 4

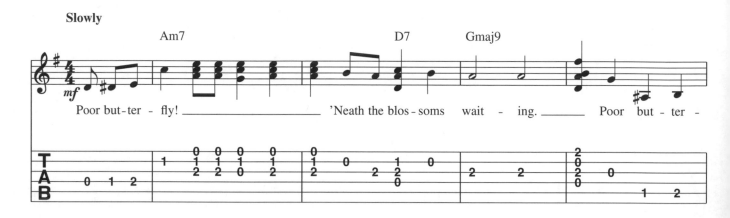

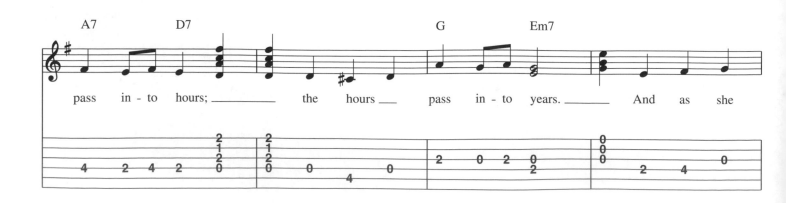

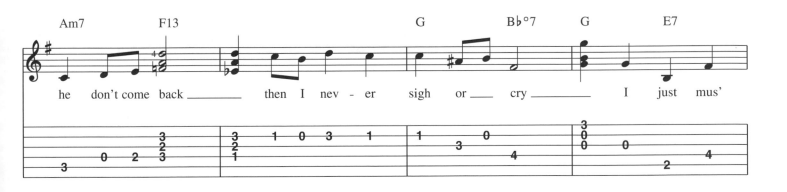

Prayer of Thanksgiving

Traditional

Strum Pattern: 7
Pick Pattern: 8

Additional Lyrics

2. Beside us, to guide us, our God with us joining,
Ordaining, maintaining His kingdom divine.
So from the beginning the fight we were winning:
Thou Lord, wast at our side, all glory be Thine.

3. We all do extol Thee, Thou leader triumphant,
And pray that Thou still our defender will be.
Let Thy congregation escape tribulation;
Thy name be ever praised! Oh Lord, make us free!

Pretty Baby

Words by Gus Kahn
Music by Egbert Van Alstyne and Tony Jackson

Strum Pattern: 2
Pick Pattern: 4

A Pretty Girl Is Like a Melody

from the 1919 Stage Production ZIEGFELD FOLLIES
Words and Music by Irving Berlin

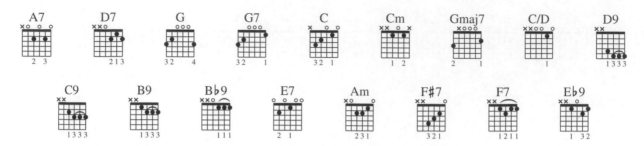

Strum Pattern: 2
Pick Pattern: 4

Verse
Moderately

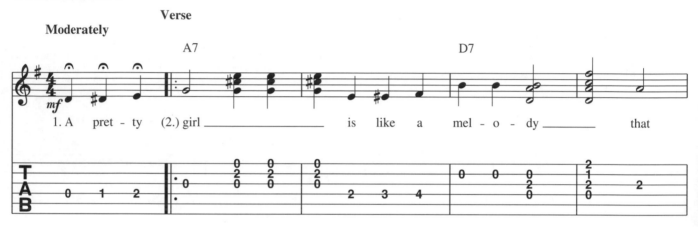

1. A pret - ty (2.) girl _____ is like a mel - o - dy _____ that

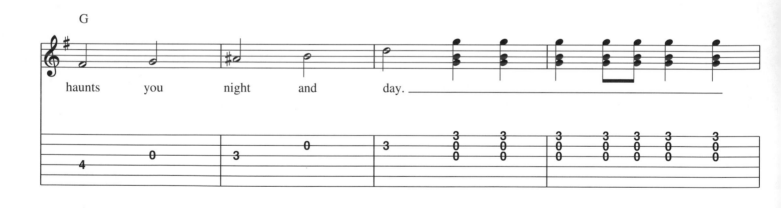

haunts you night and day. _____

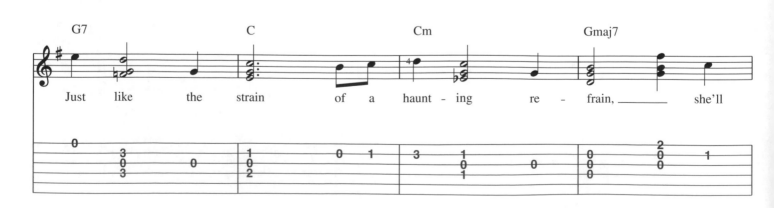

Just like the strain of a haunt - ing re - frain, _____ she'll

Put Your Arms Around Me, Honey

Words by Junie McCree
Music by Albert von Tilzer

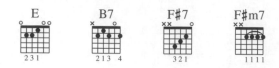

Strum Pattern: 3
Pick Pattern: 1

1. Put your arms a - round __ me, hon - ey, hold __ me
2. *See additional lyrics*

tight, _____ hud - dle up and cud - dle up with

all __ your might. _____ Oh! _____ Oh! _____

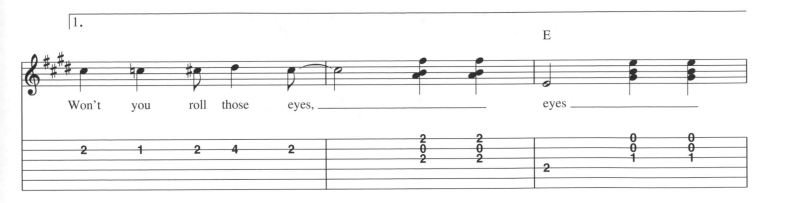

Won't you roll those eyes, _____ eyes _____

E

that _____ I just i - dol - ize? _____

B7

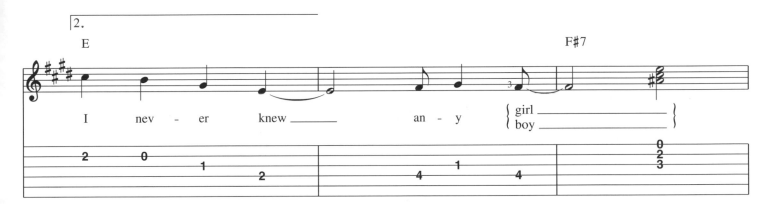

2.

E

I nev - er knew _____ an - y {girl/boy} _____

F#7

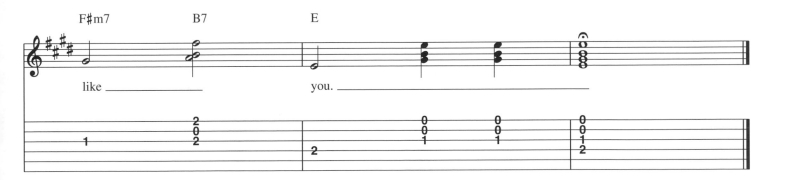

F#m7   B7   E

like _____ you. _____

Additional Lyrics

2. When they look at me, my heart begins to float,
   Then it starts a-rockin' like a motor boat.
   Oh! Oh! I never knew
   Any { girl / boy } like you.

Ragtime Cowboy Joe

Words and Music by Lewis F. Muir, Grant Clarke and Maurice Abrahams

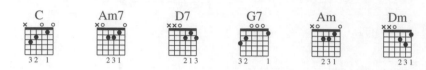

Strum Pattern: 1
Pick Pattern: 3

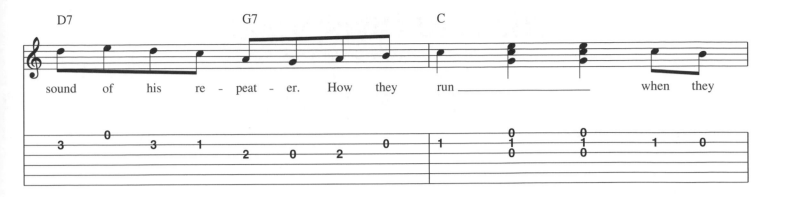

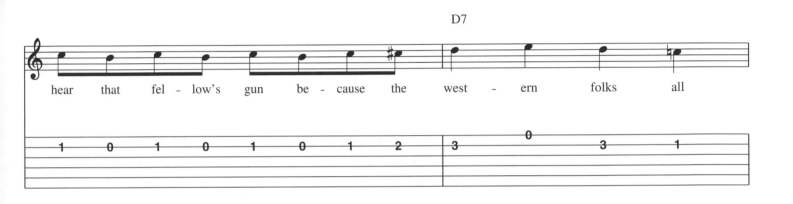

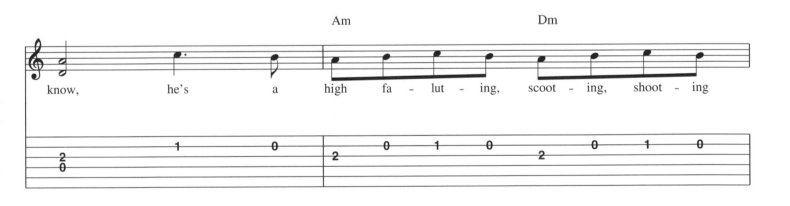

The Red River Valley

Traditional American Cowboy Song

Strum Pattern: 4
Pick Pattern: 5

Verse

Moderately

1. Come and sit by my side if you love me. _____ Do not has-ten to
2. - 4. *See additional lyrics*

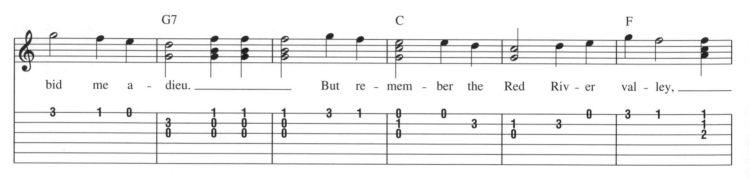

bid me a - dieu. _____ But re - mem - ber the Red Riv - er val - ley, _____

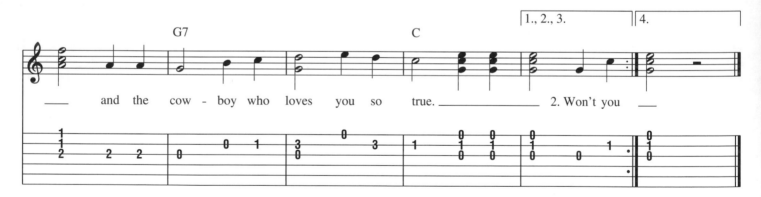

_____ and the cow - boy who loves you so true. _____ 2. Won't you _____

Additional Lyrics

2. Won't you think of this valley you're leaving?
   Oh, how lonely, how sad it will be.
   Oh, think of the fond heart you're breaking,
   And the grief you are causing me.

3. From this valley they say you are going.
   When you may your darling go, too?
   Would you leave her behind unprotected,
   When she loves no other but you?

4. I have promised you, darling, that never
   Will a word from my lips cause you pain.
   And my life, it will be yours forever,
   If you only will love me again.

Sailors Hornpipe

Sea Chantey

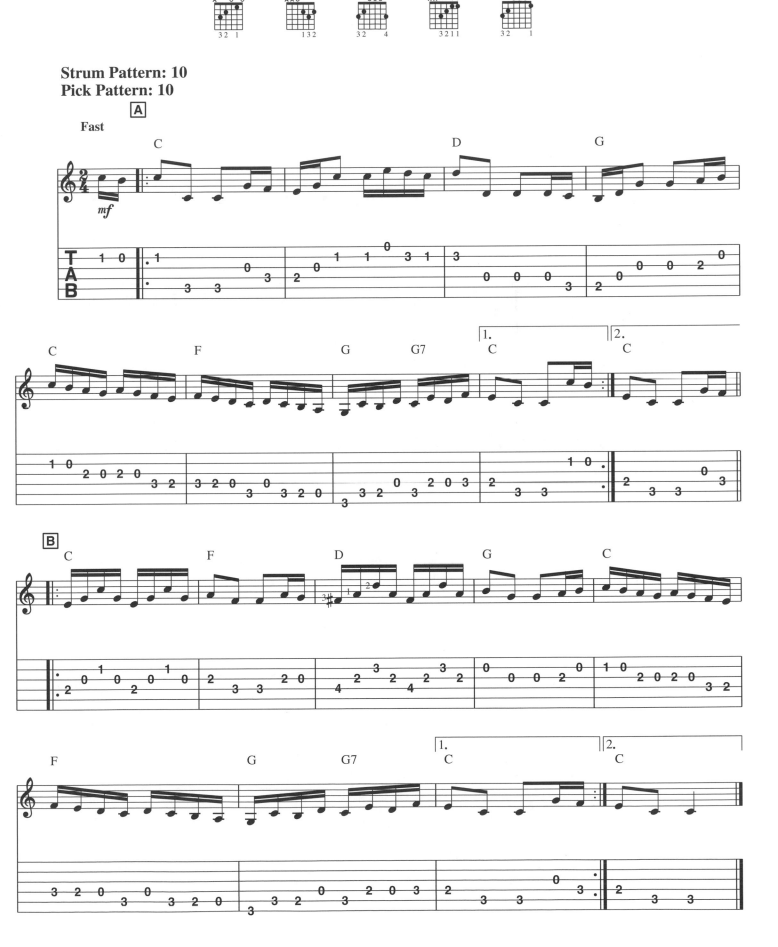

Rock Island Line
Railroad Song

Strum Pattern: 3
Pick Pattern: 3

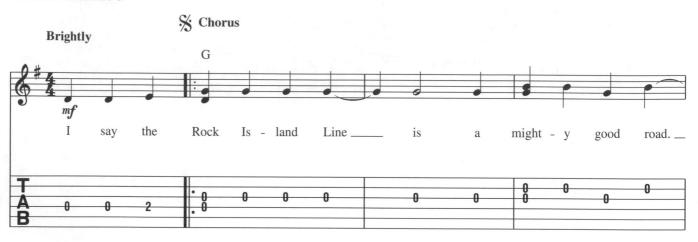

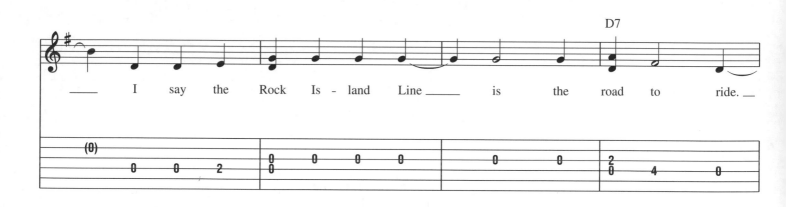

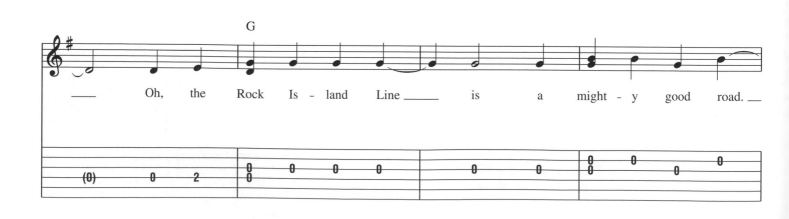

To Coda ⊕

Verse

3nd time, D.S. al Coda

Play 3 times

⊕ **Coda**

Additional Lyrics

2. Now Jesus died to save our sins,
   Glory be to God, we're going to need Him again.

3. I may be right and I may be wrong,
   I know you're gonna miss me when I am gone.

Rock-A-Bye Your Baby With a Dixie Melody

from SINBAD

Words by Sam M. Lewis and Joe Young
Music by Jean Schwartz

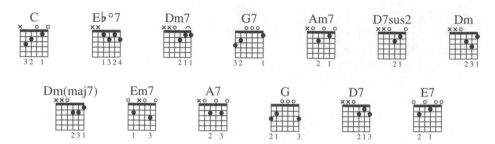

Strum Pattern: 2
Pick Pattern: 4

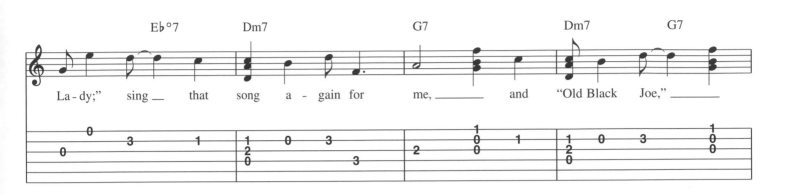

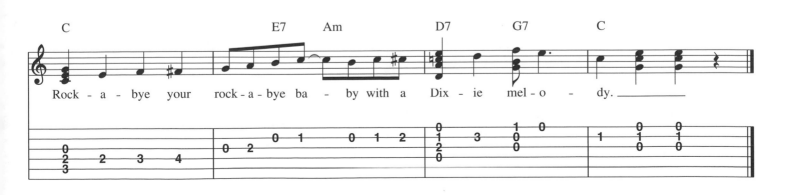

Sailing, Sailing

Words and Music by Godfrey Marks

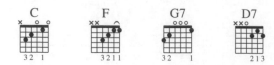

Strum Pattern: 7, 8
Pick Pattern: 7, 8

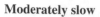

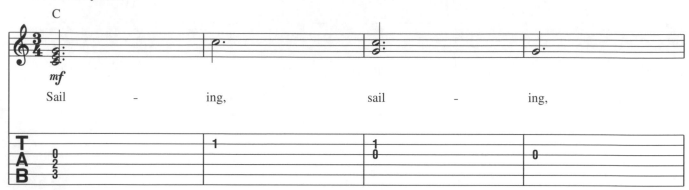

Sail - ing, sail - ing,

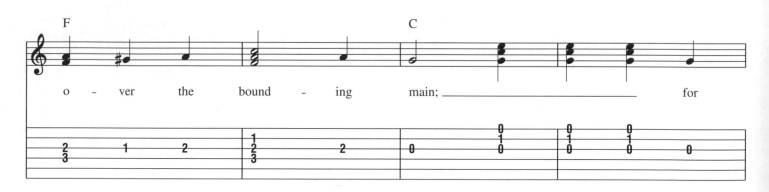

o - ver the bound - ing main; _____ for

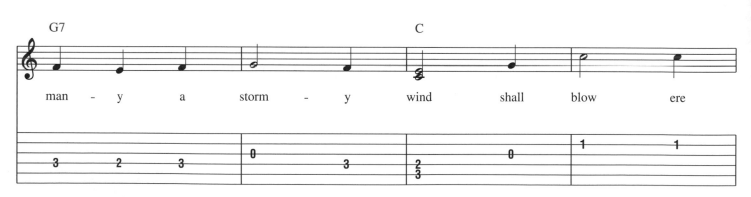

man - y a storm - y wind shall blow ere

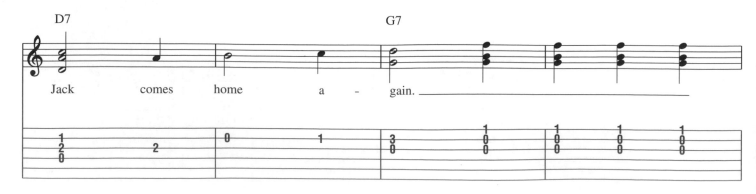

Jack comes home a - gain. _____

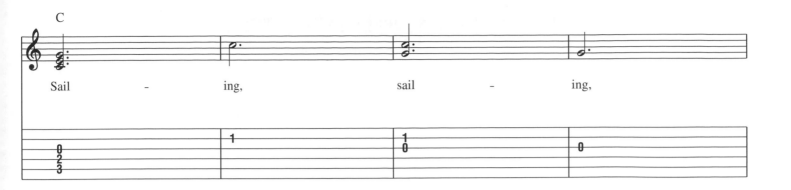

Sail - ing, sail - ing,

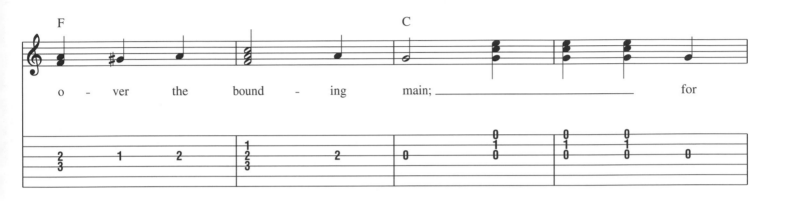

o - ver the bound - ing main; _____ for

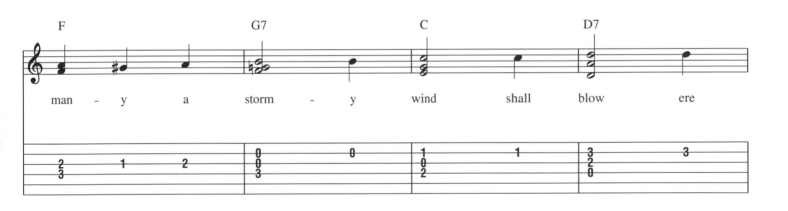

man - y a storm - y wind shall blow ere

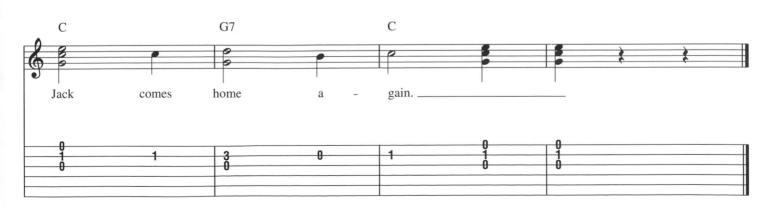

Jack comes home a - gain. _____

Saint James Infirmary

Words and Music by Joe Primrose

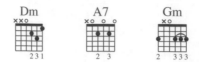

Strum Pattern: 2
Pick Pattern: 4

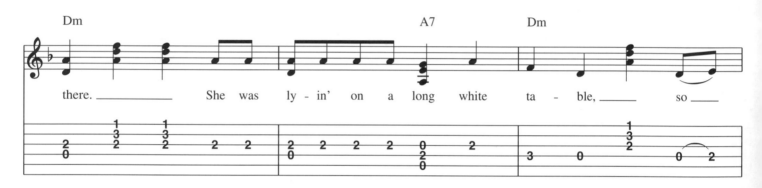

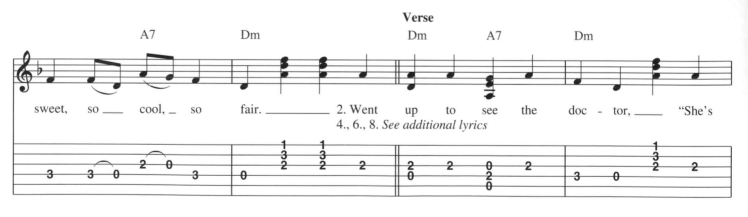

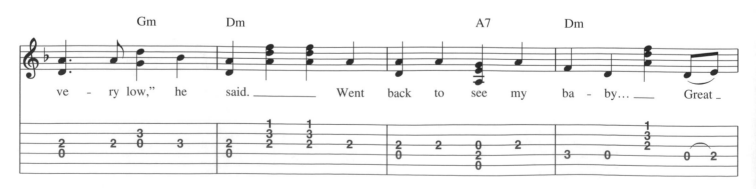

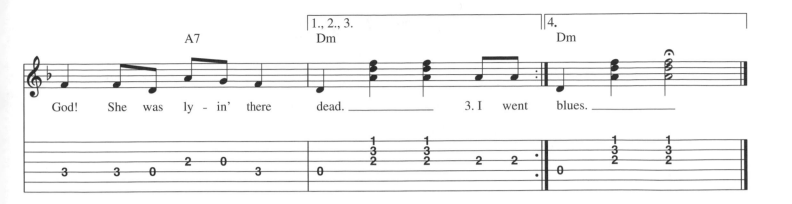

Additional Lyrics

3. I went down to old Joe's barroom,
   On the corner by the square.
   They were servin' the drinks as usual,
   And the usual crowd was there.

4. On my left stood Joe McKennedy;
   His eyes bloodshot red.
   He turned to the crowd around him,
   These are the words he said:

5. Let her go, let her go, God bless her;
   Wherever she may be.
   She may search this wide world over;
   She'll never find a man like me.

6. Oh, when I die, please bury me
   In my high-top Stetson hat;
   Put a gold piece on my watch chain
   So they'll know I died standin' pat.

7. Get six gamblers to carry my coffin.
   Six chorus girls to sing my song.
   Put a jazz band on my tail gate
   To raise hell as we go along.

8. Now that's the end of my story;
   Let's have another round of booze;
   And if anyone should ask you, just tell them
   I've got the St. James Infirmary blues.

Santa Lucia

Traditional

Strum Pattern: 8, 9
Pick Pattern: 8, 9

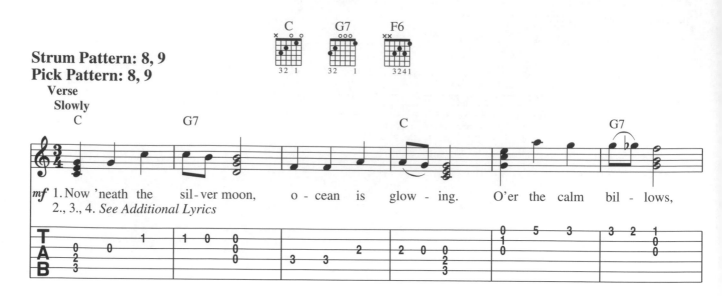

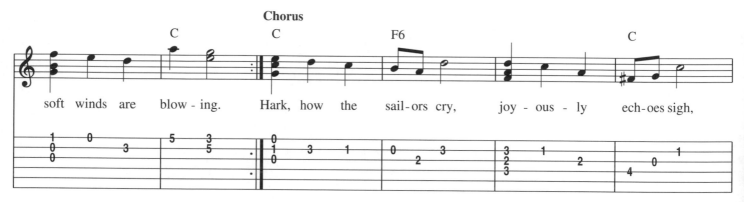

Now 'neath the sil-ver moon, o-cean is glow-ing. O'er the calm bil-lows,

soft winds are blow-ing. Hark, how the sail-ors cry, joy-ous-ly ech-oes sigh,

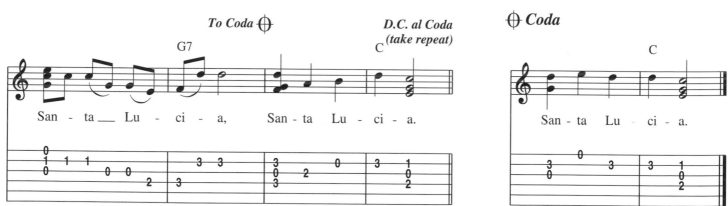

San-ta Lu-ci-a, San-ta Lu-ci-a. San-ta Lu-ci-a.

Additional Lyrics

2. Here balmy breezes blow, pure joys invite us.
   And as we gently row, all things delight us.

3. When o'er the waters, light winds are playing;
   Their spell can soothe us, all care allaying.

4. Thee, sweet Napoli, what charms are given.
   Where smiles creation, toil blessed heaven.

Scarborough Fair

Traditional English

Strum Pattern: 7
Pick Pattern: 7

Verse
Gently

mp

1. Are you go-ing to Scar-bor-ough Fair? _____ Pars-ley, sage, rose-
2. – 8. *See additional lyrics*

ma-ry and thyme. Re-mem-ber me to one who lives there, _ for

once she was a true love of mine. _____ mine. _____

Additional Lyrics

2. Tell her to make me a cambric shirt,
   Parsley, sage, rosemary and thyme,
   Without any seam or fine needlework,
   For once she was a true love of mine.

3. Tell her to wash it in yonder dry well,
   Parsley, sage, rosemary and thyme,
   Where water ne'er spring, nor drop of rain fell,
   For once she was a true love of mine.

4. Tell her to dry in on yonder thorn,
   Parsley, sage, rosemary and thyme,
   Which never bore blossom since Adam was born,
   For once she was a true love of mine.

5. Will you find me an acre of land,
   Parsley, sage, rosemary and thyme,
   Between the sea foam and the sea sand,
   For once she was a true love of mine.

6. Will you plough it with a lamb's horn,
   Parsley, sage, rosemary and thyme,
   And sow it all over with one peppercorn,
   For once she was a true love of mine.

7. Will you reap it with sickle of leather,
   Parsley, sage, rosemary and thyme,
   And tie it all up with a peacock's feather,
   For once she was a true love of mine.

8. When you're done and finished your work,
   Parsley, sage, rosemary and thyme,
   Then come to me for your cambric shirt,
   And you shall be a true love of mine.

Say It With Music

from the 1921 Stage Production MUSIC BOX REVUE
from the 20th Century Fox Motion Picture ALEXANDER'S RAGTIME BAND

Words and Music by Irving Berlin

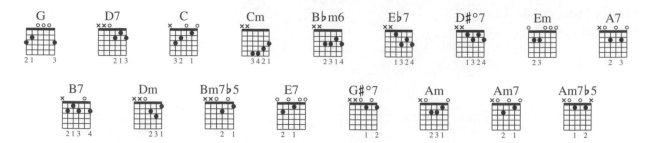

Strum Pattern: 2
Pick Pattern: 4

Verse
Moderately

1., 2. Say _____ it with mu - sic, _____ beau - ti - ful

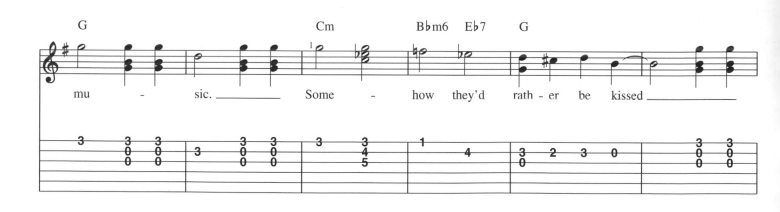

mu - sic. _____ Some - how they'd rath - er be kissed _____

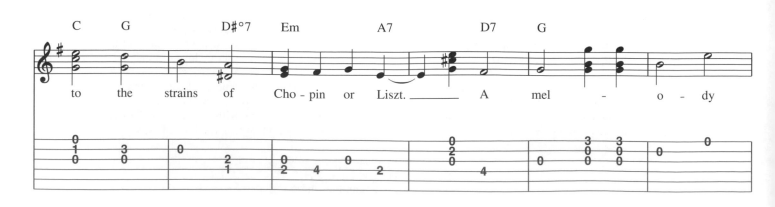

to the strains of Cho - pin or Liszt. _____ A mel - o - dy

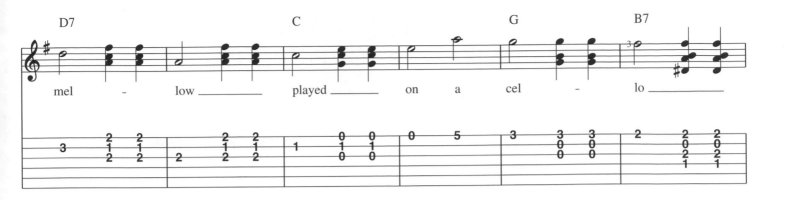

mel - low _____ played _____ on a cel - lo _____

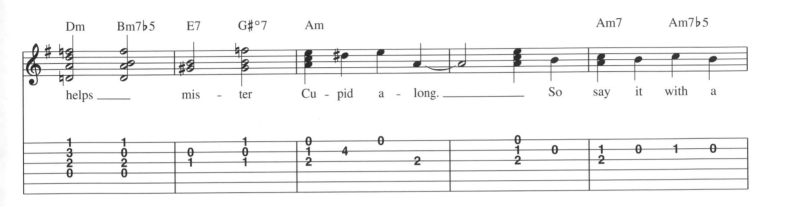

helps _____ mis - ter Cu - pid a - long. _____ So say it with a

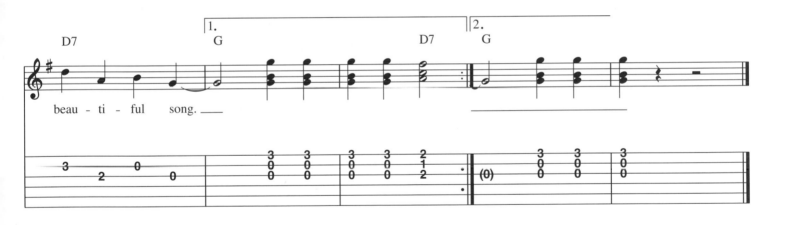

beau - ti - ful song. _____

School Days
(When We Were a Couple of Kids)

Words by Will D. Cobb
Music by Gus Edwards

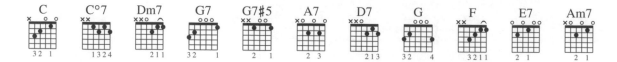

Strum Pattern: 7, 8
Pick Pattern: 8

Moderate Waltz

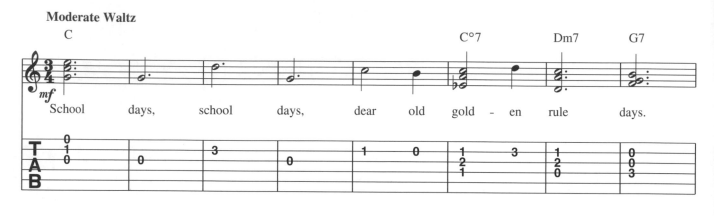

School days, school days, dear old gold - en rule days.

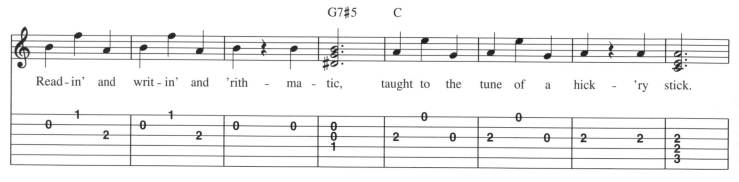

Read-in' and writ-in' and 'rith - ma - tic, taught to the tune of a hick - 'ry stick.

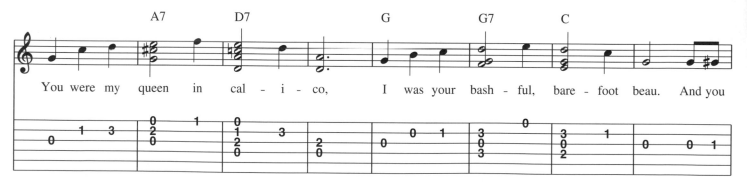

You were my queen in cal - i - co, I was your bash - ful, bare - foot beau. And you

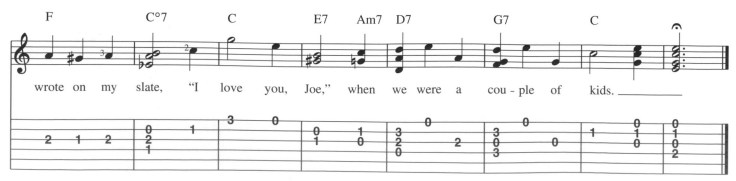

wrote on my slate, "I love you, Joe," when we were a cou - ple of kids. _____

She'll Be Comin' 'Round the Mountain

Traditional

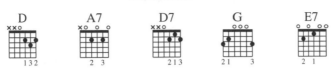

Strum Pattern: 2
Pick Pattern: 4

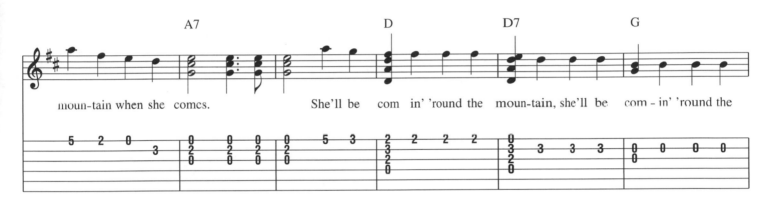

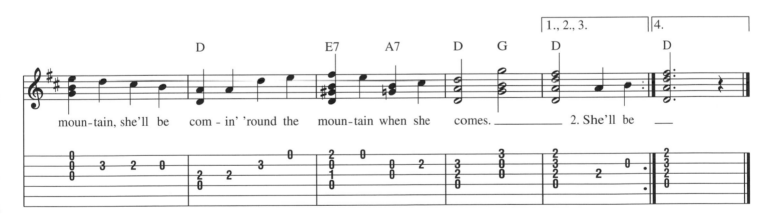

Additional Lyrics

2. She'll be drivin' six white horses when she comes.
   She'll be drivin' six white horses when she comes.
   She'll be drivin' six white horses,
   She'll be drivin' six white horses,
   She'll be drivin' six white horses when she comes.

3. Oh, we'll all go out to meet her when she comes.
   Oh, we'll all go out to meet her when she comes.
   Oh, we'll all go out to meet her,
   Oh, we'll all go out to meet her,
   Yes, we'll all go out to meet her when she comes.

4. She'll be wearin' a blue bonnet when she comes.
   She'll be wearin' a blue bonnet when she comes.
   She'll be wearin' a blue bonnet,
   She'll be wearin' a blue bonnet,
   She'll be wearin' a blue bonnet when she comes.

She Wore a Yellow Ribbon

Words and Music by George A. Norton

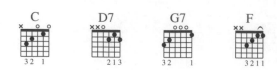

Strum Pattern: 4
Pick Pattern: 6

Moderately

'Round her neck she wore a yel - low rib - bon, she

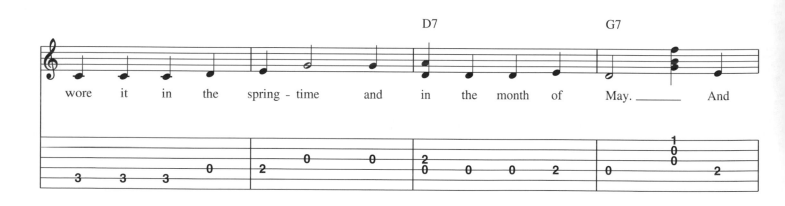

wore it in the spring - time and in the month of May. _____ And

if you asked her why the heck she wore it, she

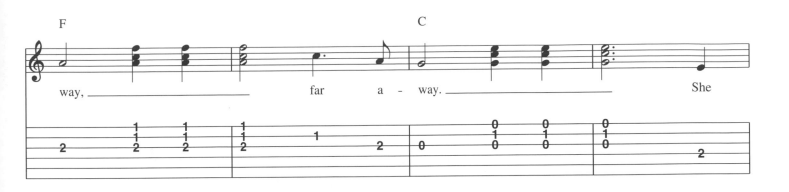

The Sheik of Araby

Words by Harry B. Smith and Francis Wheeler
Music by Ted Snyder

D   A7   D6   D°7   F#7   B7#5   E7

Strum Pattern: 2
Pick Pattern: 4

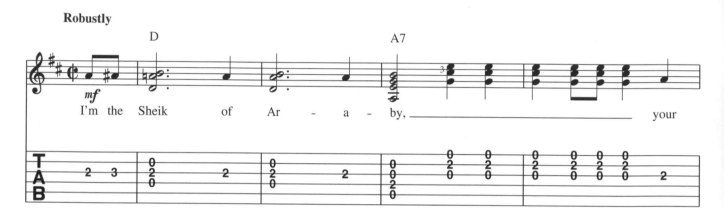

I'm the Sheik of Ar - a - by, _____ your

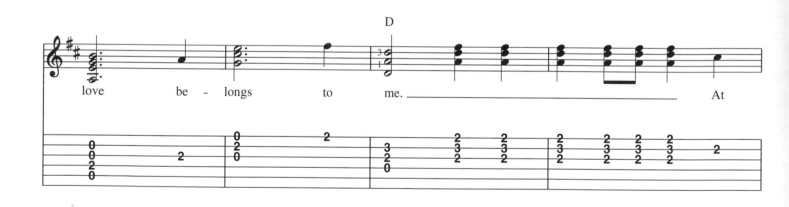

love be - longs to me. _____ At

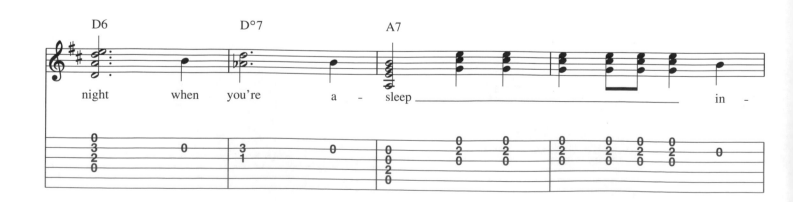

night when you're a - sleep _____ in -

to   your   tent   I'll   creep. _____ The

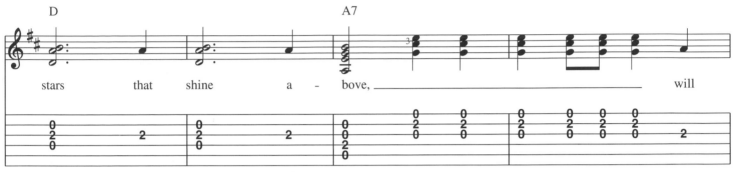

stars   that   shine   a - bove, _____ will

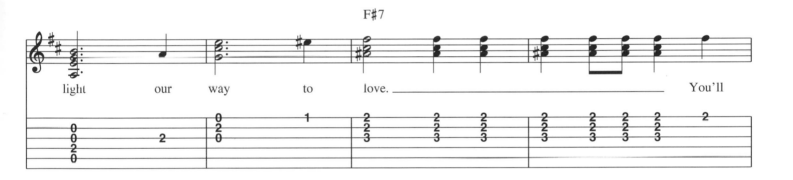

light   our   way   to   love. _____ You'll

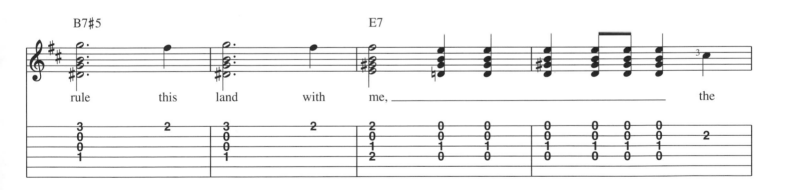

rule   this   land   with   me, _____ the

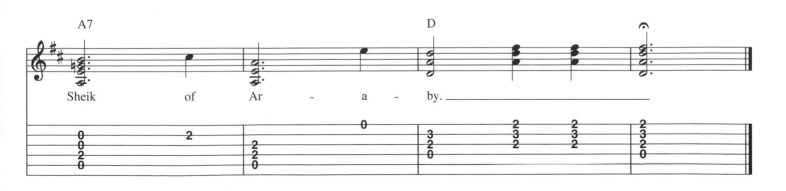

Sheik   of   Ar - a - by. _____

Shenandoah

American Folksong

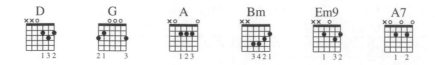

Strum Pattern: 1
Pick Pattern: 2

Verse

Moderately slow

O Shen-an-doah ____ I love to see you. A - way, _____ you roll-ing

riv - er. O Shen-an-doah, _____ I long to see you. A -

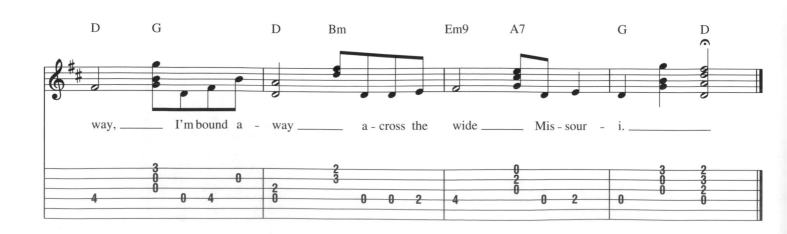

way, _____ I'm bound a - way _____ a-cross the wide _____ Mis-sour - i.

Skip to My Lou

Traditional

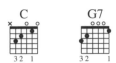

Strum Pattern: 10
Pick Pattern: 10

Chorus
Moderately fast

Skip, skip, skip to my lou, skip, skip, skip to my lou. Skip, skip, skip to my lou,

Verse

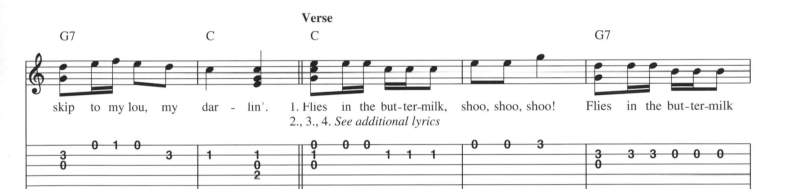

skip to my lou, my dar-lin'. 1. Flies in the but-ter-milk, shoo, shoo, shoo! Flies in the but-ter-milk
2., 3., 4. *See additional lyrics*

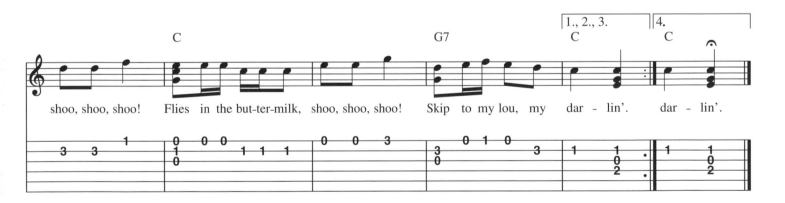

shoo, shoo, shoo! Flies in the but-ter-milk, shoo, shoo, shoo! Skip to my lou, my dar-lin'. dar-lin'.

Additional Lyrics

2. Lost my partner, what'll I do?
   Lost my partner, what'll I do?
   Lost my partner, what'll I do?
   Skip to my lou, my darlin'.

3. I'll get another one purtier than you,
   I'll get another one purtier than you,
   I'll get another one purtier than you,
   Skip to my lou, my darlin'.

4. Can't get a red bird, a blue bird'll do,
   Can't get a red bird, a blue bird'll do,
   Can't get a red bird, a blue bird'll do,
   Skip to my lou, my darlin'.

Shine On, Harvest Moon

Words by Jack Norworth
Music by Nora Bayes and Jack Norworth

Strum Pattern: 3
Pick Pattern: 3

Verse
Moderately slow

1. The night was might-y dark so you could hard-ly see, ___ for the moon re-fused to shine. ___
2. *See additional lyrics*

Cou-ple sit-ting un-der-neath a wil-low tree, ___ for love ___ they pine. ___ Lit-tle maid was kind-a 'fraid of dark-ness so ___ she said, ___ "I guess I'll go." ___ Boy be-gan to sigh, looked up at the sky, told the moon his lit-tle tale of

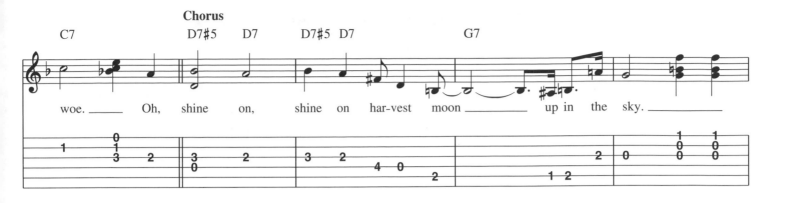

woe._____ Oh, shine on, shine on har-vest moon _____ up in the sky._____

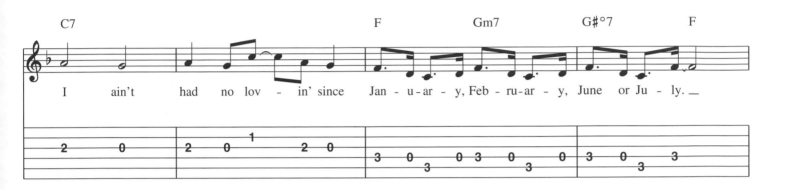

I ain't had no lov – in' since Jan – u-ar – y, Feb – ru-ar – y, June or Ju – ly.__

Snow time ain't no time to stay _____ out-doors and spoon, _____ so shine on,

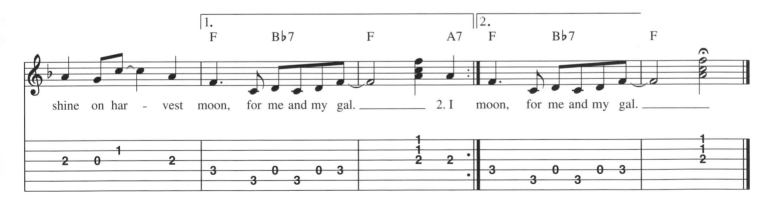

shine on har – vest moon, for me and my gal. _____ 2. I moon, for me and my gal. _____

Additional Lyrics

2. I can't see why a boy should sigh, when by his side
Is the girl he loves so true.
All he has to say is, "Won't you be my bride,
For I love you."
Why should I be telling you this secret when
I know that you can guess
Harvest Moon will smile, shine on all the while,
If this little girl should answer, "Yes."

Sidewalks of New York

Words and Music by Charles B. Lawlor and James W. Blake

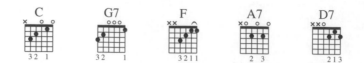

Strum Pattern: 7, 8
Pick Pattern: 7, 8

Moderately

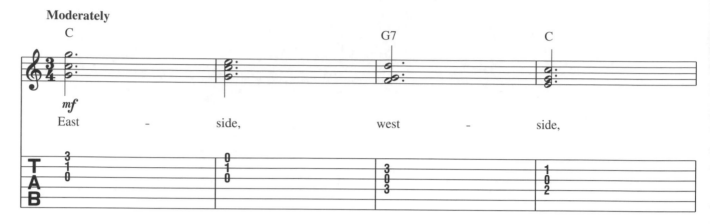

East – side, west – side,

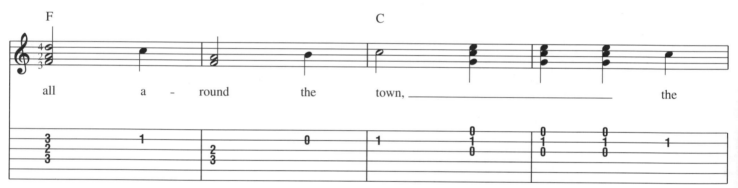

all a – round the town, _____ the

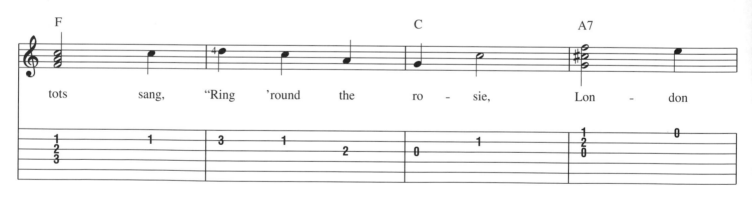

tots sang, "Ring 'round the ro – sie, Lon – don

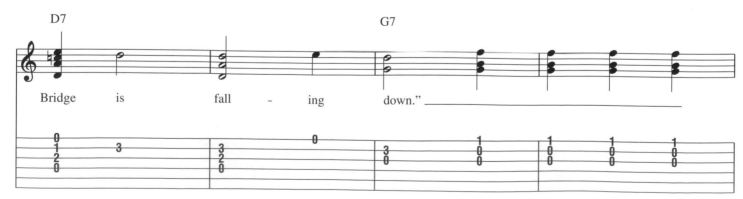

Bridge is fall – ing down." _____

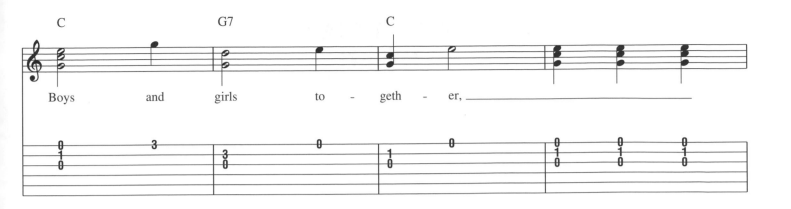

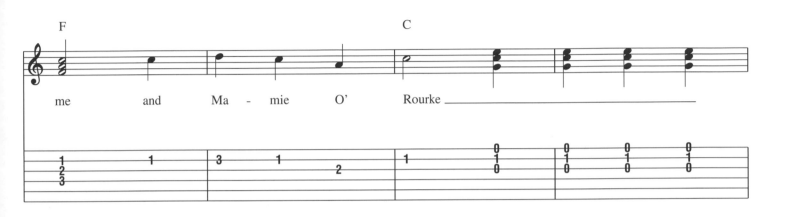

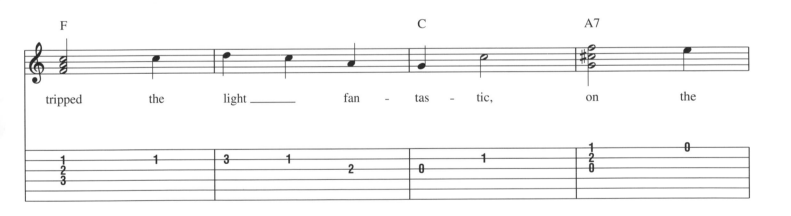

The Skaters
(Waltz)
By Emil Waldteufel

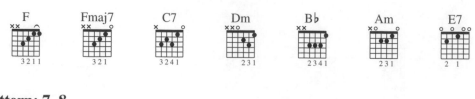

Strum Pattern: 7, 8
Pick Pattern: 8

Moderately

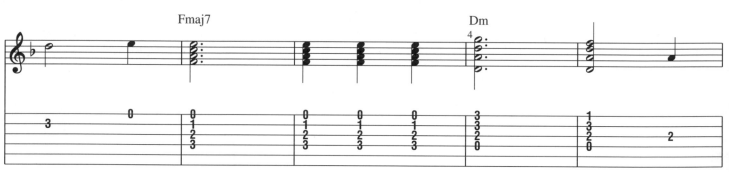

4th time, To Coda ⊕

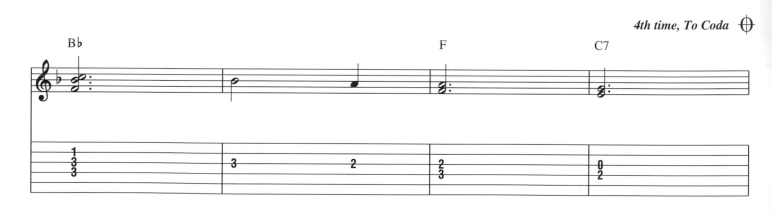

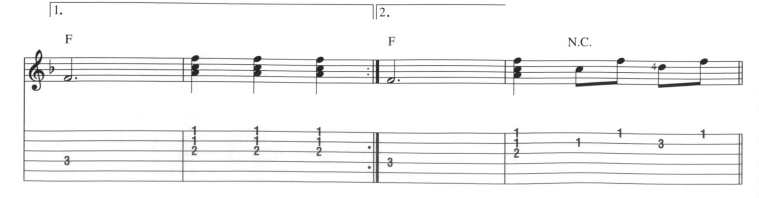

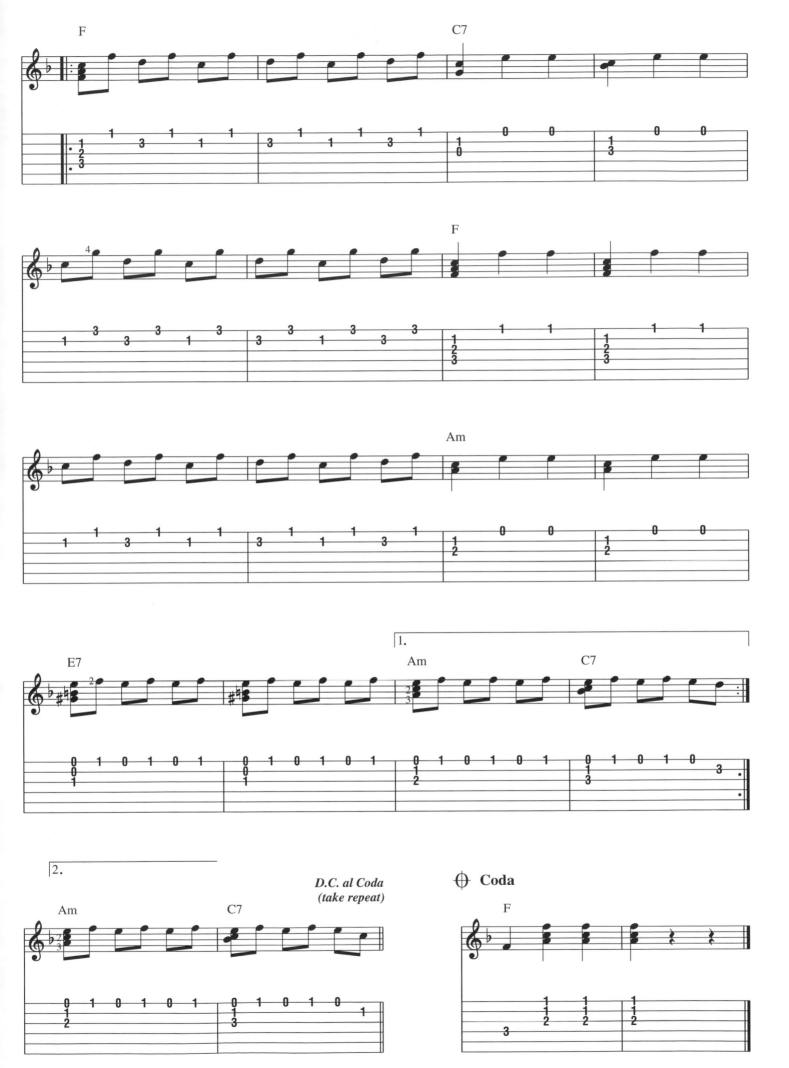

Smiles

Words by J. Will Callahan
Music by Lee S. Roberts

G7   C   E7   Am   D7   C7   A7sus4   A7   Fmaj7   F#°7

Strum Pattern: 3, 4
Pick Pattern: 1, 3

Moderately

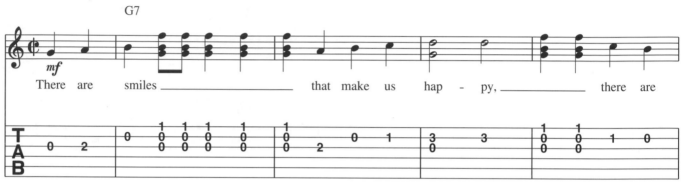

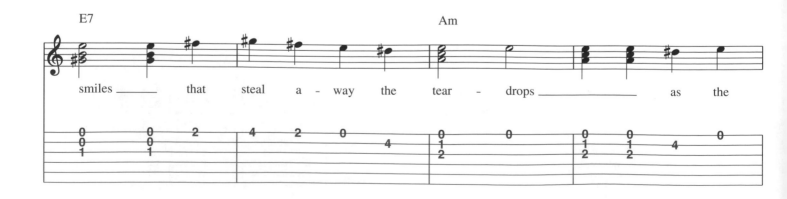

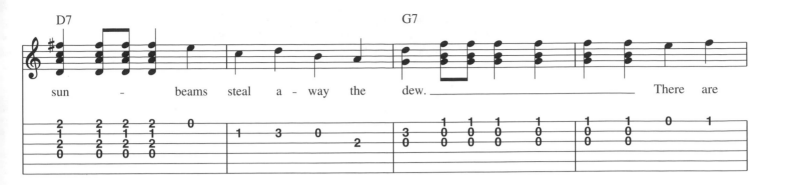

sun - beams   steal   a - way the   dew._______________________________________ There are

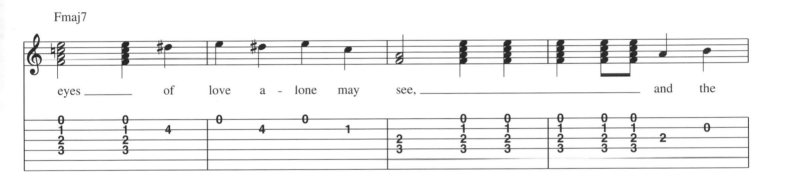

smiles_______ that have a ten - der mean - ing___________________ that the

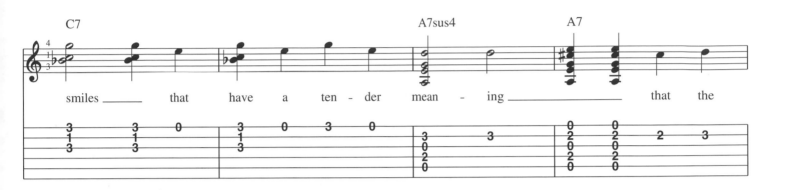

eyes_______ of love a - lone may see,_________________________ and the

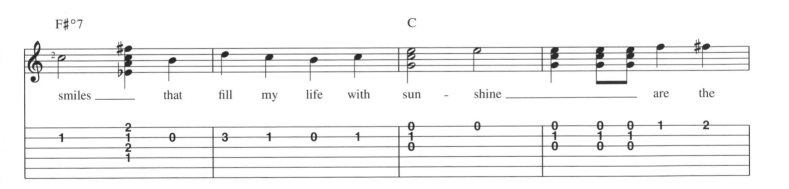

smiles_______ that fill my life with sun - shine__________________ are the

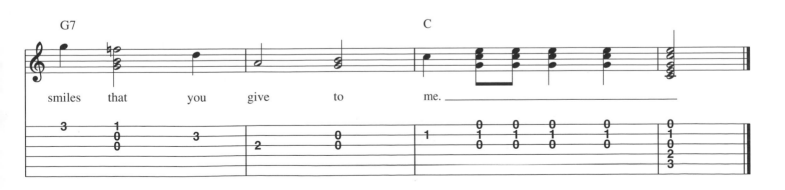

smiles that   you   give   to   me._________________

Somebody Stole My Gal

Words and Music by Leo Wood

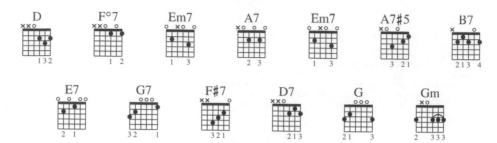

Strum Pattern: 2
Pick Pattern: 4

Verse
Brightly

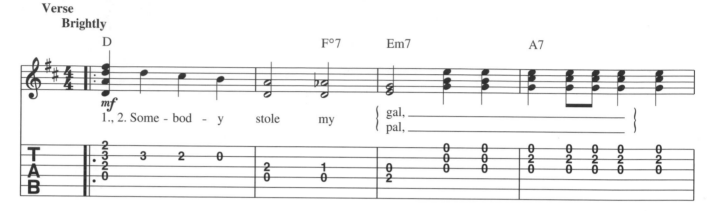

1., 2. Some - bod - y stole my { gal, _____ / pal, _____ }

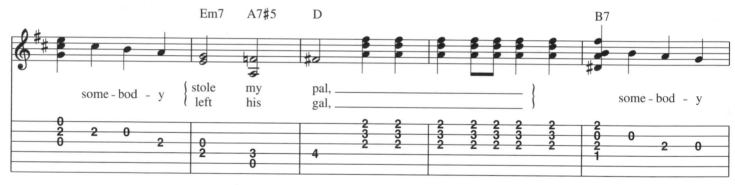

some - bod - y { stole my pal, _____ / left his gal, _____ } some - bod - y

came and took { her / him } a - way. _____ { She / He } did - n't e - ven

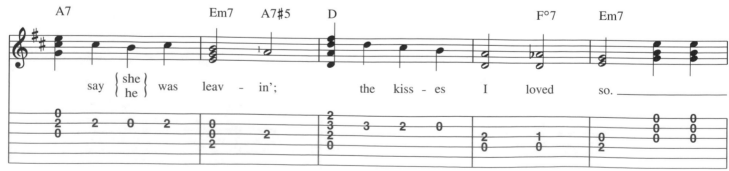

say { she / he } was leav - in'; the kiss - es I loved so. _____

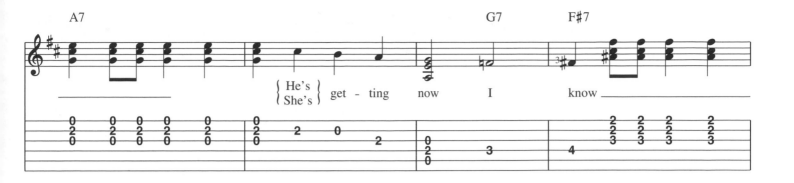

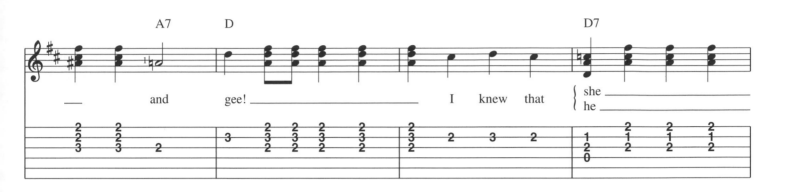

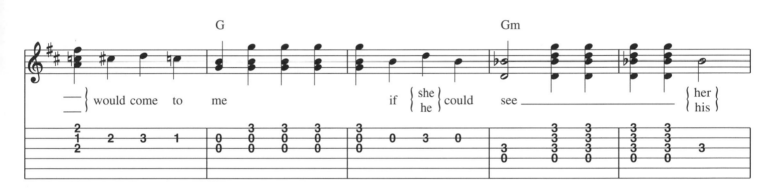

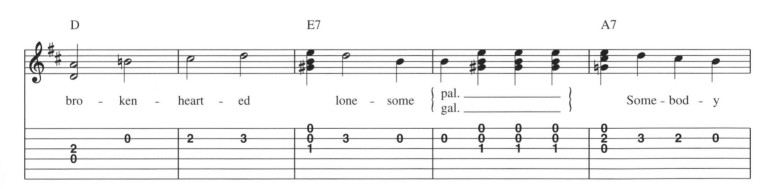

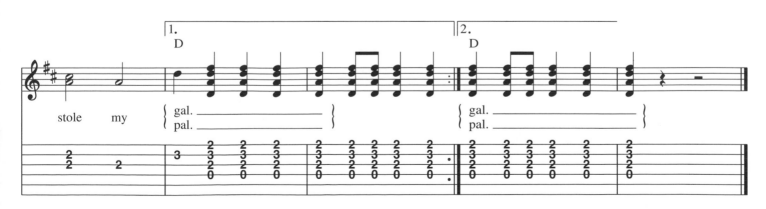

Sometimes I Feel Like a Motherless Child

African-American Spiritual

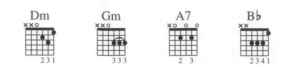

Strum Pattern: 10
Pick Pattern: 10

Verse
Moderately slow

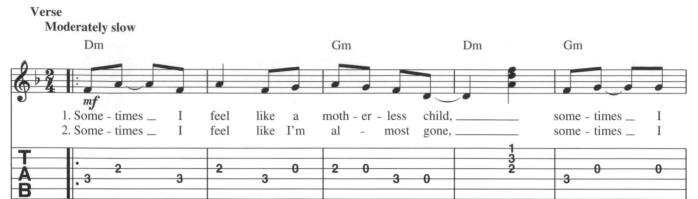

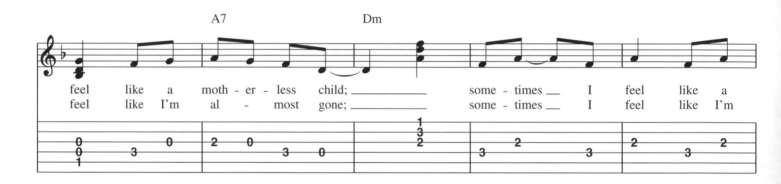

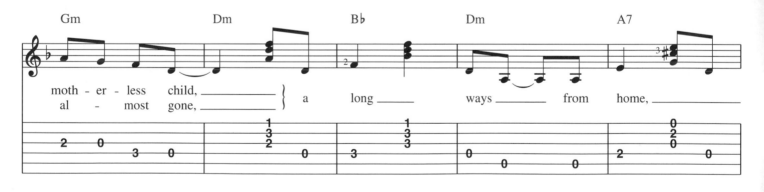

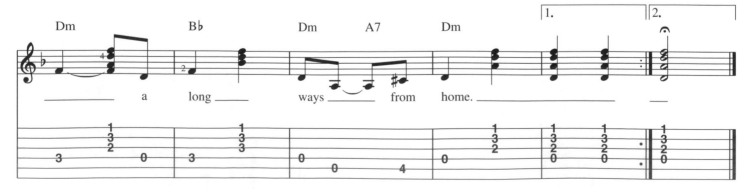

Song of the Islands

Words and Music by Charles E. King

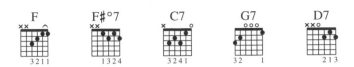

Strum Pattern: 2
Pick Pattern: 4

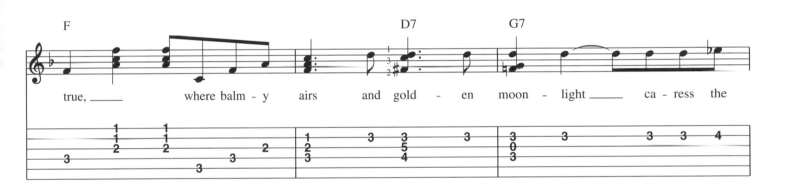

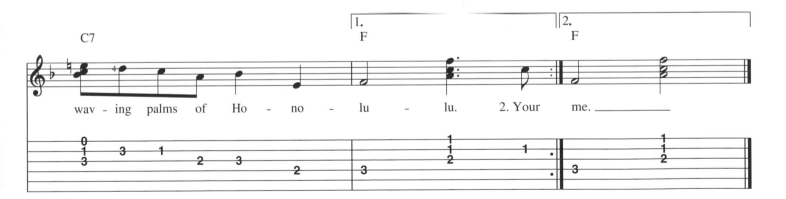

Additional Lyrics

2. Your valleys with their rainbows;
   Your mountains green, the azure sea.
   Your fragrant flow'rs enchanting music;
   Unite and sing aloha oe to me.

St. Louis Blues

from BIRTH OF THE BLUES

Words and Music by W.C. Handy

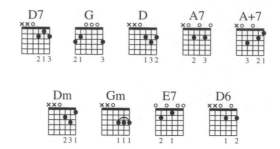

Strum Pattern: 4, 5
Pick Pattern: 4, 5

Verse
Moderately

1. I hate to see __ de eve-nin' sun go down. __
3., 5. *See Additional Lyrics*

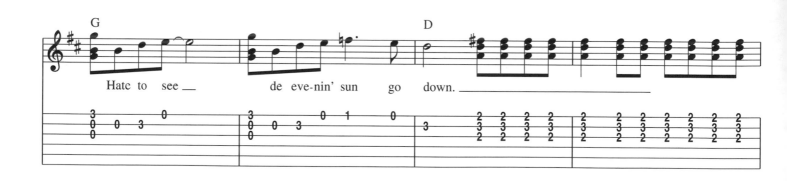

Hate to see __ de eve-nin' sun go down. __

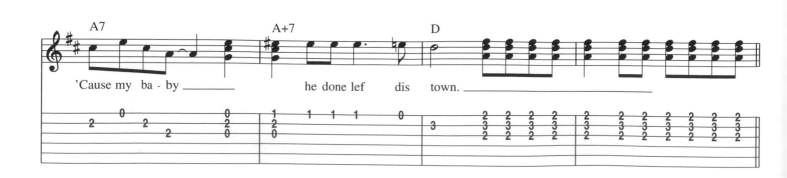

'Cause my ba-by _____ he done lef dis town. __

Verse

2. Feel-in' to-mor - row lak __ Ah feel to - day, _____

4., 6. *See Additional Lyrics*

feel to-mor - row lak __ Ah feel to - day. _____

I'll pack my trunk, _____ make ma get - a - way. _____ 1. St. Lou - is

Pre-Chorus

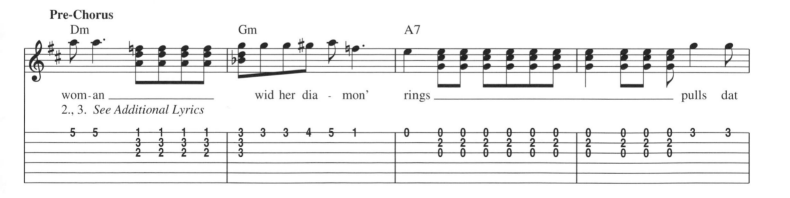

wom-an _____ wid her dia - mon' rings _____ pulls dat

2., 3. *See Additional Lyrics*

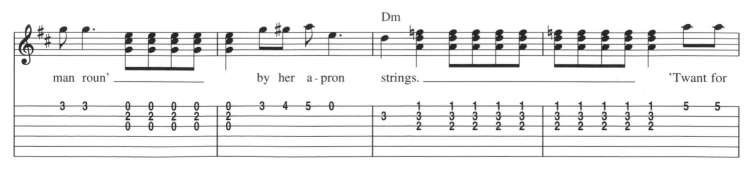

man roun' _____ by her a-pron strings. _____ 'Twant for

pow - der _____ an' for store _ bought hair _____ de

man I love _____ would not gone no - where. _____ 1. Got de

Chorus

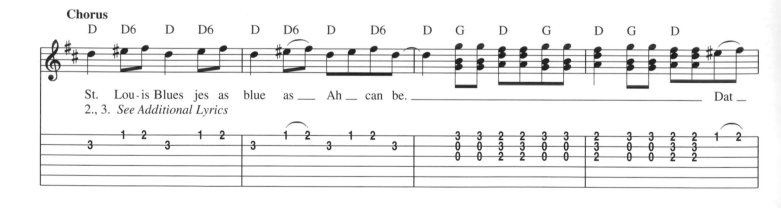

St. Lou - is Blues jes as blue as __ Ah __ can be. _____ Dat __

2., 3. *See Additional Lyrics*

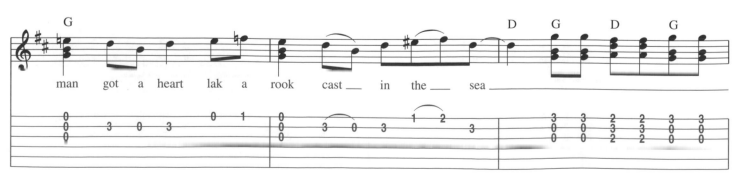

man got a heart lak a rook cast __ in the __ sea ___

or ___ else ___ he ___ would-n't have gone ___ so ___ far ___ from _ me. _

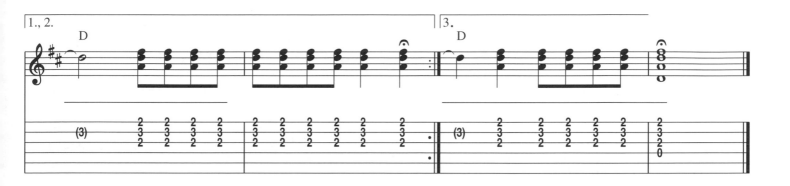

Additional Lyrics

3. Been to de Gypsy to get ma fortune tole,
   To de Gypsy done got ma fortune tole.
   'Cause I'm most wile 'bout ma Jelly Roll.

4. Gypsy done tole me, "Don't you wear no black."
   Yes, she done tole me, "Don't you wear no black.
   Go to St. Louis, you can win him back."

Pre-Chorus 2. Help me to Cairo, make St. Louis by maself.
   Git to Cairo, find ma ole friend Jeff.
   Gwine to pin maself close to his side.
   If Ah flag his train, I sho' can ride.

Chorus 2. I loves dat man lak a school boy loves his pie.
   Lak a Kentucky Col'nel loves his mint an' rye.
   I'll love ma baby till the day Ah die.

5. You ought to see dat stove-pipe brown of mine,
   Lak he owns de Dimon' Joseph line.
   He'd make a cross-eyed o' man go stone blind.

6. Blacker than midnight, teeth lak flags of truce.
   Blackest man in de whole St. Louis.
   Blacker de berry, sweeter is the juice.

Pre-Chorus 3. About a crap game he knows a pow'ful lot,
   But when work time comes he's on de dot.
   Gwine to ask him for a cold ten spot,
   What it takes to git it he's cert'nly got.

Chorus 3. A black-headed gal make a freight train jump the track.
   Said a black-headed gal make a freight train jump the track.
   But a red-headed woman makes a preacher ball the Jack.

Optional Choruses

Lawd, a blonde-headed woman makes a good man leave the town,
I said a blonde-headed woman makes a good man leave the town,
But a red-head woman makes a boy slap his papa down.

O ashes to ashes and dust to dust,
I said ashes to ashes and dust to dust,
If my blues don't get you my jazzing must.

The Star-Spangled Banner

Words by Francis Scott Key
Music by John Stafford Smith

Strum Pattern: 8
Pick Pattern: 8

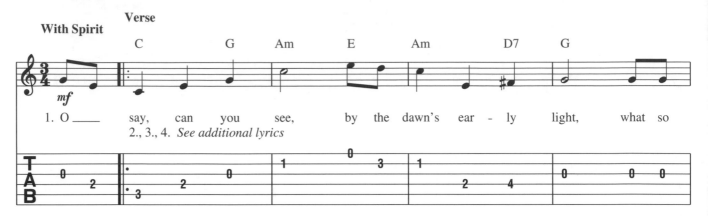

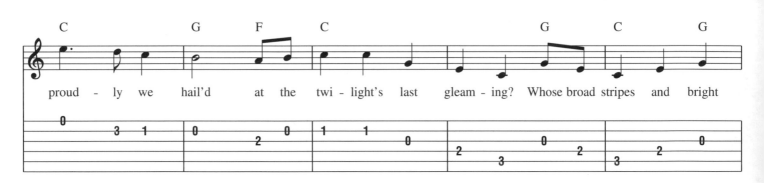

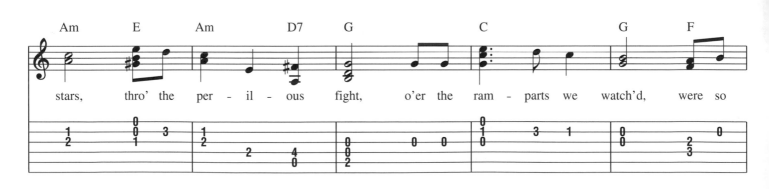

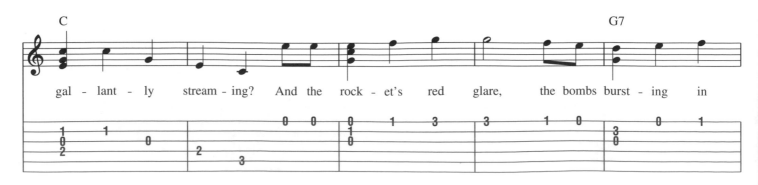

Additional Lyrics

2. On the shore dimly seen thro' the mists of the deep,
   Where the foe's haughty host in dread silence reposes,
   What is that which the breeze, o'er the towering steep,
   As it fitfully blows, half conceals, half discloses?
   Now it catches the gleam of the morning's first beam,
   In full glory reflected now – shines in the stream.
   'Tis the star-spangled banner, o long may it wave
   O'er the land of the free and the home of the brave.

3. And where is the band who so dauntingly swore,
   'Mid the havoc of war and the battle's confusion.
   A home and a country they'd leave us no more?
   Their blood has wash'd out their foul footstep's pollution.
   No refuge could save the hireling and slave
   From the terror of flight or the gloom of the grave.
   And the star-spangled banner in triumph doth wave
   O'er the land of the free and the home of the brave.

4. O thus be it ever when free man shall stand,
   Between their loved homes and the war's desolation.
   Blest with the vic'try and peace, may the heav'n rescued land
   Praise the Power that hath made and preserved us a nation!
   Then conquer we must when our cause it is just,
   And this be our motto, "In God is our trust!"
   And the star-spangled banner in triumph shall wave
   O'er the land of the free and the home of the brave.

Stars and Stripes Forever

By John Philip Sousa

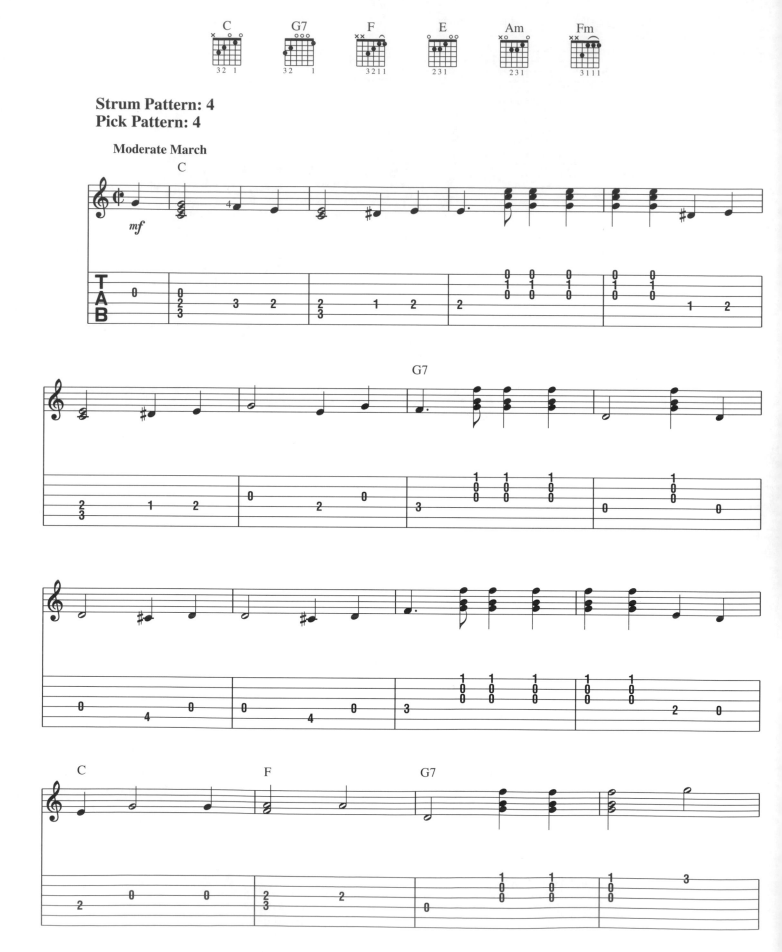

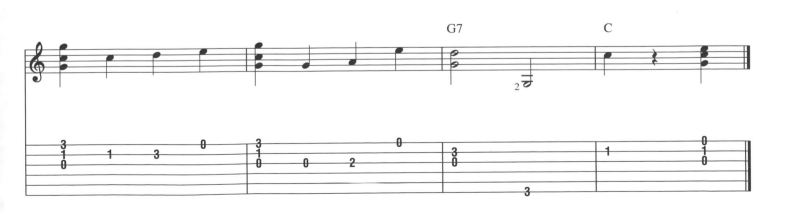

Streets of Laredo

American Cowboy Song

Strum Pattern: 8
Pick Pattern: 8

Additional Lyrics

2. "I see by your outfit that you are a cowboy."
These words, he did say as I proudly stepped by,
"Come sit beside me and hear my sad story,
Got shot in the breast and I know I must die."

Sweet Adeline
(You're the Flower of My Heart, Sweet Adeline)

Words and Music by Richard H. Gerard and Henry W. Armstrong

Strum Pattern: 4
Pick Pattern: 3

Sugar Blues

Words by Lucy Fletcher
Music by Clarence Williams

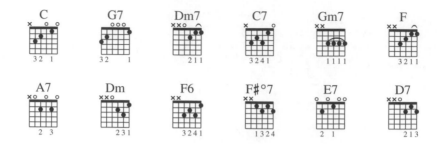

Strum Pattern: 2
Pick Pattern: 4

Verse
Moderate Blues

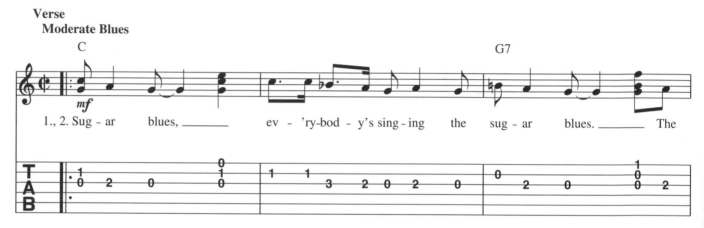

1., 2. Sug - ar blues, _____ ev - 'ry-bod - y's sing - ing the sug - ar blues. _____ The

whole town is ring - ing. My lov - in' man's _ sweet as he can be, ____ but the
I love my cof - fee, I love my tea, ____ but the

Chorus

dog - gone fool turned so - ur on me. _____
dog - gone cream turned so - ur on me. _____ I'm so un-hap-py, I feel so bad _ I could

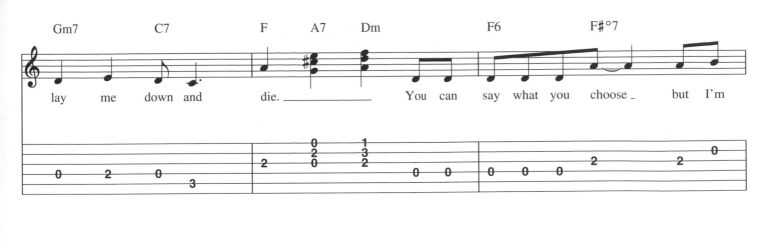

lay me down and die. _____ You can say what you choose _ but I'm

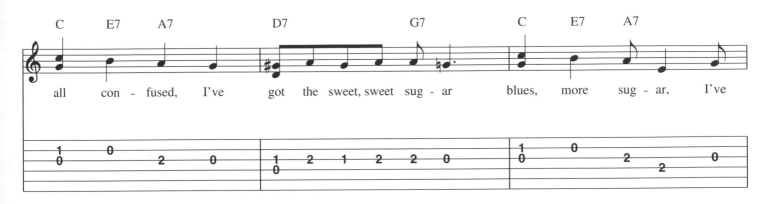

all con - fused, I've got the sweet, sweet sug - ar blues, more sug - ar, I've

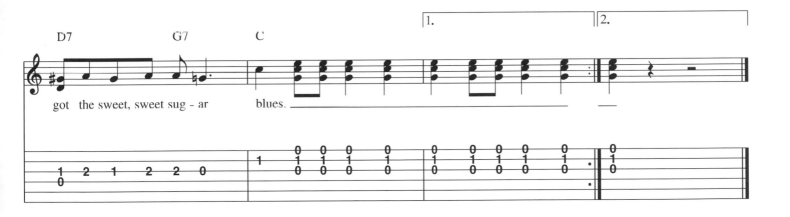

got the sweet, sweet sug - ar blues. _____

Swanee

Words by Irving Caesar
Music by George Gershwin

Strum Pattern: 2
Pick Pattern: 4

Verse
Moderately

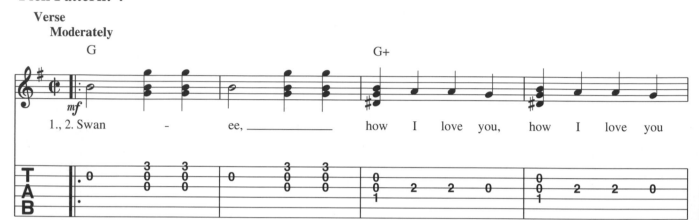

1., 2. Swan - ee, _____ how I love you, how I love you

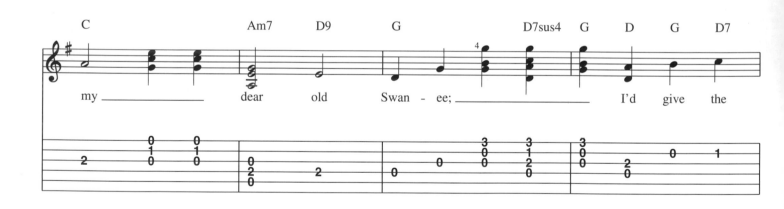

my _____ dear old Swan - ee; _____ I'd give the

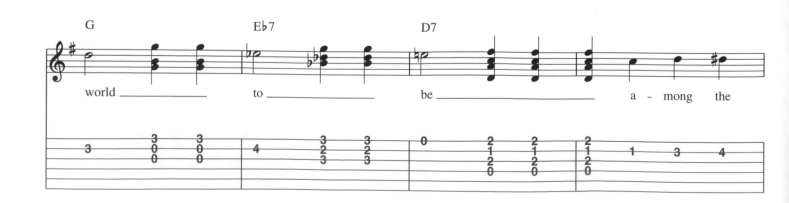

world _____ to _____ be _____ a - mong the

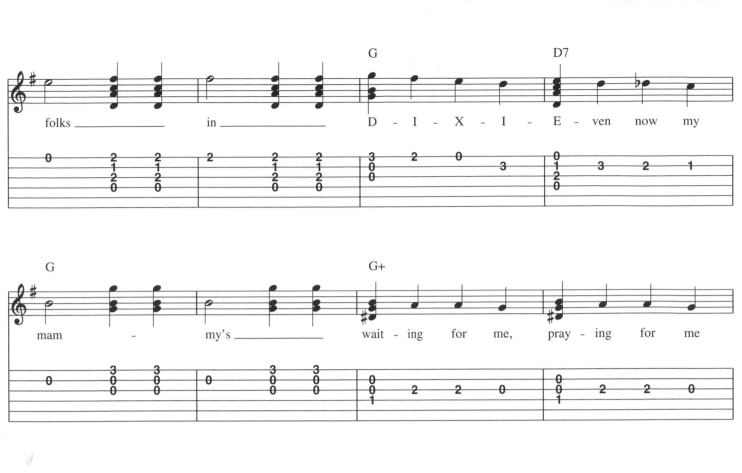

folks _____ in _____ D - I - X - I - E - ven now my

mam - my's _____ wait - ing for me, pray - ing for me

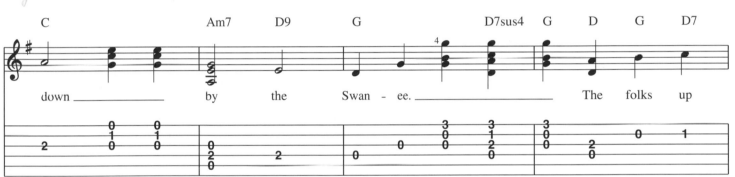

down _____ by the Swan - ee. _____ The folks up

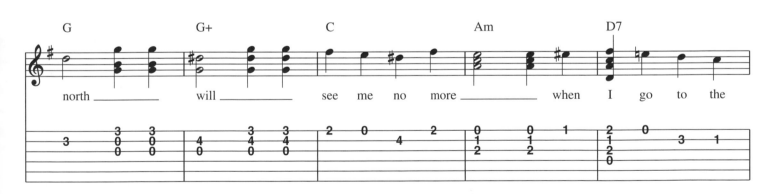

north _____ will _____ see me no more _____ when I go to the

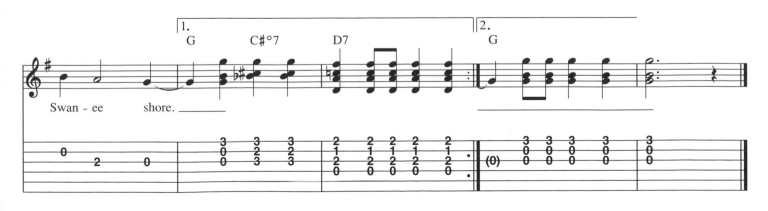

Swan - ee shore. _____

Sweet Betsy from Pike

American Folksong

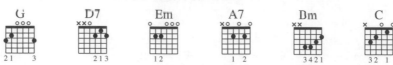

Strum Pattern: 7
Pick Pattern: 9

Additional Lyrics

2. One evening quite early they camped on the Platte,
   'Twas near by the road on a green shady flat
   Where Betsy, quite tired, lay down to repose
   While with wonder Ike gazed on his Pike County rose.

3. They stopped at Salt Lake to inquire the way,
   Where Brigham declared that sweet bets should stay.
   But Betsy got frightened and ran like a deer,
   While Brigham stood pawing the ground like a steer.

The Sweetheart of Sigma Chi

Words by Byron D. Stokes
Music by F. Dudleigh Vernor

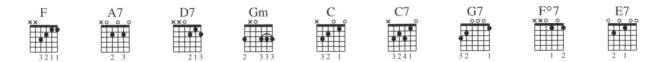

Strum Pattern: 8
Pick Pattern: 8

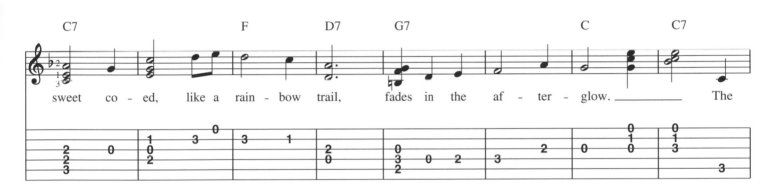

Sweethearts

Words by Robert B. Smith
Music by Victor Herbert

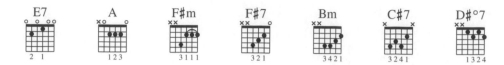

Strum Pattern: 7, 8
Pick Pattern: 7, 8

Slowly

Sweet-hearts make love their ver-y own, ___ sweet-hearts can live on love a-lone. ___

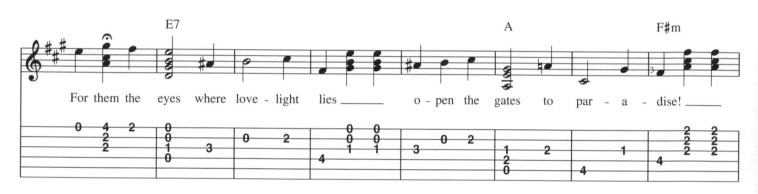

For them the eyes where love-light lies ___ o-pen the gates to par-a-dise! ___

All oth-er love is doomed to fade, ___ it is like sun-shine veiled in shade. ___

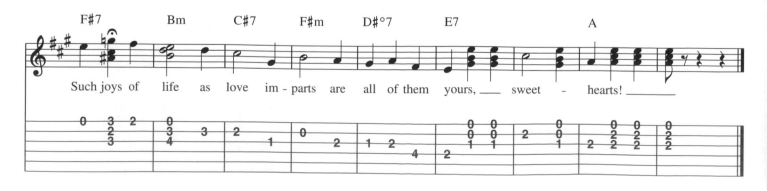

Such joys of life as love im-parts are all of them yours, ___ sweet-hearts! ___

Swing Low, Sweet Chariot

Traditional Spiritual

Strum Pattern: 2
Pick Pattern: 4

Ta-Ra-Ra-Boom-Der-E

Words and Music by Henry J. Sayers

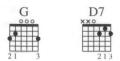

Strum Pattern: 10
Pick Pattern: 10

Verse

Moderately slow

A smart and styl - ish girl you see, Belle of good so - ci - e - ty,

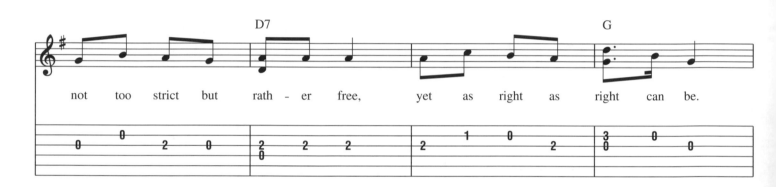

not too strict but rath - er free, yet as right as right can be.

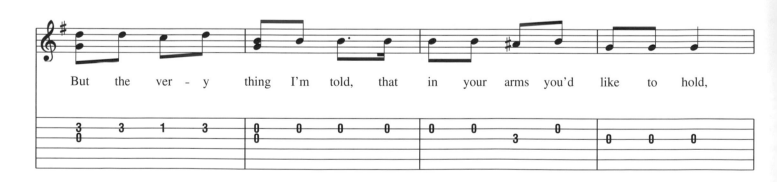

But the ver - y thing I'm told, that in your arms you'd like to hold,

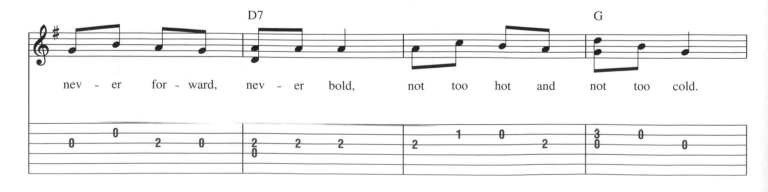

nev - er for - ward, nev - er bold, not too hot and not too cold.

Chorus

Take Me Out to the Ball Game

Words by Jack Norworth
Music by Albert Von Tilzer

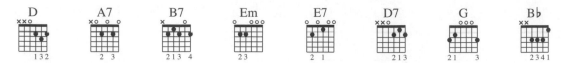

Strum Pattern: 8
Pick Pattern: 8

Spirited Waltz

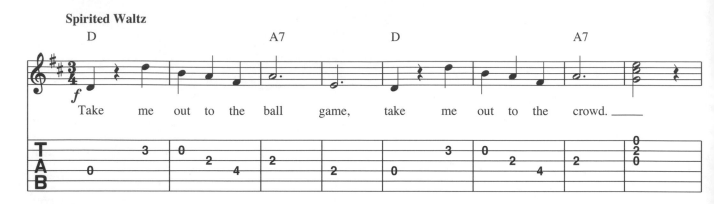

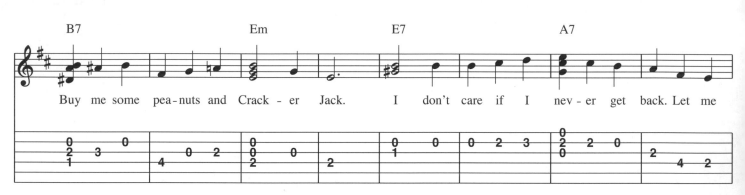

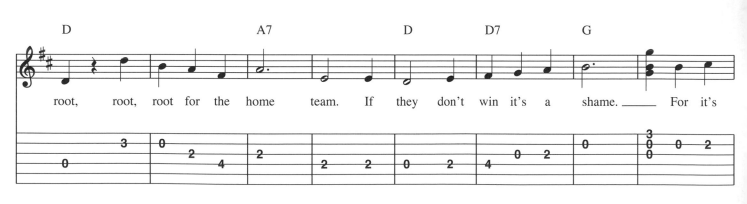

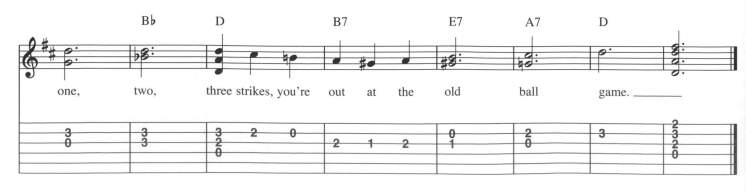

That's a Plenty

Words by Ray Gilbert
Music by Lew Pollack

338

339

Tarantella

Traditional

There Is a Tavern in the Town

Traditional Drinking Song

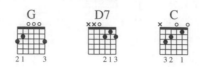

Strum Pattern: 3, 4
Pick Pattern: 1, 3

Moderately slow

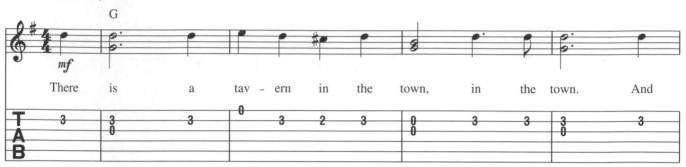

There is a tav - ern in the town, in the town. And

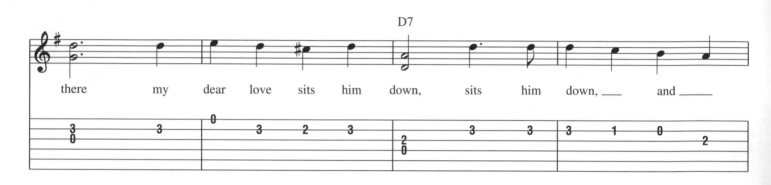

there my dear love sits him down, sits him down, ___ and ___

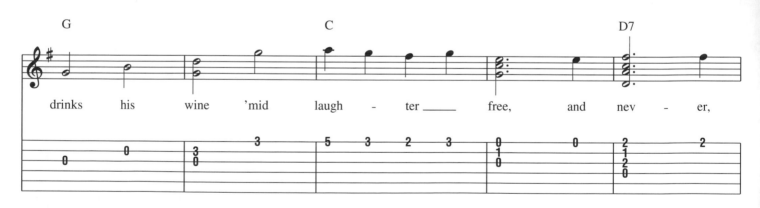

drinks his wine 'mid laugh - ter ___ free, and nev - er,

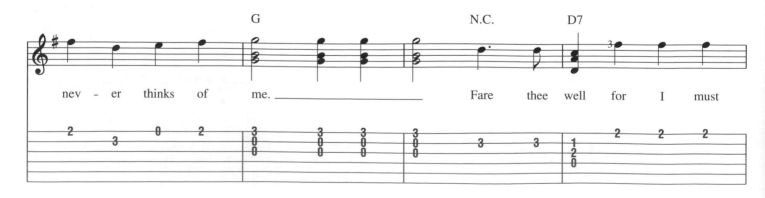

nev - er thinks of me. _____ Fare thee well for I must

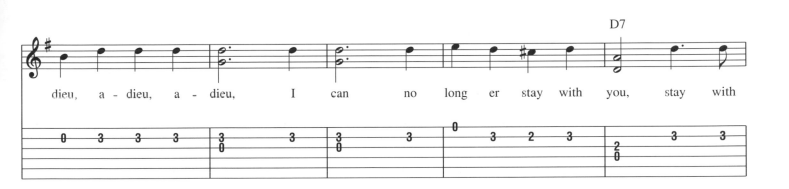

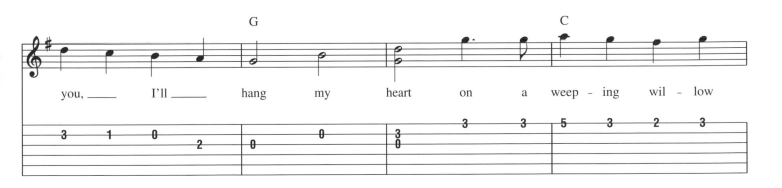

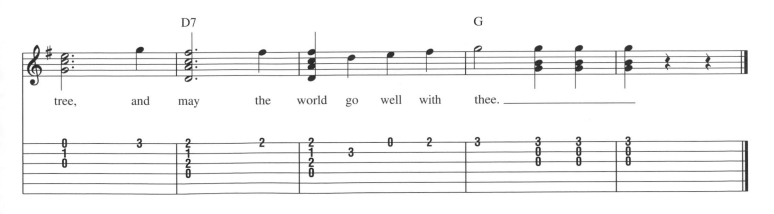

There's a Hole in the Bucket

Traditional

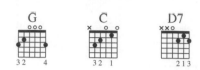

Strum Pattern: 8
Pick Pattern: 8

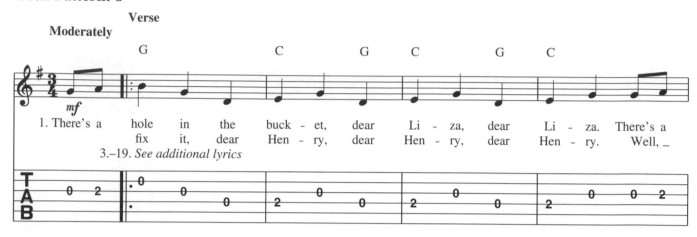

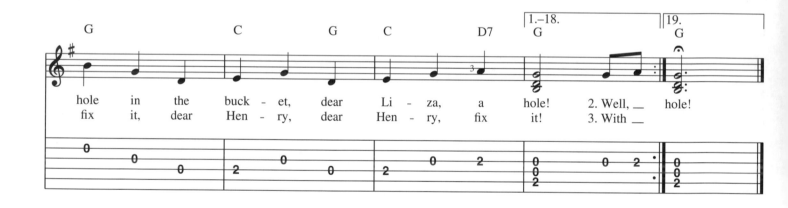

Additional Lyrics

3. With what shall I fix it, dear Liza, etc.
4. With a straw, dear Henry, etc.
5. But the straw is too long, dear Liza, etc.
6. Then cut it, dear Henry, etc.
7. With what shall I cut it, dear Liza, etc.
8. With a knife, dear Henry, etc.
9. But the knife is too dull, dear Liza, etc.
10. Then sharpen it, dear Henry, etc.
11. With what shall I sharpen it, dear Liza, etc.
12. With a stone, dear Henry, etc.
13. But the stone is too dry, dear Liza, etc.
14. Then wet it, dear Henry, etc.
15. With what shall I wet it, dear Liza, etc.
16. With water, dear Henry, etc.
17. In what shall I carry it, dear Liza, etc.
18. In a bucket, dear Henry, etc.
19. There's a hole in the bucket, dear Liza, etc.

This Train

Traditional

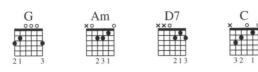

Strum Pattern: 2
Pick Pattern: 4

Additional Lyrics

2. This train don't carry no gamblers, this train.
   This train don't carry no gamblers, this train.
   This train don't carry no gamblers,
   No hypocrites, no midnight ramblers.

3. This train don't carry no liars, this train.
   This train don't carry no liars, this train.
   This train don't carry no liars,
   No hypocrites and no high flyers.

4. This train is build for speed now, this train.
   This train is built for speed now, this train.
   This train is built for speed now,
   Fastest train you ever did see.

5. This train you don't pay no transportation, this train.
   This train you don't pay no transportation, this train.
   This train you don't pay no transportation,
   No Jim Crow and no discrimination.

6. This train don't carry no rustlers, this train.
   This train don't carry no rustlers, this train.
   This train don't carry no rustlers,
   Sidestreet walkers, two-bit hustlers.

This Little Light of Mine

African-American Spiritual

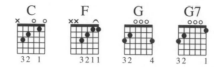

Strum Pattern: 2, 4
Pick Pattern: 5, 4

Chorus
Moderately

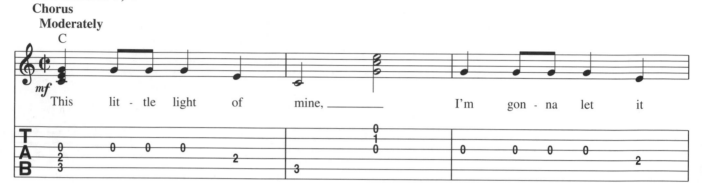

This lit - tle light of mine, _____ I'm gon - na let it

shine. _____ This lit - tle light of mine, _____ I'm gon - na let it

shine, let it shine, let it shine, let it shine! _____

Verse

1. Hide it un - der a bush - el, no!
2., 3. *See additional lyrics*

I'm gon - na let it shine. _____ Hide it un - der a bush - el, no!

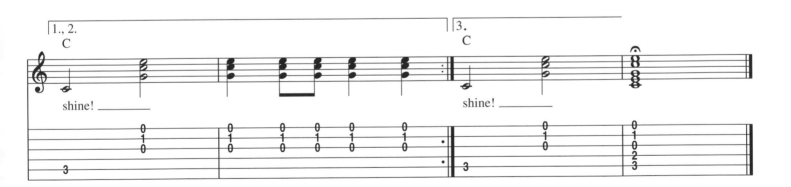

I'm gon - na let it shine, let it shine, let it shine, let it

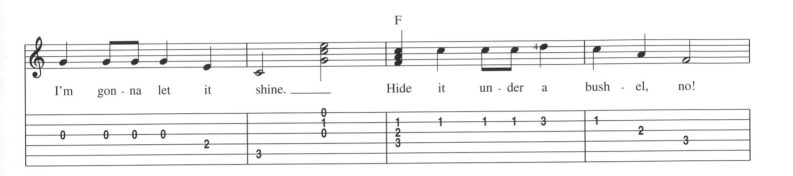

1., 2.

shine! _____

3.

shine! _____

Additional Lyrics

2. Don't let Satan (blow) it out,
I'm gonna let it shine.
Don't let Satan (blow) it out,
I'm gonna let it shine, let it shine,
Let it shine, let it shine!

3. Let it shine till Jesus comes,
I'm gonna let it shine.
Let it shine till Jesus comes,
I'm gonna let it shine, let it shine,
Let it shine, let it shine!

Three O'Clock in the Morning

Words by Dorothy Terriss
Music by Julian Robledo

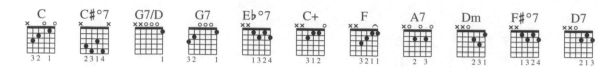

Strum Pattern: 7, 8
Pick Pattern: 7, 8

Slowly

It's three o' clock in the morn - ing,

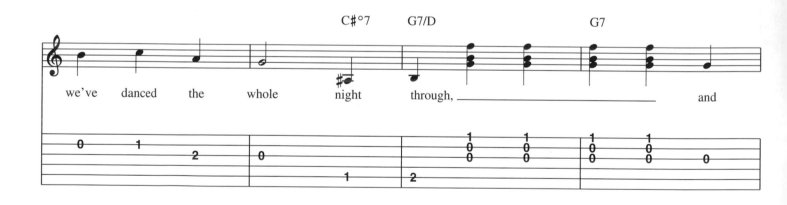

we've danced the whole night through, _____ and

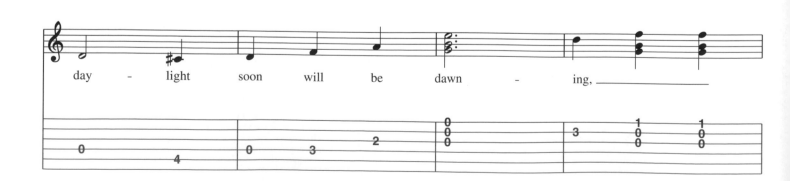

day - light soon will be dawn - ing, _____

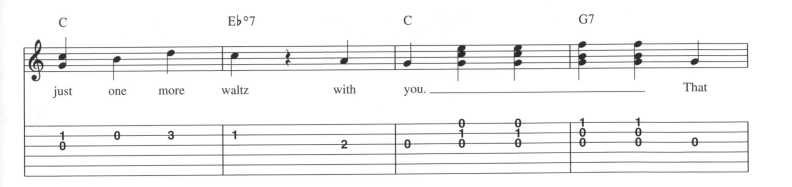

just one more waltz with you. _____ That

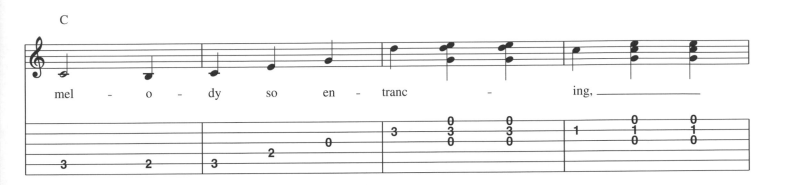

mel - o - dy so en - tranc - ing, _____

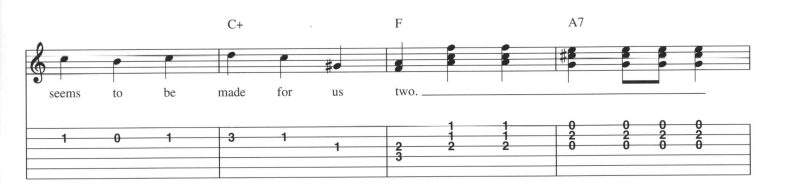

seems to be made for us two. _____

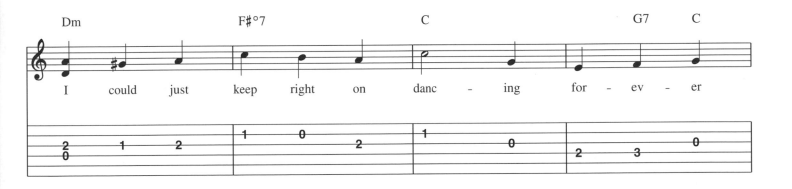

I could just keep right on danc - ing for - ev - er

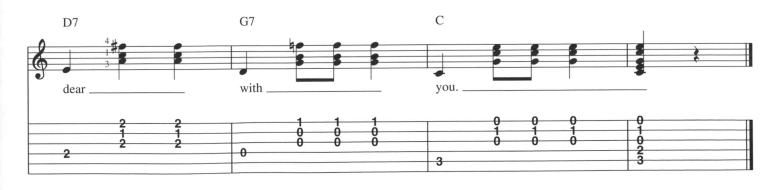

dear _____ with _____ you. _____

Tiger Rag
(Hold That Tiger)

Words by Harry DeCosta
Music by Original Dixieland Jazz Band

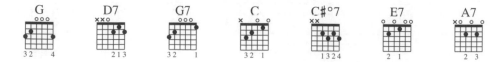

Strum Pattern: 2
Pick Pattern: 4

Verse
Fast

1., 2. Where's that ti - ger! Where's that ti - ger!

Where's that ti - ger! Where's that ti - ger!

Hold that ti - ger! Hold that ti - ger!

Hold that ti - ger! Choke him, poke him, kick him and soke him!

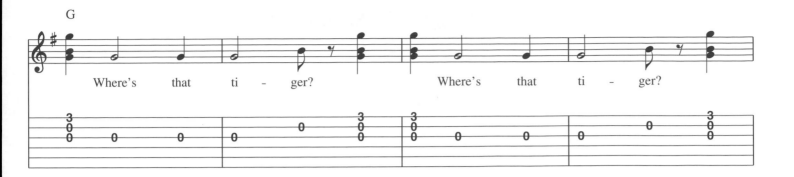

Where's that ti - ger? Where's that ti - ger?

Where, _____ oh, where ___ can he be? _____

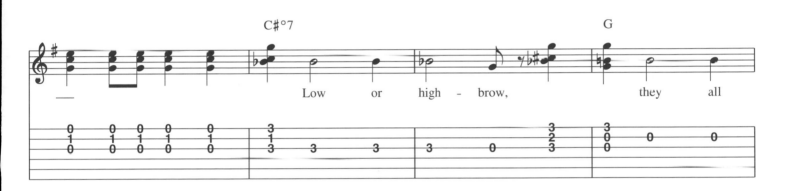

___ Low or high - brow, they all

cry now: "Please play that Ti - ger Rag ___ for

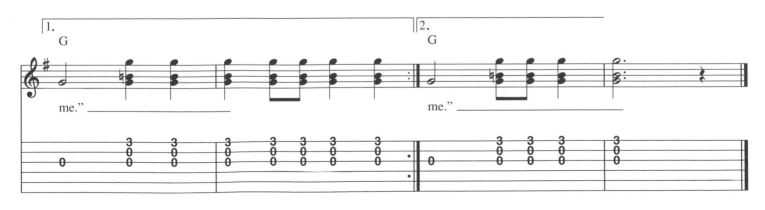

me." _____ me." _____

Tom Dooley

Traditional Folksong

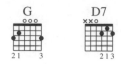

Strum Pattern: 3, 4
Pick Pattern: 1, 3

Chorus

Moderately

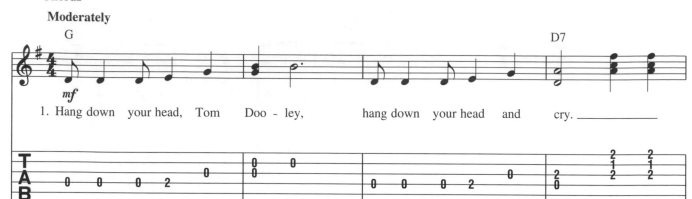

1. Hang down your head, Tom Doo - ley, hang down your head and cry. _____

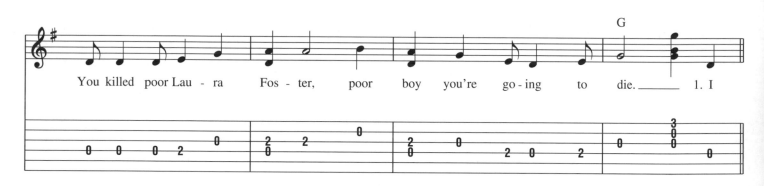

You killed poor Lau - ra Fos - ter, poor boy you're go - ing to die. _____ 1. I

Verse

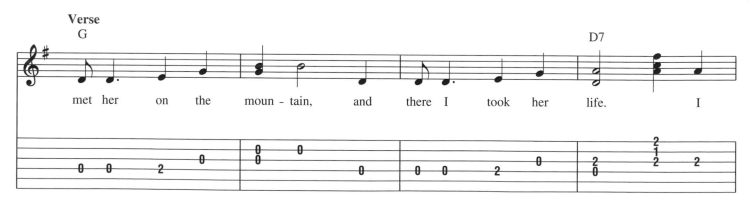

met her on the moun - tain, and there I took her life. I

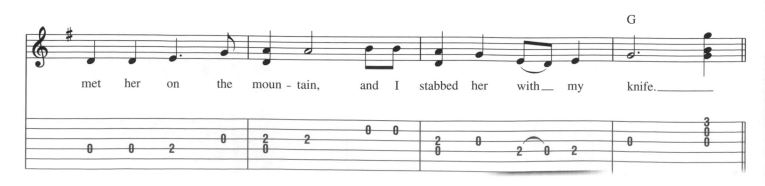

met her on the moun - tain, and I stabbed her with__ my knife._____

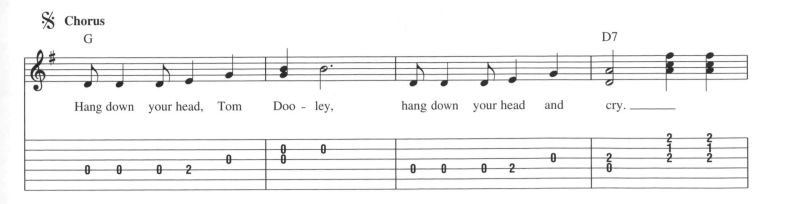

Chorus

Hang down your head, Tom Doo - ley, hang down your head and cry. _____

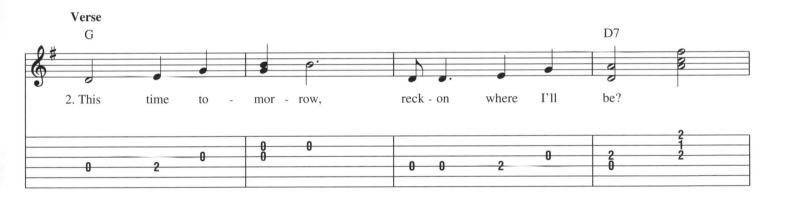

You killed poor Lau - ra Fos - ter, poor boy you're go - ing to die. _____

Fine

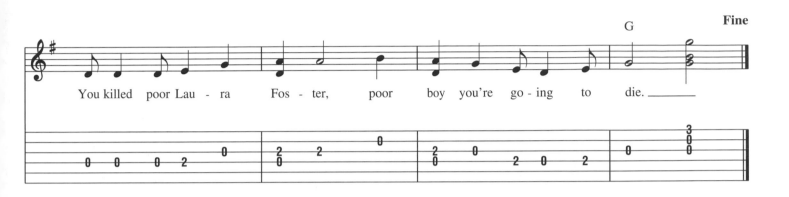

Verse

2. This time to - mor - row, reck - on where I'll be?

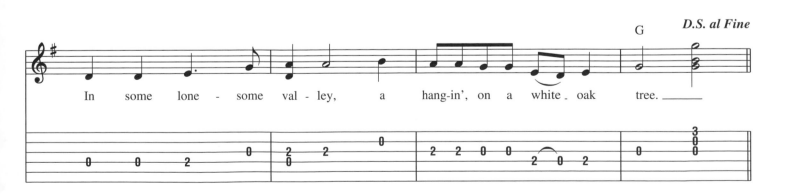

D.S. al Fine

In some lone - some val - ley, a hang-in', on a white oak tree. _____

Too-Ra-Loo-Ra-Loo-Ral
(That's an Irish Lullaby)
from GOING MY WAY
Words and Music by James R. Shannon

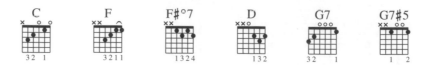

Strum Pattern: 10
Pick Pattern: 10

Toyland

(from Babes in Toyland)

Music by Victor Herbert

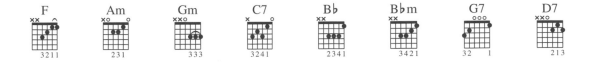

Strum Pattern: 8
Pick Pattern: 8

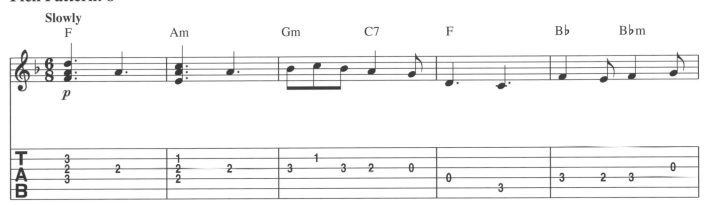

Toreador Song
from CARMEN
By Georges Bizet

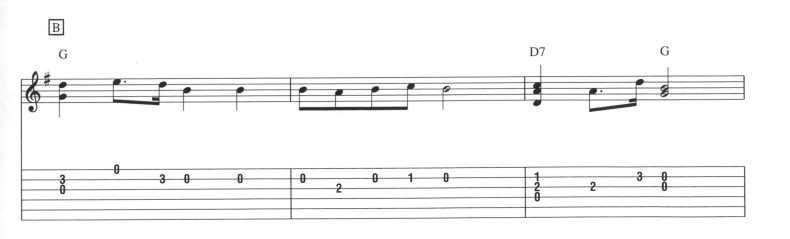

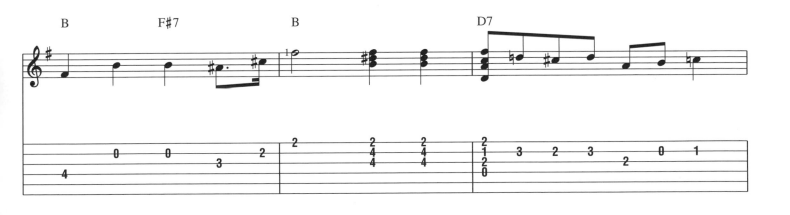

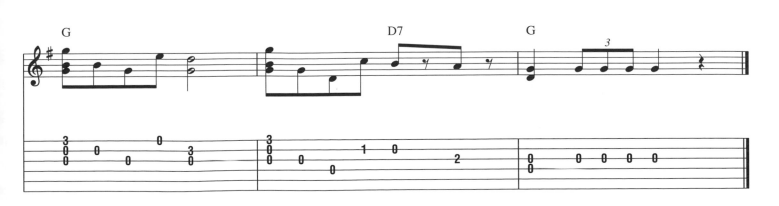

Tramp! Tramp! Tramp!

Words and Music by George F. Root

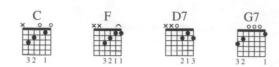

Strum Pattern: 3
Pick Pattern: 3

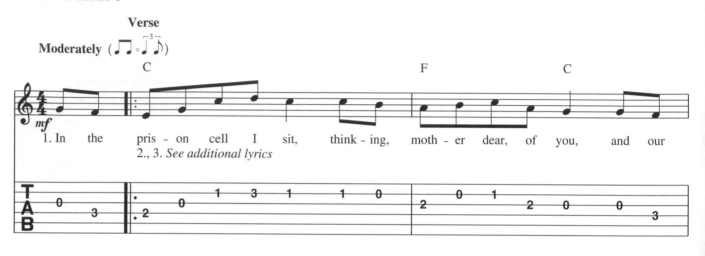

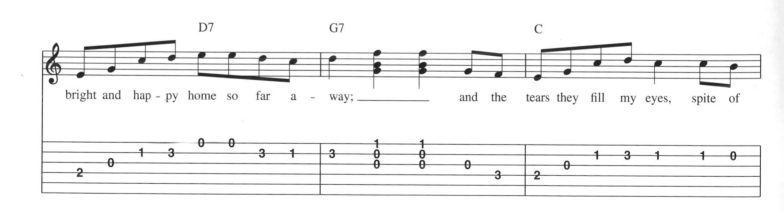

Chorus

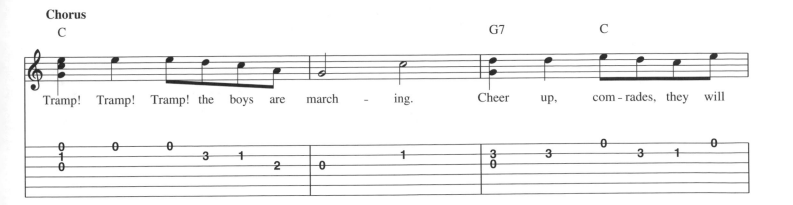

Tramp! Tramp! Tramp! the boys are march - ing. Cheer up, com - rades, they will

come, _____ and be - neath the star - ry flag we shall breathe the air a - gain of the

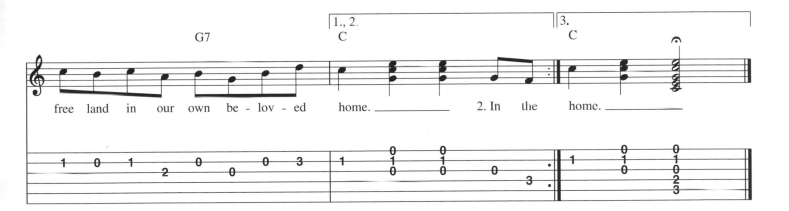

free land in our own be - lov - ed home. _____ 2. In the home. _____

Additional Lyrics

2. In the battle front we stood when their fiercest charge they made,
   And they swept us off a hundred men or more;
   But before we reached their lines, they were beaten back, dismayed,
   And we heard the cry of vict'ry o'er and o'er.

3. So, within the prison cell, we are waiting for the day
   That shall come to open wide the iron door,
   And the hollow eye grows bright, and the poor heart almost gay,
   As we think of seeing home and friends once more.

Twelfth Street Rag

By Euday L . Bowman

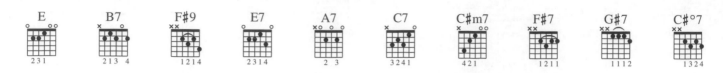

Strum Pattern: 3
Pick Pattern: 1

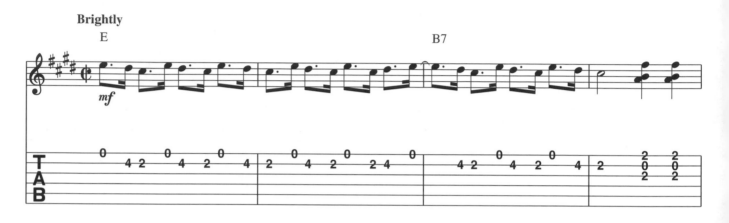

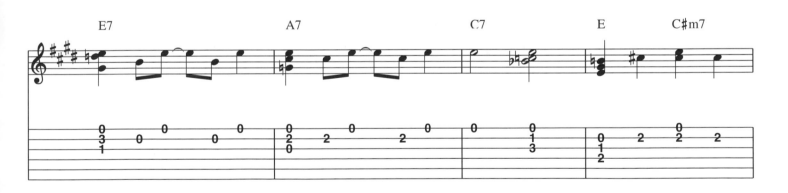

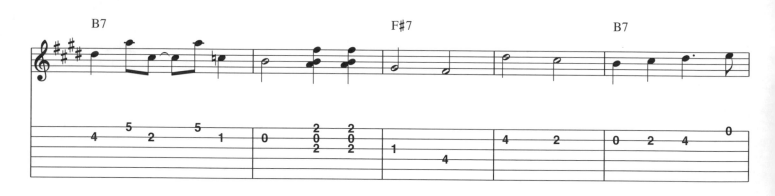

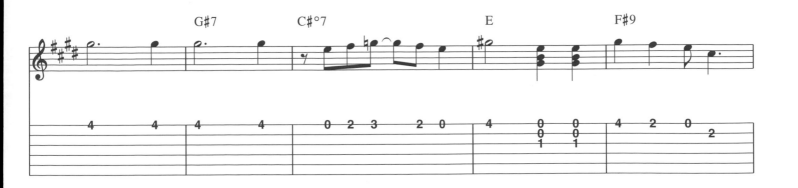

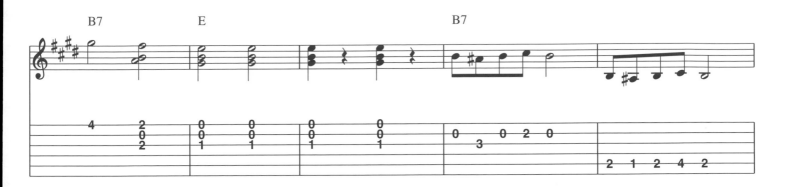

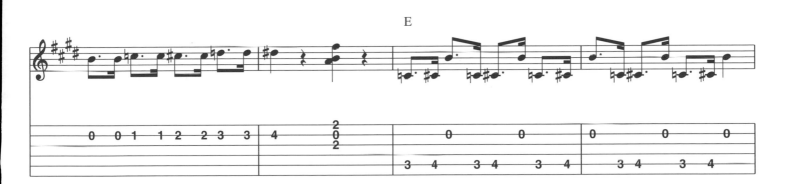

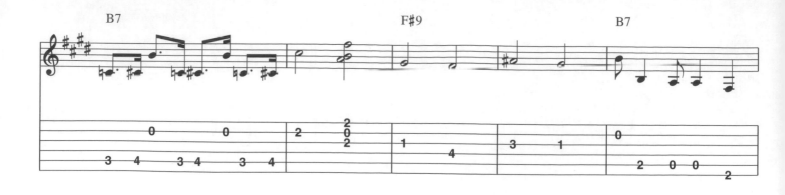

Two Guitars

Russian Gypsy Song

Strum Pattern: 10
Pick Pattern: 10

Vive L'Amour

Traditional

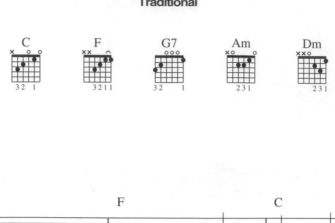

Strum Pattern: 7, 8
Pick Pattern: 7, 8

Verse
Moderately

1. Let ev - 'ry good fel - low now fill up his glass,
2. *See additional lyrics*

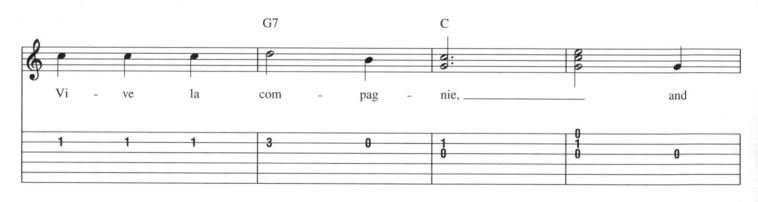

Vi - ve la com - pag - nie, _____ and

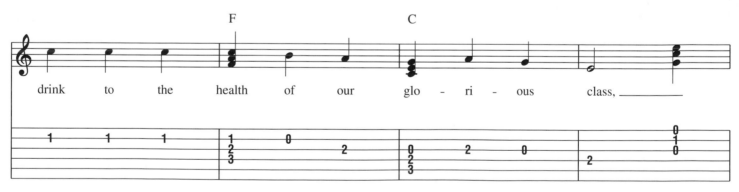

drink to the health of our glo - ri - ous class, _____

Vi - ve la com - pag - nie.

Chorus

Vi - ve la, vi - ve la, vi - ve l'a - mour,

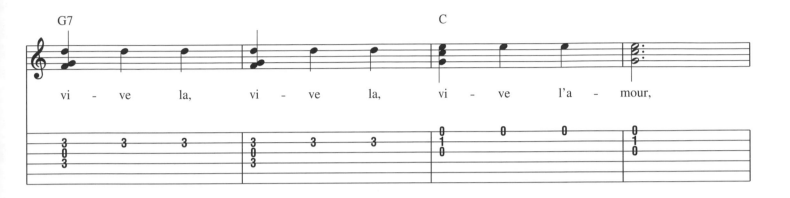

vi - ve la, vi - ve la, vi - ve l'a - mour,

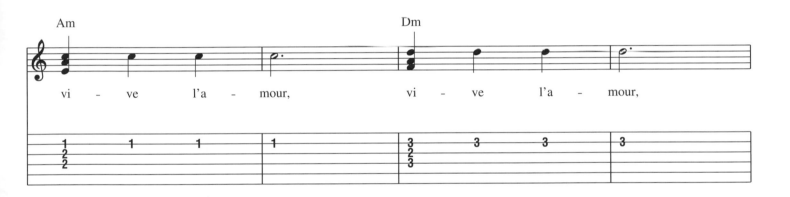

vi - ve l'a - mour, vi - ve l'a - mour,

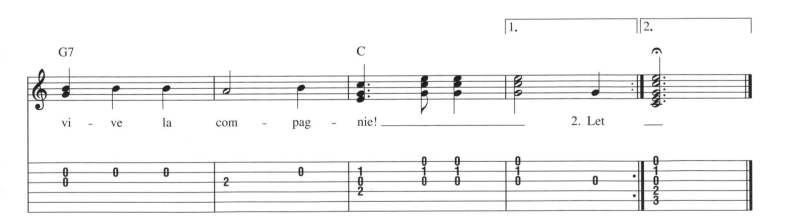

vi - ve la com - pag - nie! _____ 2. Let ___

Additional Lyrics

2. Let every married man drink to his wife,
   Viva la compagnie.
   The joy of his bosom and plague of his life,
   Viva la compagnie.

Volga Boat Song

Traditional

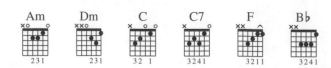

Strum Pattern: 3, 4
Pick Pattern: 3, 4

Verse
Slowly

1. Yo, ___ heave ho! ___ Yo, ___ heave ho! ___ Once more, once more.
2., 3. *See Additional Lyrics*

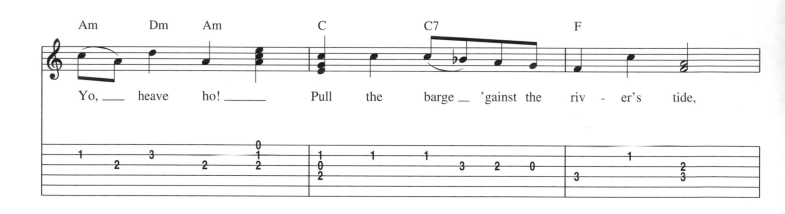

Yo, ___ heave ho! ___ Pull the barge ___ 'gainst the riv - er's tide,

Chorus

Vol - ga riv - er stretch - ing far and wide. Ai, da, da, ai, da,

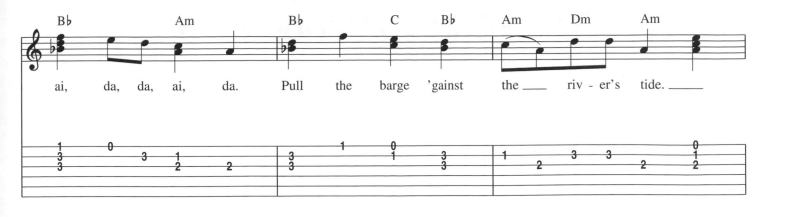

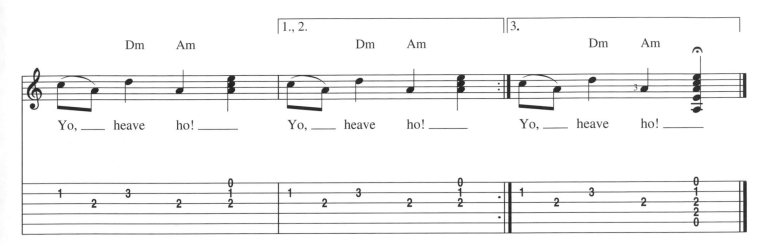

Additional Lyrics

2. Yo, heave ho! Yo, heave ho!
   Once more, once more. Yo, heave ho!
   As the barges float along,
   To the sun we sing our song…

3. Yo, heave ho! Yo, heave ho!
   Once more, once more. Yo, heave ho!
   Volga, Volga our pride,
   Mighty stream so deep and wide.

The Wabash Cannon Ball

Hobo Song

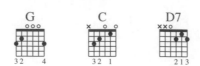

Strum Pattern: 4
Pick Pattern: 5

Verse
Moderately

1. I stood on the At-lan-tic O-cean, on the wide Pa-cif-ic shore, __ saw the queen of flow-ing
2., 3., 4. *See additional lyrics*

riv-ers might-y moun-tain by the score. __ She's long and she's tall and hand-some, yes, she's loved by one and

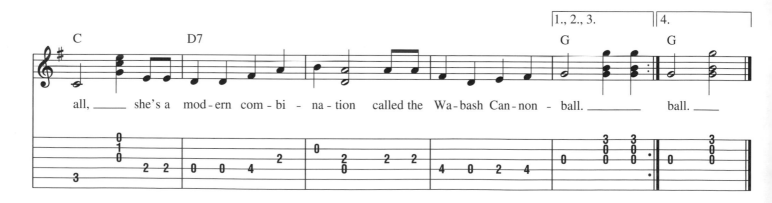

all, __ she's a mod-ern com-bi-na-tion called the Wa-bash Can-non-ball. __ ball. __

Additional Lyrics

2. Listen to the jingle, the rumble and the roar.
   Riding through the woodlands, to the hills and by the shore.
   Hear the mighty rush of the engine, hear the lonesome hobo squall,
   Riding through the jungle on the Wabash Cannonball.

3. Eastern states are dandies so the Western people say.
   From New York to St. Louis and Chicago by the way.
   Through the hills of Minnesota where the rippling waters fall,
   No chances can be taken on the Wabash Cannonball.

4. Here's to Daddy Claxton, may his name forever stand.
   May he ever be remembered through the parts of all our land.
   When his earthly race is over and the curtain 'round him fall,
   We'll carry him to glory on the Wabash Cannonball.

Waiting for the Robert E. Lee

Words by L . Wolfe Gilbert
Music by Lewis F. Muir

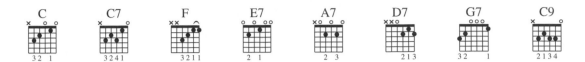

Strum Pattern: 3
Pick Pattern: 3

Verse
Brightly

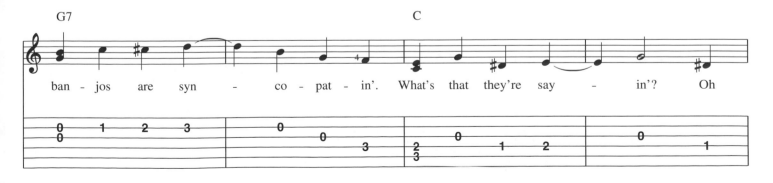

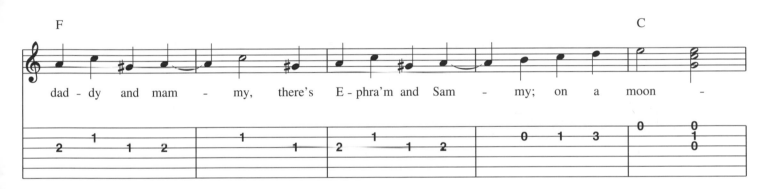

what's that they're say - in'? The while they keep play - in', I'm hum - min' and sway -

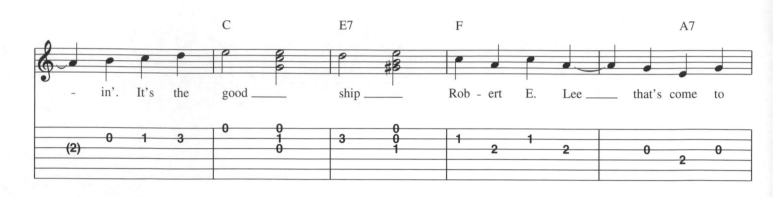

- in'. It's the good ____ ship ____ Rob - ert E. Lee ____ that's come to

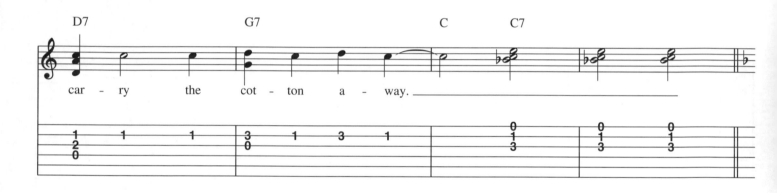

car - ry the cot - ton a - way. ____

Chorus

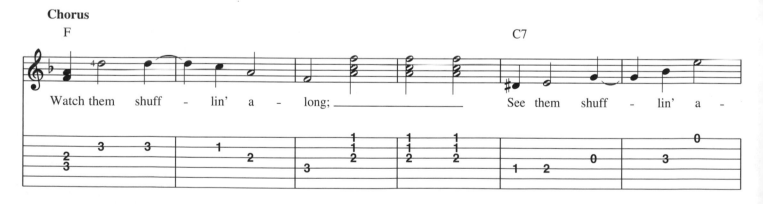

Watch them shuff - lin' a - long; ____ See them shuff - lin' a -

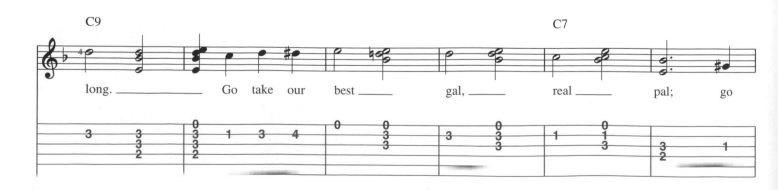

long. ____ Go take our best ____ gal, ____ real ____ pal; go

down to the lev - ee, I said to the lev - ee! And then join that shuf -

- lin' throng. _____ Hear that mu - sic and song; _____

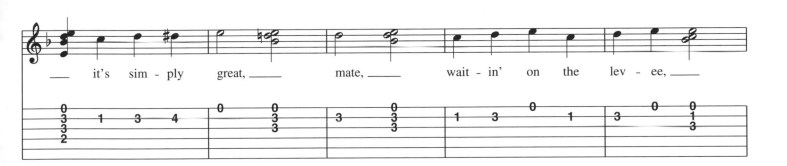

___ it's sim - ply great, ___ mate, ___ wait - in' on the lev - ee, ___

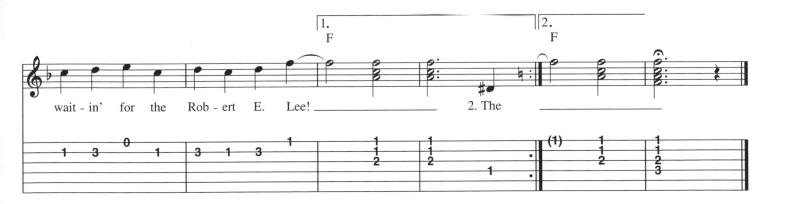

wait - in' for the Rob - ert E. Lee! _____ 2. The

Additional Lyrics

2. The whistles are blowin', the smokestacks are showin',
   The ropes they are throwin'. Excuse me, I'm goin'
   To the place where all is harmonious.
   Even the preacher, they say, is the dancin' teacher.
   Have you been down there? Say, were you aroun' there?
   If you ever go there, you'll always be found there.
   Why "dog-gone" here comes my baby
   On the good old ship Robert E. Lee

Wait 'Til the Sun Shines, Nellie

Words by Andrew B. Sterling
Music by Harry von Tilzer

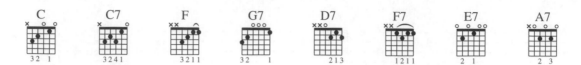

Strum Pattern: 3, 4
Pick Pattern: 1, 3

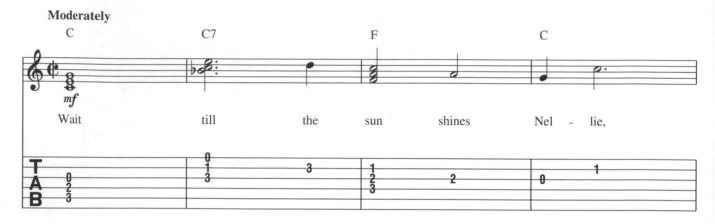

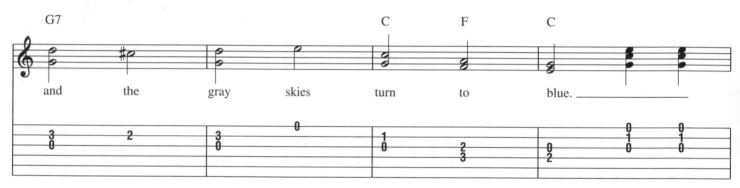

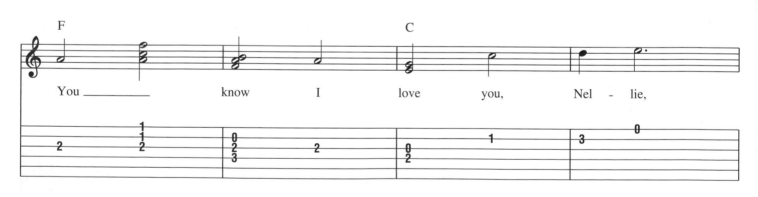

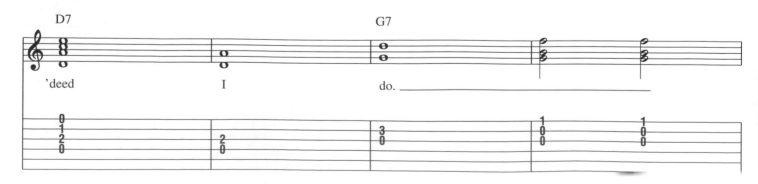

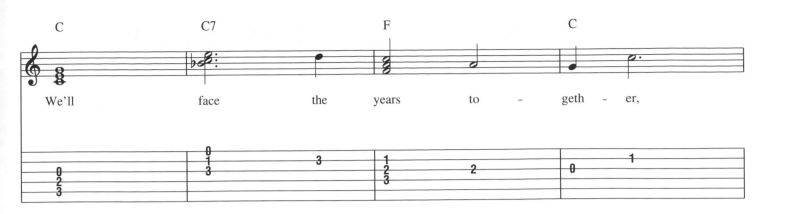

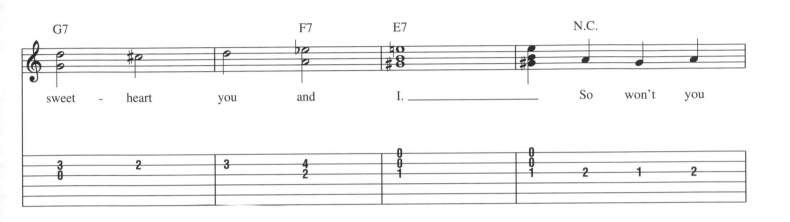

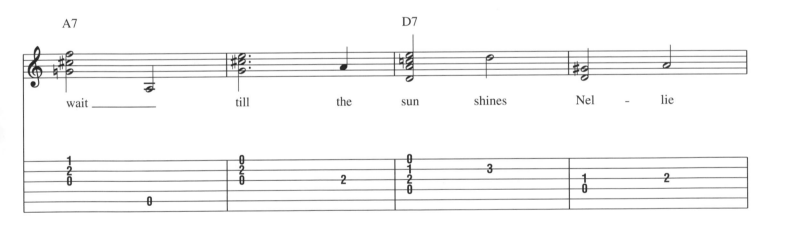

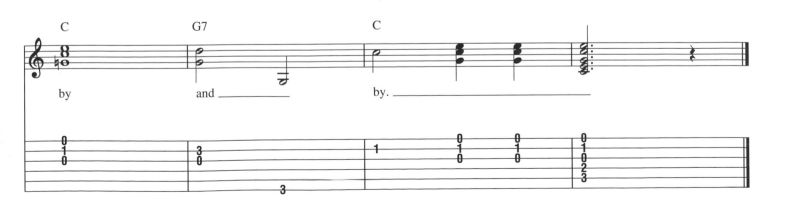

'Way Down Yonder in New Orleans

Words and Music by Henry Creamer and J. Turner Layton

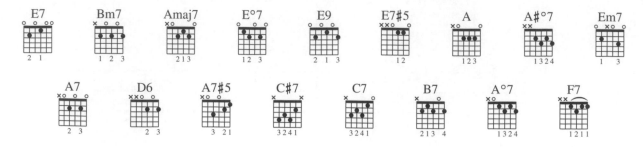

Strum Pattern: 2
Pick Pattern: 4

Verse
Moderate bounce

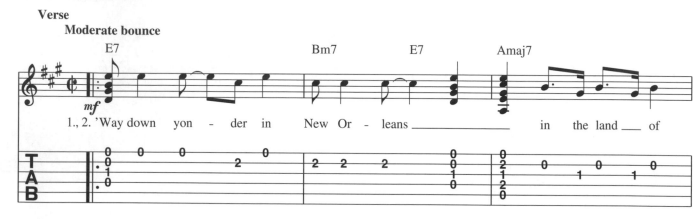

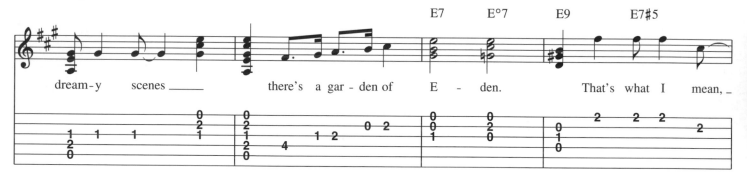

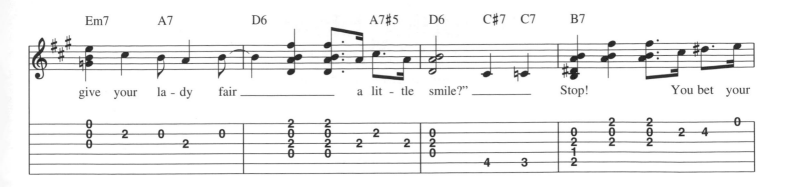

give your la-dy fair _____ a lit-tle smile?" _____ Stop! You bet your

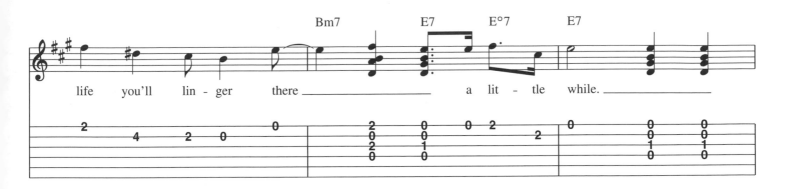

life you'll lin-ger there _____ a lit-tle while. _____

There is heav - en right here on earth _____ with those beau - ti-ful
They've got an - gels right here on earth _____ wear-ing lit - tle blue

queens _____ 'way down yon - der in New Or -
jeans _____

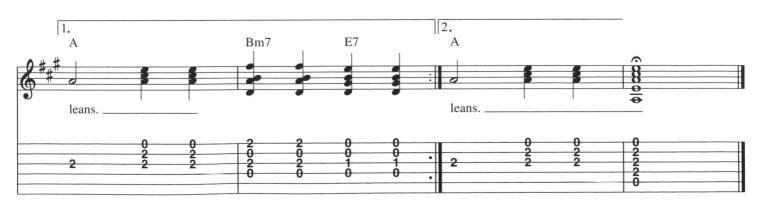

leans. _____   leans. _____

Wedding March
(Bridal Chorus)
from the opera LOHENGRIN
By Richard Wagner

Strum Pattern: 3, 4
Pick Pattern: 1, 3

When Johnny Comes Marching Home

Words and Music by Patrick Sarsfield Gilmore

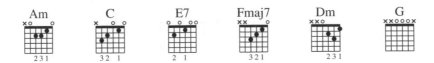

Strum Pattern: 8
Pick Pattern: 8

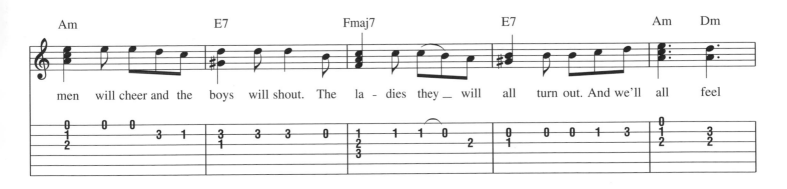

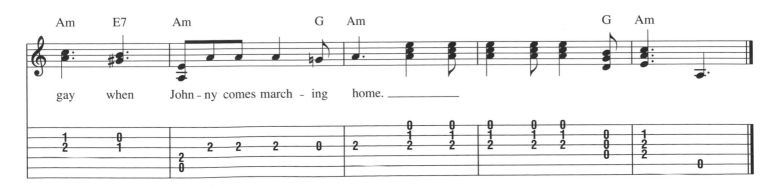

When Irish Eyes Are Smiling

Words by Chauncey Olcott and George Graff, Jr.
Music by Ernest R. Ball

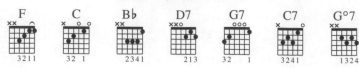

Strum Pattern: 7, 9
Pick Pattern: 8

Moderately

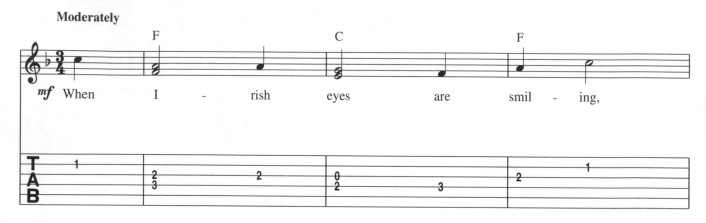

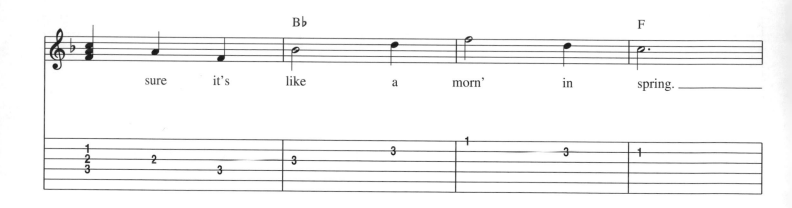

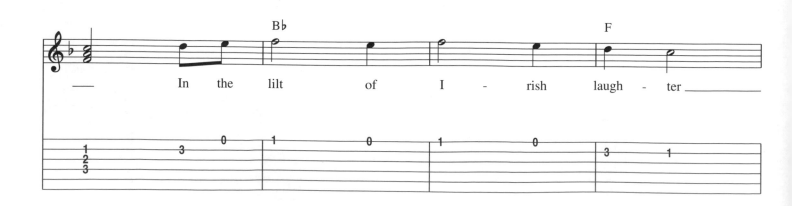

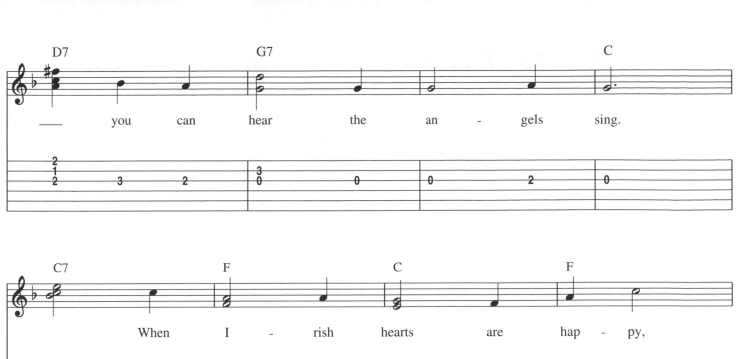

you can hear the an - gels sing.

When I - rish hearts are hap - py,

all the world seems bright and gay.

And when I - rish eyes are smil -

ing, sure they steal ___ your heart a - way.

When My Baby Smiles At Me

Words and Music by Harry von Tilzer, Andrew B. Sterling, Bill Munro and Ted Lewis

Strum Pattern: 3, 4
Pick Pattern: 1, 3

Moderately

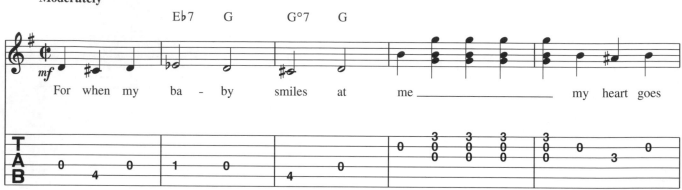

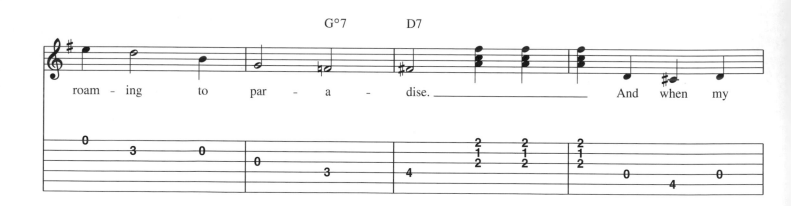

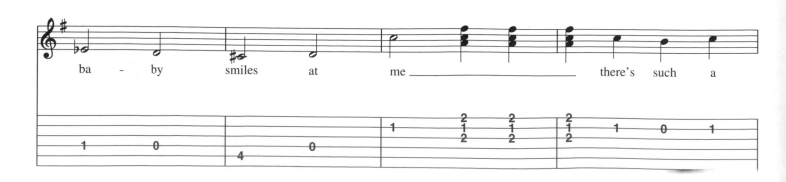

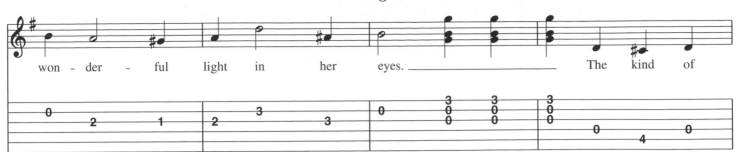

won - der - ful light in her eyes. _____ The kind of

light that means just love, _____ the kind of

love _____ that brings sweet har - mon - y _____ I

sigh, _____ I cry. _____ It's just a glimpse of heav - en when my

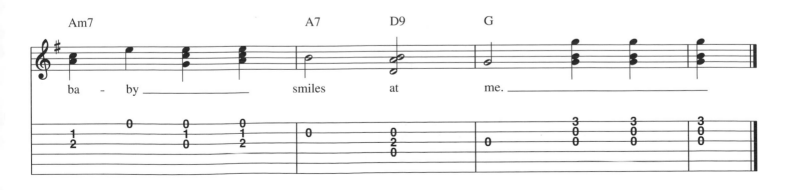

ba - by _____ smiles at me.

When the Saints Go Marching In

Words by Katherine E. Purvis
Music by James M. Black

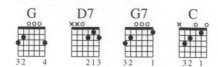

Strum Pattern: 1
Pick Pattern: 2

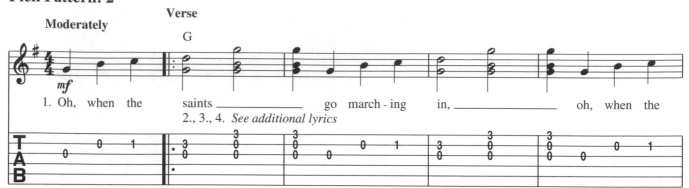

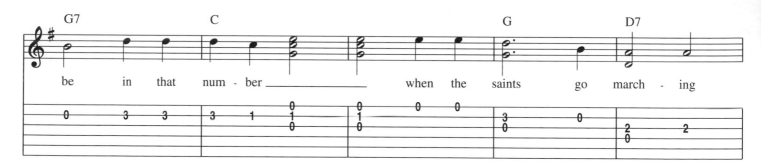

Additional Lyrics

2. Oh, when the sun refuse to shine,
Oh, when the sun refuse to shine,
Oh Lord, I want to be in that number,
When the sun refuse to shine.

3. Oh, when they crown Him Lord of all,
Oh, when they crown Him Lord of all,
Oh Lord, I want to be in that number,
When they crown Him Lord of all.

4. Oh, when they gather 'round the throne,
Oh, when they gather 'round the throne,
Oh Lord, I want to be in that number,
When they gather 'round the throne.

When You Wore a Tulip
(And I Wore a Big Red Rose)

Words by Jack Mahoney
Music by Percy Wenrich

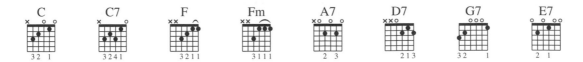

Strum Pattern: 3, 4
Pick Pattern: 3, 4

While Strolling Through the Park One Day

Words and Music by Ed Haley and Robert A. Keiser

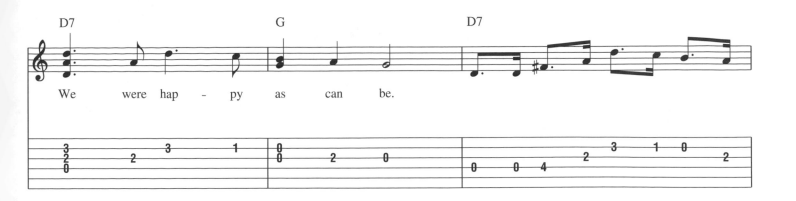

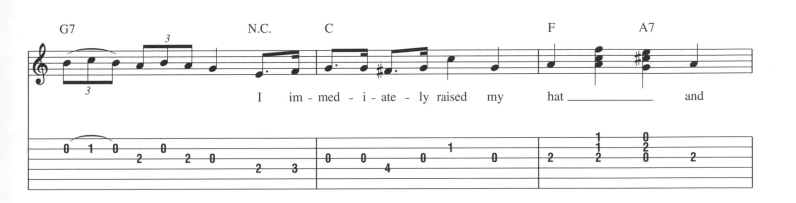

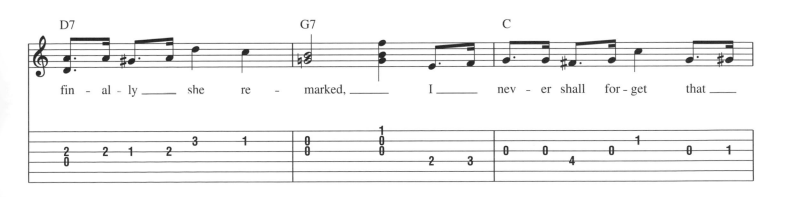

Whispering

Words and Music by Richard Coburn, John Schonberger and Vincent Rose

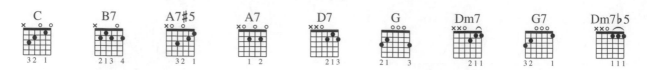

Strum Pattern: 3, 5
Pick Pattern: 3, 4

Verse
Moderately

1., 3. Whis - per - ing while you cud - dle near me,

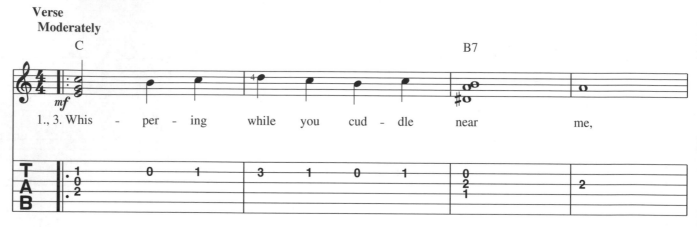

whis - per - ing so no one can hear ____ me. ____

Each lit - tle whis - per seems to cheer ____ me. ____

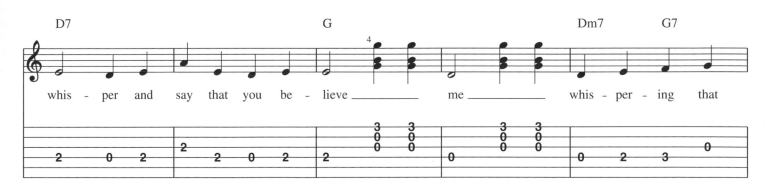

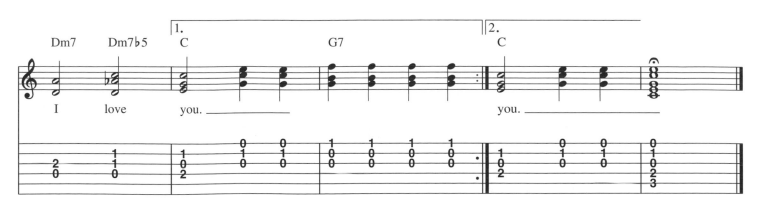

Whispering Hope

Words and Music by Alice Hawthorne

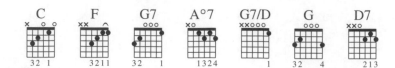

Strum Pattern: 8
Pick Pattern: 8

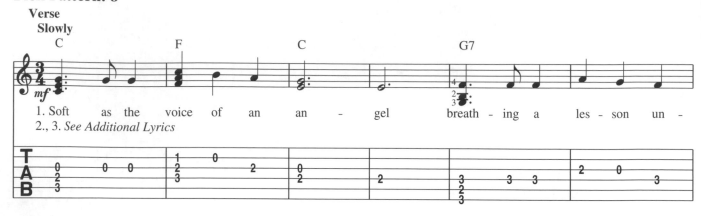

1. Soft as the voice of an an - gel breath - ing a les - son un -
2., 3. *See Additional Lyrics*

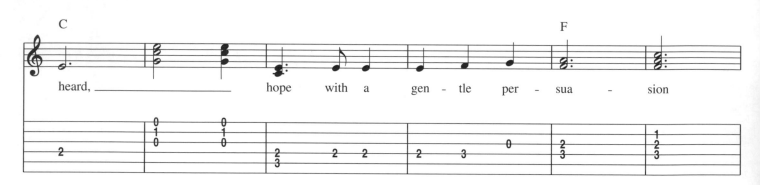

heard, _____ hope with a gen - tle per - sua - sion

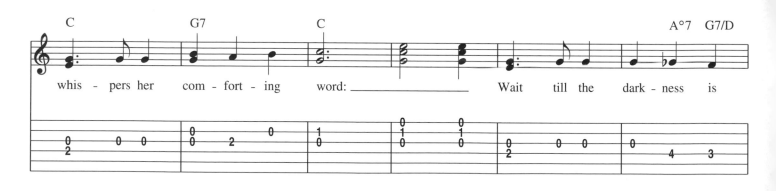

whis - pers her com - fort - ing word: _____ Wait till the dark - ness is

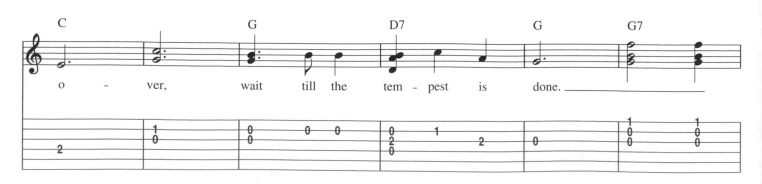

o - ver, wait till the tem - pest is done. _____

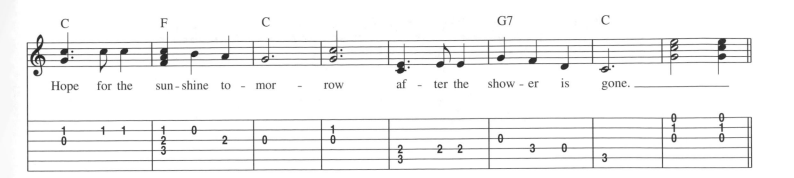

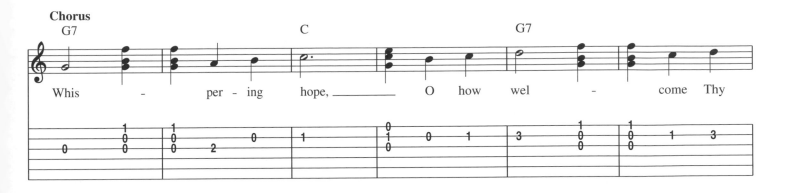

Chorus

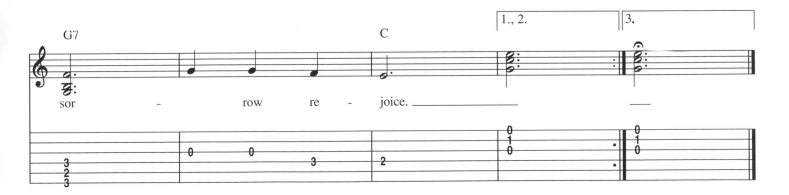

Additional Lyrics

2. If, in the dusk of the twilight,
   Dim be the region afar,
   Will not the deepening darkness
   Brighten the glimmering star?
   Then when the night is upon us,
   Why should the heart sink away?
   When the dark midnight is over,
   Watch for the breaking of day.

3. Hope, as an anchor so steadfast,
   Rends the dark veil for the soul,
   Whither the Master has entered,
   Robbing the grave of its goal.
   Come then, O come, glad fruition,
   Come to my sad, weary heart.
   Come, O Thou blest hope of glory,
   Never, O never depart.

Will the Circle Be Unbroken

Words by Ada R. Habershon
Music by Charles H. Gabriel

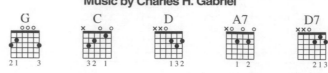

Strum Pattern: 3
Pick Pattern: 3

Verse
Moderately slow

1. I was stand-ing ___ by my win-dow, ___ on one cold and cloud-y day. ___ When I
2., 3. *See additional lyrics*

saw the ___ hearse come roll-ing, for to take my moth-er a-way. ___ Will the

Chorus

cir-cle ___ be un-brok-en, ___ by and by, Lord, by and by? ___ There's a

bet-ter home a-wait-ing, ___ in the sky, in the sky. ___ 2. Oh, I sky. ___

Additional Lyrics

2. Oh, I told the undertaker,
   "Undertaker please drive slow,
   For this body you are hauling,
   Lord, I hate to see her go."

3. I will follow close behind her,
   Try to hold up and be brave.
   But I could not hide my sorrow,
   When they laid her in her grave.

The World Is Waiting for the Sunrise

Words by Eugene Lockhart
Music by Ernest Seitz

Strum Pattern: 2
Pick Pattern: 4

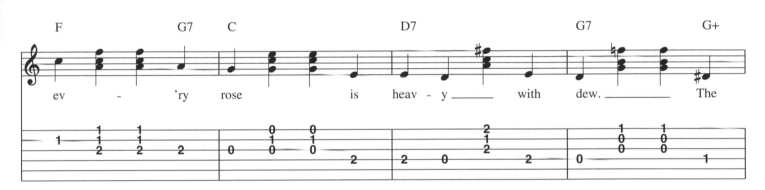

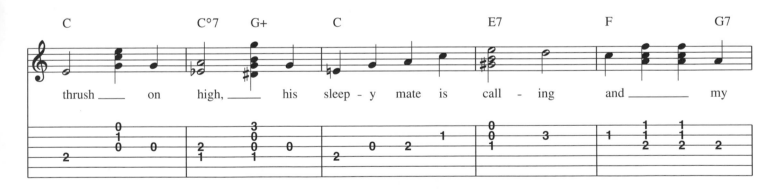

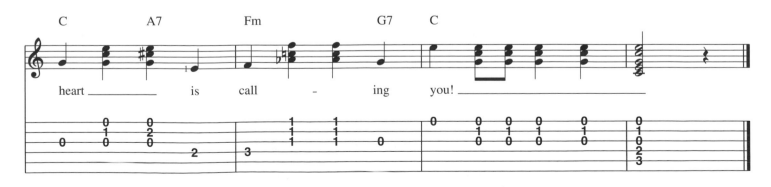

Worried Man Blues

Traditional

Strum Pattern: 3
Pick Pattern: 1

Additional Lyrics

2. I went across the river and I lay down to sleep.
I went across the river and I lay down to sleep.
I went across the river and I lay down to sleep;
When I woke up, had shackles on my feet.

Yankee Doodle

Traditional

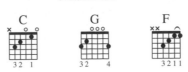

Strum Pattern: 10
Pick Pattern: 10

Verse
Moderately

1. Fath'r and I went down to camp a - long with Cap - tain Good - 'in and there we saw the
2. - 10. *See additional lyrics*

Chorus

men and boys as thick as has - ty pud - din'. Yan - kee Doo - dle keep it up, Yan - kee Doo - dle

dan - dy. Mind the mu - sic and the step, and with the girls be han - dy. 2. And han - dy.

Additional Lyrics

2. And there we see a thousand men
   As rich as Squire David.
   And what they wasted ev'ry day
   I wish it could be saved.

3. And there was Captain Washington
   Upon a slapping stallion
   A-giving orders to his men,
   I guess there was a million.

4. And then the feathers on his hat,
   They looked so very fine, ah!
   I wanted peskily to get
   To give to my Jemima.

5. And there I see a swamping gun,
   Large as a log of maple,
   Upon a mighty little cart,
   A load for father's cattle.

6. And ev'ry time they fired it off,
   It took a horn of powder.
   It made a noise like father's gun,
   Only a nation louder.

7. An' there I see a little keg,
   Its head all made of leather.
   They knocked upon't with little sticks
   To call the folks together.

8. And Cap'n Davis had a gun,
   He kind o'clapt his hand on't
   And stuck a crooked stabbing-iron
   Upon the little end on't.

9. The troopers, too, would gallop up
   And fire right in our faces.
   It scared me almost half to death
   To see them run such races.

10. It scared me so I hooked it off
    Nor stopped, as I remember,
    Nor turned about till I got home,
    Locked up in mother's chamber.

Yankee Doodle Boy

from LITTLE JOHNNY JONES
Words and Music by George M. Cohan

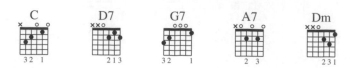

Strum Pattern: 3, 4
Pick Pattern: 3, 4

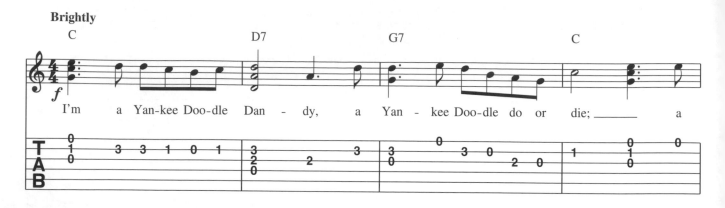

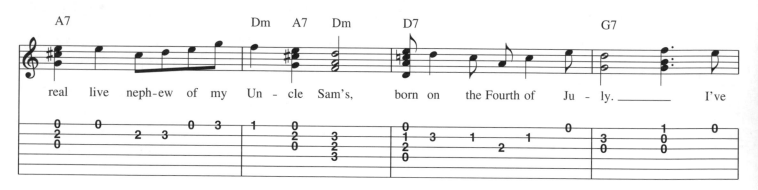

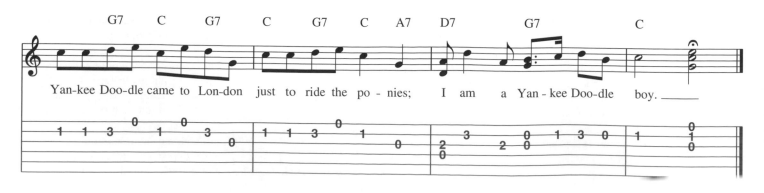

You Tell Me Your Dream

Words by Seymour Rice and Albert H. Brown
Music by Charles N. Daniels

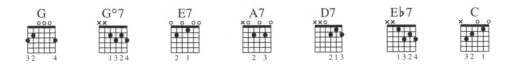

Strum Pattern: 7
Pick Pattern: 8

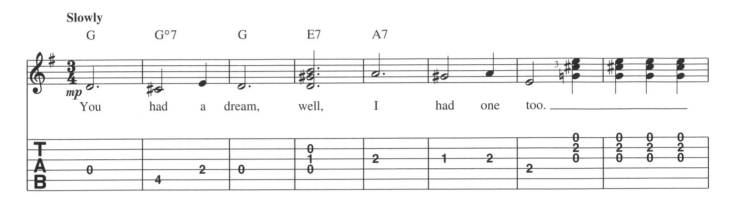

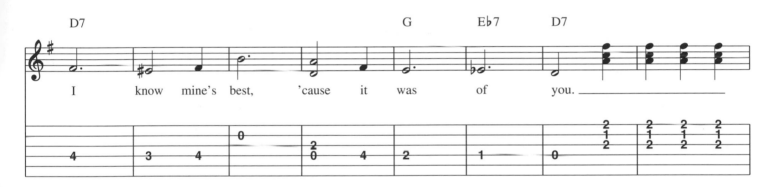

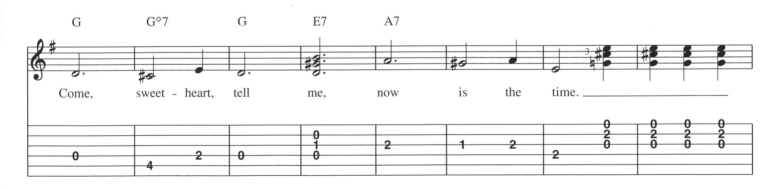

The Yellow Rose of Texas

Traditional Folksong

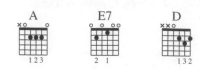

Strum Pattern: 3
Pick Pattern: 3

1. There's a yel - low rose in Tex - as that I am goin' to see, _____ no
3. *See additional lyrics*

oth - er fel - low loves her, _____ no - bod - y, on - ly me. _____ She

cried so when I left her, it like to broke my heart, _____ and

if I ev - er find _____ her, we nev - er - more will part. _____ 2. She's the
4. *See additional lyrics*

Verse

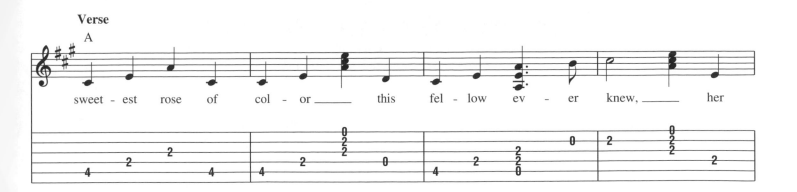

sweet - est rose of col - or _____ this fel - low ev - er knew, _____ her

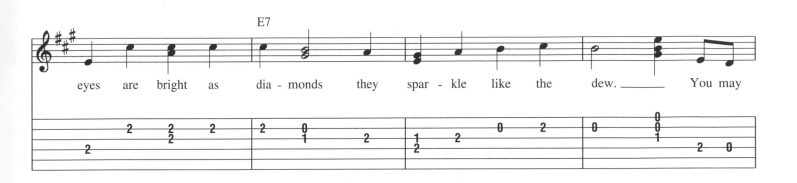

eyes are bright as dia - monds they spar - kle like the dew. _____ You may

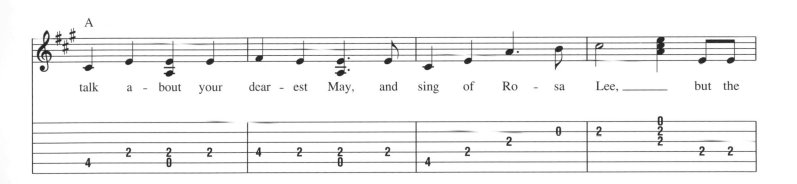

talk a - bout your dear - est May, and sing of Ro - sa Lee, _____ but the

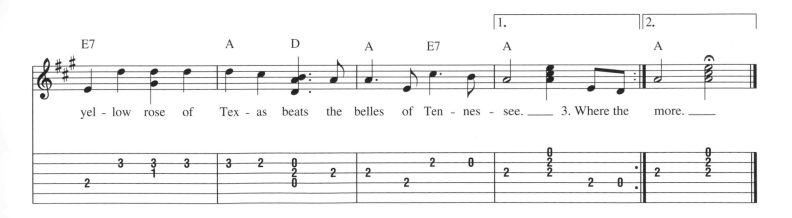

yel - low rose of Tex - as beats the belles of Ten - nes - see. _____ 3. Where the   more. _____

Additional Lyrics

3. Where the Rio Grande is flowing,
   And the starry skies are bright,
   She walks along the river,
   In the quiet summer night,
   She thinks, if I remember,
   When we parted long ago,
   I promised to come back again,
   And not to leave her so.

4. Oh, now I'm going to find her,
   For my heart is full of woe,
   And we'll sing the song together,
   That we sang so long ago,
   We'll play the banjo gaily
   And we'll sing the songs of yore,
   And the yellow rose of Texas
   Shall be mine forevermore.

You're a Grand Old Flag

from GEORGE WASHINGTON, JR.

Words and Music by George M. Cohan

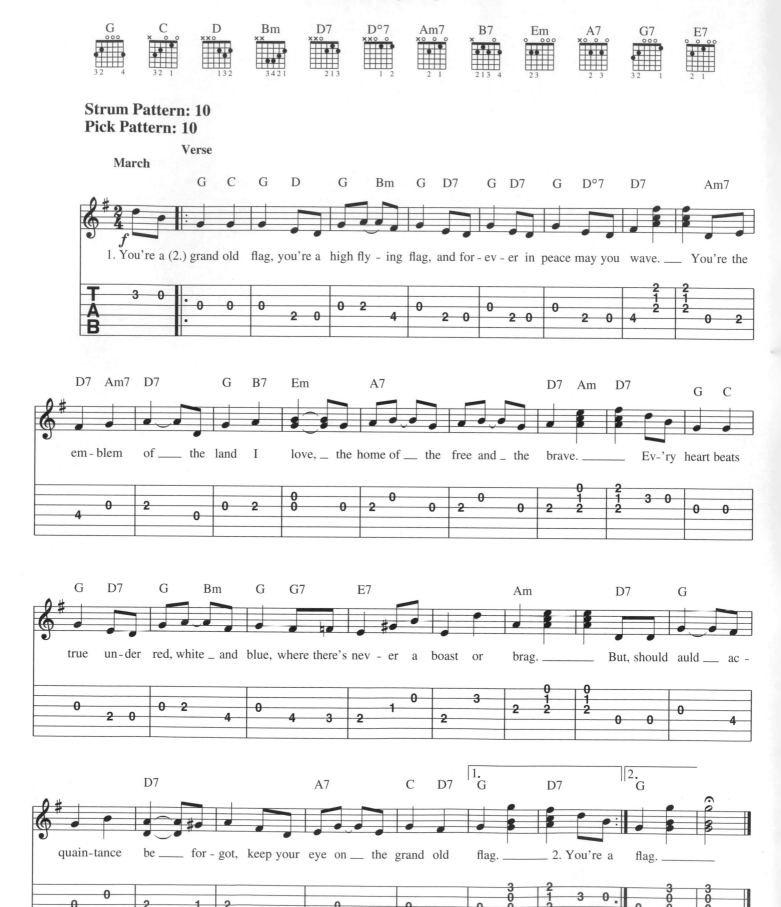

Strum Pattern: 10
Pick Pattern: 10